Impact Assessment and Sustainable Development

EVALUATING SUSTAINABLE DEVELOPMENT

Series Editors: André Martinuzzi, *Research Institute for Managing Sustainability, Vienna University of Economics and Business Administration, Vienna, Austria* and Peter Hardi, *Chair, Department of Business and Society and Director, Center for the Social Foundations of Business, Central European University Business School, Budapest, Hungary.*

The objective of this series is to provide a bridge between academic and applied research, and present results directly relevant to policy makers. It will establish a baseline of practical approaches and highlight the stages involved in the development of best practice, providing research material and references for further academic work. The series will address methodological challenges, facilitate an exchange of experience between disciplines and practitioners, and contribute to capacity building for evaluation. The volumes will comprise of selected papers presented at the five international EASY-ECO conferences organized by a consortium of seven leading European universities and research institutes.

Titles in the series include:

Impact Assessment and Sustainable Development

European Practice and Experience

Edited by

Clive George

Senior Research Fellow, Impact Assessment Research Centre, Institute for Development Policy and Management, School of Environment and Development, University of Manchester, UK

Colin Kirkpatrick

Hallsworth Professor of Development Economics, and Director of the Impact Assessment Research Centre, Institute for Development Policy and Management, School of Environment and Development, University of Manchester, UK

EVALUATING SUSTAINABLE DEVELOPMENT

Edward Elgar
Cheltenham, UK • Northampton, MA, USA

Published by
Edward Elgar Publishing Limited
Glensanda House
Montpellier Parade
Cheltenham
Glos GL50 1UA
UK

Edward Elgar Publishing, Inc.
William Pratt House
9 Dewey Court
Northampton
Massachusetts 01060
USA

A catalogue record for this book
is available from the British Library

Library of Congress Control Number: 2006934140

ISBN 978 1 84542 787 0

Printed and bound in Great Britain by MPG Books Ltd, Bodmin, Cornwall

Contents

Figures

Tables

Contributors

Tom Bauler works on issues related to the institutionalisation of sustainable development (SD) into policy-making.

Alessandro Bonifazi is currently a Ph.D candidate in Planning and Urban Studies at the Politecnico di Bari, Italy.

Matthew Cashmore is a Lecturer in Environmental Management based within the School of Environmental Sciences at the University of East Anglia, UK.

Wouter de Ridder is a Policy Researcher working for the Netherlands Environmental Assessment Agency (MNP).

Geert P.J. Draaijers is Senior Secretary at the Netherlands Commission for Environmental Impact Assessment.

Sebastian Elbe is a Spatial Planner and Partner/Co-Founder of SPRINT.

Clive George is a Senior Research Fellow in the Institute for Development Policy and Management at the University of Manchester, UK.

Mojca Golobic is a Researcher at the Urban Planning Institute of the Republic of Slovenia and Associated Professor at Ljubljana University.

Benjamin Görlach is a Fellow and Environmental Economist with Ecologic.

Peter Hardi is Director of the Center for the Social Foundations of Business at the Central European University Business School, Hungary.

Alex Haxeltine is a leader of the Climate Policy research programme at the Tyndall Centre in the University of East Anglia, UK.

Julia Hertin is a Senior Research Fellow at Environmental Policy Research Centre, Freie Universität Berlin.

Eduard Interwies is engaged in environmental economic research and policy consulting at Ecologic with a focus on the use of economic instruments in environmental policy.

Klaus Jacob is Senior Research Fellow and Research Director at the Environmental Policy Research Centre, Freie Universität Berlin.

Martin Jänicke is Director of the Environmental Policy Research Center at the Freie Universität Berlin.

Helen Johns is an Environmental Economist with EFTEC.

Andrew Jordan is Reader and Philip Leverhulme Prize Fellow in the School of Environmental Sciences at the University of East Anglia, UK

Colin Kirkpatrick is Hallsworth Professor of Development Economics and Director of the Impact Assessment Research Centre in the Institute for Development Policy and Management, School of Environment and Development, University of Manchester, UK.

Wolfgang Meyer is the Senior Scientist and Project-Coordinator of the Working Area 'Labour Market and Environmental Evaluation' at the Center for Evaluation at Saarland University, Germany.

Jodi Newcombe is a Senior Economist with URS Australia Pty Ltd in their Economics and Policy Department.

Joe Ravetz is Deputy Director at the Centre for Urban & Regional Ecology (CURE) at the University of Manchester, UK.

Jan Rotmans is a Professor at Erasmus University Rotterdam in the Netherlands.

Serban Scrieciu is a Research Associate for the Cambridge Centre for Climate Change Mitigation Research, Department of Land Economy, University of Cambridge, UK.

Benoit Simon works as a Director of Planète Publique, Paris, France.

Jean-Pierre Sivignon is at the French Ministry of Ecology and Sustainable Development in the Office of National Strategy on Sustainable Development.

Katarína Staroňová is a Lecturer in the Institute of Public Policy at Comenius University in Bratislava, Slovakia.

John Turnpenny is a Senior Research Associate in the Tyndall Centre and CSERGE at the University of East Anglia, UK.

Marjan van Herwijnen is a Senior Researcher at the Institute for Environmental Studies of the Vrije Universiteit, Amsterdam, in the Netherlands.

Rob Verheem is Adjunct-Secretary of the Netherlands Commission for Environmental Assessment.

Axel Volkery is project manager for scenario and policy analysis at the European Environment Agency.

Marco Wäktare is a Master's student at the U.L.B. in International Politics, Brussels.

Paul Weaver is a Senior Researcher at the Wolfson Research Institute, Director of the Centre for Eco-Efficiency and Enterprise, and Visiting Professor at the University of Paris.

Franc Zakrajšek is a mathematician and consultant for governmental and international projects.

Preface

The translation of the principle of sustainable development into policy and practice, and the evaluation of the outcomes of these strategic interventions, are some of the most pressing challenges facing policy makers in Europe and beyond. The chapters in this volume contribute to the debate on these issues by exploring the conceptual and methodological issues relating to the evaluation of sustainable development, and by analysing European practice and experience.

The chapters were first presented at an international conference entitled 'Impact assessment for a new Europe and beyond', which was held at the University of Manchester, as part of a series of conferences and training courses (EASY-ECO 2005-07) supported by the European Commission's Marie Curie Initiative under the 6th Research Framework. The conference was also supported by the United Nations Environment Programme. The University of Manchester's School of Environment and Development (SED) is a co-partner in the project, which is led by the Vienna University of Economics and Business Administration, Austria. The other co-partners are the International Institute for Sustainable Development (IISD), Canada; the Centre for Evaluation, Saarland University, Germany; the Regional Environmental Centre (REC), Hungary; the Regional Environmental Centre, Slovakia; the Sendzimir Foundation, Poland; and the National Centre for Sustainable Development (NCSD), Romania.

We are grateful to the European Commission and UNEP for supporting the conference that led to the final production of the chapters in this volume. Nevertheless, the views and conclusions expressed by the authors are entirely their own and should not be attributed to the conference sponsors.

We are grateful to the contributing authors for making available to us their original papers and for agreeing to revise the papers for publication in this volume; also to our colleagues at the Vienna University of Economics and Business Administration for having invited us to contribute this volume to the Evaluating Sustainable Development Series. We also owe a large debt of gratitude to our colleagues in the School of Environment and Development at Manchester University for their assistance. Debra Whitehead, Lyn Currie and Marion Fahy were responsible for organizing the conference and for the administrative and financial management of the project, and Serban Scrieciu, Lindsay Stringer and Jennifer Franz provided us with excellent support in preparing the papers for publication.

Finally, we thank the commissioning and editing staff at Edward Elgar for their patience, encouragement during the preparation stage and for their efficiency in the preparation of the manuscript for final publication.

Clive George
Colin Kirkpatrick

1. Impact assessment and sustainable development: an introduction

Clive George and Colin Kirkpatrick

I. INTRODUCTION

The United Nations (UN) Conference on Environment and Development in 1992 successfully established the concept of sustainable development as an underlying principle for strategic policy and planning. But the translation of the principle of sustainable development into practice has presented new challenges in finding workable solutions to the complex trade-offs that can arise between the different, and often conflicting, dimensions of sustainable development.

The growing complexity of policy-making in terms of the goal of sustainable development has encouraged a growing interest among researchers and practitioners in developing a practical and evidence based approach to public policy appraisal and evaluation. As a result, impact assessment, defined as the systematic assessment of the potential or actual effects of a public intervention on the economic, social and environmental 'pillars' of sustainable development, is now used as a tool for policy-making in the European Commission, most member states of the European Union (EU), other OECD countries, and in a growing number of developing countries and transitional economies.[1]

II. IMPACT ASSESSMENT AND SUSTAINABLE DEVELOPMENT

The last decade has seen a growing international interest in the development and use of evidence-informed policy and practice across a wide range of public policy issues. While the design and implementation of public policy has always been of concern to public sector researchers and policy makers, the importance of good regulation has come to the forefront today because of the rise of the 'regulatory state' (Majone 1994, 1997), in which government's role is perceived to be that of regulating the market economy.

State regulation that promotes economic and social welfare needs to be both effective and efficient: effective in the sense of achieving its planned goals, and efficient in the sense of achieving these goals at least cost, in terms of government administration costs and the costs imposed on the economy in terms of complying with regulations. There is, therefore, a compelling case for the systematic appraisal of the positive and negative impacts of any proposed or actual regulatory change. The purpose of impact assessment (often referred to as regulatory impact assessment, RIA) is to 'explain the objectives of the [regulatory] proposal, the risks to be addressed and the options for delivering the objectives. In doing so it should make transparent the expected costs and benefits of the options for the different bodies involved, such as other parts of Government and small businesses, and how compliance with regulatory options would be secured and enforced' (NAO 2002, p. 51). The appraisal should encompass the likely economic, environmental, social and distributional consequences of a regulatory measure, thereby providing a comprehensive analysis of its impact.

The underlying rationale for RIA is that regulations need to be assessed on a case-by-case basis, to see whether they contribute to strategic policy goals. RIA has the potential to strengthen regulation efficiency and effectiveness by examining the possible impacts arising from planned government actions and communicating this information to decision makers in a way that allows them to consider (ideally) the full range of positive and negative effects (benefits and costs) that are associated with a proposed regulatory change. Equally, RIA has the potential to improve the monitoring of existing regulatory policies. This might lead to revisions to an existing regulation to improve its performance or even the outright cancellation of a regulation. Both *ex ante* and *ex post* RIA help to constrain damaging regulatory discretion and expose cases of regulatory conflict (e.g. between government agencies).

Impact assessment (IA) can contribute to both the *outcome* and the *process* dimensions of national objectives. The outcome contribution of IA can be assessed against the economic, social and environmental goals of government. The process contribution of IA can be assessed in terms of the principles of 'good governance'. There is a broad consensus that these principles encompass consistency in decision-making to avoid uncertainty, accountability for regulatory actions and outcomes, and transparency in decision-making. IA encourages public consultation to identify and measure benefits and costs and thereby has the potential to improve the transparency of governmental decision-making. It can promote government accountability by reporting on the information used in decision-making and by demonstrating how the regulation will impact on society. In these ways IA can contribute to improved regulatory governance, and the result should be an improved and more consistent regulatory environment for both producers and consumers. The contribution of IA to better policy-making therefore rests on the systematic assessment of the impacts of a regulatory measure, and the adherence to the principles of accountability, transparency and consistency.

Where IA is adopted at the national level, the precise form it takes can be expected to vary between countries. Equally, we should expect the government policy decisions to which it is applied and the pace of adoption both to vary. At the same time, however, a number of principles seem to be universal.

Firstly, IA needs the development of skills within the government machinery, including skills in evaluating the problem that is being addressed and enumerating the relevant costs and benefits. Generally, qualitative effects will involve much judgmental or subjective evaluation, and physical units introduce serious problems of aggregation. There may be a temptation, therefore, to diminish the IA to include only an evaluation of measurable financial costs and benefits. Or, the assessment could be reduced to looking solely at the cheapest way of achieving the regulatory outcome (in effect providing a *cost effectiveness* study only) in which the benefits are taken as given. This lesser form of IA risks ignoring important differential benefits from differing forms of regulation.

Secondly, IA requires the extension of consultation procedures to ensure that appropriate information is collected and analysed in reaching a view on the regulatory impact. There may be little tradition of consulting widely in a country before undertaking regulation, or those chosen for consultation in the past may not have been representative of the relevant stakeholders. Consultation is an essential part of the IA process.

Thirdly, IA will need to be championed across government if it is to be used consistently and become a normal feature of regulatory policy-making. It therefore needs clear and powerful political support if it is to overcome bureaucratic and political inertia.

IA requires an explicit statement of the goals of government regulatory policy, since these goals will determine the criteria for assessing impacts. In practice, sustainable development is widely used as the ultimate goal for all regulatory interventions, and IA is designed, therefore, to assess the full range of economic, social and environmental results of a particular regulatory measure or policy.

In the EU, as a result of the Göteborg European Council meeting in June 2001 which committed the Commission to promote sustainable development and to establish mechanisms for the assessment of all European policy proposals (EC 2001a),[2] there are now procedures in place to ensure that each major legislative proposal is informed by an assessment of the potential impacts of the measure, both inside and outside the European Union.

Following the 2001 European Council meeting, the Commission proposed that 'a coherent method for impact analysis' be introduced for all major commission proposals by the end of 2002 (EC 2001b). The 2002 Communication of the European Commission on Impact Assessment committed the Commission to undertake an IA of all major policy proposals in order 'to improve the quality and coherence of the policy development process', . . . (and to) . . . 'contribute to an effective and efficient regulatory environment and further, to a more coherent implementation of the European Strategy for Sustainable Development' (EC 2002).

In 2003, the Commission began implementing the new integrated system for the systematic use of IA. In 2005 it issued new guidelines for integrated assessment, 'based on the principle of sustainable development and designed to allow policy makers to make choices on the basis of careful analysis of the potential economic, social and environmental impacts of new legislation' (EC 2005: 5). All initiatives set out in the Commission's Legislative and Work Programme, which covers key legislative proposals as well as the most important cross-cutting policy-defining non-legislative proposals, are now subject to an integrated form of IA.

The use of IA in the Commission has so far been confined to ex ante assessment. However, it is proposed to develop ex post monitoring and evaluation procedures, using a common set of indicators to assess progress in improving the quality of the regulatory environment at the EU level (EC 2005).

III.   EVALUATING SUSTAINABLE DEVELOPMENT

The 1992 UN Conference on Environment and Development (the Rio Conference) established the principle of integrating sustainable development considerations into strategic development planning and policy, and as one of the key mechanisms for achieving this, it was agreed that each government should adopt a national sustainable development strategy (NSDS), in order to implement the goals of Agenda 21 (UN 1992, paragraph 8.7). Agenda 21 established that the overall objective of an NSDS is 'to improve or restructure the decision-making process so that consideration of socio-economic and environmental issues is fully integrated and a broader range of public participation assured' (paragraph 8.3). An effective NSDS will be distinguished therefore, by adherence to a set of principles for strategic planning and sustainable development, and a coordinated set of measures to ensure its implementation.

The basic principles for an NSDS are well established. The OECD Development Assistance Committee has developed a set of principles intended mainly for developing countries, and the UN Department for Economic and Social Affairs has developed similar principles appropriate for all countries (OECD/DAC 2001; UNDESA 2002). Both sets of principles are accompanied by guidance on implementation, and further work by OECD, UNDP and the International Institute for Environment and Development (IIED) has led to the preparation of a resource book for NSDS, giving in-depth information on possible approaches and methodologies (Dalal-Clayton and Bass 2002).

All of the guidance recommends that a country's NSDS should be developed from its existing strategic planning mechanisms, through a process of continual improvement. The starting point should also include the country's established mechanisms of social and economic planning. These mechanisms typically consist of the national budgeting process, national development plans and other national planning processes, and interdepartmental coordinating processes, with links to sub-national and local strategy processes (Swanson et al 2004). In many developing countries they also include internationally recognized poverty reduction strategies.

By 2003, most EU countries had implemented a recognized NSDS (UNDESA 2004). However, many other countries had not, including the United States (US) and several other high-income countries. Only 12 percent of UN member states were implementing national strategies, while a further 2 percent had received government approval. Some were developing an NSDS, but most reported only that components of a sustainable development strategy were in place. This was despite the call for accelerated action agreed to at the UN World Summit on Sustainable Development, urging states to 'take immediate steps to make progress in the formulation and elaboration of national strategies for sustainable development and begin their implementation by 2005' (UN 2002, paragraph 162).

How should a country's NSDS be evaluated?[3] A country's existing strategic planning mechanisms need to be reviewed, to measure the extent to which they already comply with NSDS principles, and to highlight any shortcomings. In order to strengthen the continual improvement aspect of NSDS development, a focus is needed on the actual achievements of operational planning systems, in relation to internationally agreed objectives. In the preparations for the 2002 World Summit on Sustainable Development, a methodology was developed for assessing countries' existing strategic planning mechanisms, to identify areas that need to be improved in order to comply with NSDS principles (Cherp, George and Kirkpatrick 2004). The methodology is based on principles of sustainable development and corresponding principles of strategic planning and management, as interpreted for NSDS by OECD and UNDESA. The OECD principles and UN principles are grouped under five core principles, derived from sustainable development principles and more general principles of strategic planning and management.[4]

The assessment methodology measures the degree to which national strategic planning processes adhere to the five core principles and the related NSDS principles. A set of criteria for each of the five principles is used as the basis for a qualitative scoring system (IDPM 2001). The outcome of an assessment against these criteria provides policy makers and other interested parties with a clear indication of the effectiveness of the planning process, so that areas where improvement is needed can be identified.

IV. THE CHAPTERS OF THE VOLUME

The remaining chapters in the volume share a common concern with IA and evaluation of sustainable development policy and practice. The book is structured into two main parts. This introductory chapter is followed by the chapters in Part I, which discuss various conceptual and methodological issues relating to IA and sustainable development. Part II explores the practice and experience of IA and sustainable development in the European context.

The focus of the chapter by Peter Hardi is on the need for a common interpretation of sustainable development (SD) in the context of evaluation. The starting assumption is that evaluation, its content, methods and results, will change with the differences in the definition of SD. In other words, evaluation as a process is not independent of the content: it depends on and changes with the definition of SD.

Martin Jänicke gives a general evaluation of the governance model standing behind the strategic concept of SD. He argues that the Rio governance model was remarkably successful in so far as it was a knowledge-based model of steering – not based on power and legal obligation – but requires constant revision and evaluation, drawing on forces that are independent from, but supportive to, the strategy of SD.

Wolfgang Meyer and Sebastian Elbe discuss capacity building for SD in the context of local network governance. Based on the Agenda 21 principles, they argue that a multi-level governance structure for vertical integration from the global to the local level was intended to synchronize the development and execution of policy strategies. New participatory approaches are indispensable for 'good regional governance', which itself is needed for establishing 'SD' at the local level. The chapter concludes with some general observations based on German experience, of steering SD at the regional level.

The chapter by Joe Ravetz is concerned with evaluation in the context of the widening of 'regional development' to 'regional sustainable development' ('RSD'), with a more integrated economic, social and environmental agenda. The chapter is based on the evaluation strand of a project that brings together best practice in RSD across Europe. It reviews two contrasting examples of evaluation methods in development. One concerns the modelling of 'tangibles' of environmental flows and impacts; the other is focused on the 'intangibles' of evaluation of regional innovation strategy. Each example demonstrates the need for more integrated approaches, and the management of complexity and uncertainty in a practical process.

The chapter by Klaus Jacob, Julia Hertin and Axel Volkery analyses the relationship between environmental assessment and integrated IA by comparing IA systems in Australia, Canada, the EU, Italy, the Netherlands, the United Kingdom (UK) and the US. They then examine whether integrated IA is beneficial to the goals of environmental policy integration or hampers their implementation. The chapter concludes by drawing a number of conclusions regarding procedural and substantial requirements to ensure a balanced treatment of environmental aspects in integrated IA.

The contribution by Matt Cashmore critically assesses the widespread perception that environmental impact assessment (EIA) is failing to achieve its potential in practice. Rather than focusing on the more tangible limitations of EIA practices, it is argued that the underlying reason it is failing is because the relationship between EIA and SD is inadequately conceptualized. Cashmore suggests, however, that one way in which EIA makes a significant contribution is by providing a forum in which societal interpretations of sustainability can be debated and that a richer conception of their relationship can still be developed, by examining causation in EIA. It is postulated that EIA can be considered to be operating as a 'front-line' tool in operationalizing SD, but in a markedly different manner to conventional expectations.

Serban Scrieciu provides an evaluation of the use of computable general equilibrium (CGE) modelling as a tool for predicting possible sustainability outcomes from policy proposals. Although some of the restrictive assumptions of CGE models have been relaxed in recent CGE modelling studies, further research needs to be undertaken in order to bring model specifications closer to realistic behavioural relationships. CGE models also tend to focus on alternative equilibrium outcomes and rarely deal with the adjustment process or regulation measures needed to realistically bring the economy into the desired new equilibrium stance. Scrieciu concludes that while CGE models may provide some useful information on individual, particularly economic, impacts of policy reform appraisal, it may be inappropriate and even misleading to rely extensively on their use in sustainability evaluation studies.

The chapter by Paul Weaver, Jan Rotmans, John Turnpenny, Alex Haxeltine and Andrew Jordan describes a major European research project which aims to develop a common conceptual framework for integrated sustainability assessment (ISA), development, implementation and evaluation. This is related to the assessment of the current status of ISA and its pattern of use in relation to different domains and contexts, including institutional factors that play a key role at the science-policy interface.

Marjan van Herwijnen and Wouter de Ridder report on a project to assemble an inventory and evaluation of tools commonly used in sustainability impact assessments (SIAs). A large set of tools is evaluated for their ability to support certain policy processes, their ability to address various aspects of SD and for certain specific operational aspects. A case study on bio-fuel is used to further deepen the evaluation and, based on concrete policy decisions, to investigate promising combinations of tools.

Part II concentrates on European practice and experience in IA and SD evaluation. The first chapter in this section, by Benjamin Görlach, Eduard Interwies, Jodi Newcombe and Helen Johns summarizes the main results of a project on the cost-effectiveness of environmental policies carried out on behalf of the European Environment Agency. The chapter first provides a review of legal requirements for ex post cost effectiveness analysis (CEA) in European environmental policy, then presents an overview of existing guidance documents and manuals for carrying out ex post CEAs, and finally gives a summary of the current practice in EU member states with regard to ex post CEA of environmental policies.

The chapter by Benoit Simon and Jean-Pierre Sivignon presents the results of a study to develop a monitoring and evaluation system for the French national strategy for SD. The paper is focused on the evaluation of sustainability on three axes: a reflection on the framework of the national strategy for SD; a discussion on the methodology used to elaborate indicators; and a reflection on difficulties encountered during the process.

The chapter by Katarína Staroňová evaluates the type and quality of information on IAs contained in the explanatory memoranda of draft legislation adopted by the government of Slovakia. The study is based on normative content analysis of a sample of 93 government-initiated draft laws and their explanatory memoranda that were submitted for government consideration during the period after EU accession. The results indicate that the system is not yet fully developed, and most of the draft laws reviewed have only a formal approach towards the assessment of impacts, with the aim of formally complying with the requirements.

The chapter by Mojca Golobic and Franc Zakrajšek argues that sustainability concerns should be ideally integrated in all fields of public action and regulation, above all in spatial planning and environment protection. The authors discuss the options for the implementation of sustainability by spatial planning process and (strategic) EIA. The experience from Slovenia is used to show that integrative tools, such as spatial vulnerability studies and evaluation of alternatives from the aspects of environmental impacts, impacts on urban and regional development and social acceptability, have been successfully used as optimization tools in decision support.

Geert Draaijers and Rob Verheem consider how sustainability assessment (SA) has been operationalized in the Dutch NSDS. Drawing on twenty years of Dutch experience with strategic environmental assessment (SEA), they show how experiments with SA were conducted. At the same time experience with SA was gained from SEAs in which sustainability issues were raised. Based on these experiences, the authors discuss some key elements for effective SA.

Tom Bauler, Marco Wäktare and Alessandro Bonifazi discuss the Belgian experience in institutionalizing a federal level evaluation scheme for the Belgian SD agenda. The authors explore whether and how such an SIA scheme could be applied to the federal level of Belgian government. More specifically, the chapter addresses issues related to the supply and the demand sides of SIAs. The supply side is covered through an analysis of major points to take into account when designing such an assessment. Issues related to the demand side are identified through face-to-face interviews which aimed at gaining knowledge of the understanding, dangers and opportunities, experiences and expertise, as well as institutional challenges perceived both by stakeholders and civil servants.

NOTES

1. For a comprehensive review of country-level experience and practice with RIA, see Kirkpatrick and Parker (2006).
2. The Communication stated that 'sustainable development should become the central objective of all sectors and policies . . . careful assessment of the full effects of a policy proposal must include estimates of its economic, environmental and social impacts inside and outside the EU' (EC 2001a).
3. Individual countries have used a variety of methods for assessing their own NSDS. In varying degrees, all these evaluations examine the extent to which the NSDS is integrated into a country's operational strategic planning mechanisms, with a view to making the NSDS itself fully operational and effective. However, they generally refrain from establishing clear benchmarks against which shortcomings may be judged, and through which progress towards rectifying them may be monitored. These different assessment methods are compared in George and Kirkpatrick (2006). See also, OECD (2005) and UNDESA (2004).

4. The five principles are shown in Table 1.1. Groups A and B may be regarded as sustainable development principles, while groups C, D and E are more general principles of strategic planning and management.

Table 1.1   NSDS principles

Core principles	OECD principles	UN principles
A. Integration of economic, social and environmental objectives	Comprehensive and integrated. People centred.	Integration and balanced across sectors and territories.
B. Participation and consensus	Consensus on long-term vision. Effective participation.	Shared strategic and pragmatic vision. Link the short to the medium and long terms. Ensure continuity of the strategy development process. Participatory and the widest possible participation ensured.
C. Country ownership and commitment	Country led and nationally owned. High-level government commitment and influential lead institutions.	Nationally owned and country-driven process. Strong political commitment at the national and local levels. Spearheaded by a strong institution.
D. Comprehensive and coordinated policy process	Based on comprehensive and reliable analysis. Building on existing processes and strategies. Link national and local levels.	Anchor the strategy process in sound technical analysis. Build on existing processes and strategies. Link national and local priorities and actions.
E. Targeting, resourcing and monitoring	Targeted with clear budgetary priorities. Incorporate monitoring, learning and improvements. Develop and build on existing capacity.	Set realistic but flexible targets. Coherence between budget and strategy priorities. Build mechanisms for monitoring follow-up, evaluation and feedback.

Source: Derived from OECD (2001) and UNDESA (2002).

REFERENCES

Cherp, A, George, C and Kirkpatrick, C (2004), 'A methodology for assessing national sustainable development strategies', *Environment and Planning C*, 22, 913–26.

Dalal-Clayton, B and Bass, S (2002), *Sustainable Development Strategies: A Resource Book*, Earthscan, London.

European Commission (EC) (2001a), *Communication: A Sustainable Europe for a Better World: A European Union Strategy for Sustainable Development*, COM(2001)264 Final, Brussels.

European Commission (EC) (2001b), *Communication: Simplifying and Improving the Regulatory Environment*, COM (2001) 726.

European Commission (EC) (2002), *Communication from the Commission on Impact Assessment*, COM (2002) 276 Final, Brussels.

European Commission (EC) (2005), *Communication from the Commission to the Council and the European Parliament, Better Regulation for Growth and Jobs in the European Union*, COM(2005) 97 final.

George, C and Kirkpatrick, C (2006), 'Assessing national sustainable development strategies: strengthening the link to operational policy', *Natural Resources Forum*, 30 (2), 146–56.

IDPM (2001), *Development of Criteria to Assess the Effectiveness of National Strategies for Sustainable Development*. Report prepared for the UK Department for International Development, Institute for Development Policy and Management, University of Manchester.

Kirkpatrick, C and Parker, D (eds) (2006), *Regulatory Impact Assessment: Towards Better Regulatory Governance?*, Edward Elgar, Cheltenham.

Majone, G (1994), 'The emergence of the regulatory state in Europe', *West European Politics*, vol. 17, pp. 77–101.

Majone, G (1997), 'From the positive to the regulatory state', *Journal of Public Policy*, 17 (2), 139–67.

NAO (National Audit Office) (2002), *Better Regulation: Making Good Use of Regulatory Impact Assessments*. Report by the Comptroller and Auditor General, HC 329 Session 2001–2002, November, London.

OECD/DAC (2001), *Strategies for Sustainable Development: Practical Guidance for Development Co-operation*, OECD, Paris.

OECD (2005), *National Strategies for Sustainable Development: Good Practices in OECD Countries*, SG/SD(2005)6, OECD, Paris.

Swanson, D, Pintér, L, Bregha, F, Volkery, A and Jacob, K (2004), *National Strategies for Sustainable Development: Challenges, Approaches and Innovations in Strategic and Co-ordinated Action*, International Institute for Sustainable Development and Deutsche Gesellschaft für Technische Zusammenarbeit, Winnipeg and Eschborn.

UNDESA (2002), *Report of an Expert Forum on National Strategies for Sustainable Development*, Accra, Ghana, 7–9 November 2001, Department of Economic and Social Affairs, United Nations, New York.

UNDESA (2004), *Assessment Report on National Sustainable Development Strategies*, Department of Economic and Social Affairs, United Nations, New York.

United Nations (1992), *Report of the United Nations Conference on Environment and Development* (Rio de Janeiro, 3–14 June 1992) A/CONF.151/26, United Nations, New York.

United Nations (2002), *Report of the World Summit on Sustainable Development* (Johannesburg, 26 August–4 September 2002), A/CONF.199/20, United Nations, New York.

PART I

Evaluation and sustainable development:
concepts and methods

2. The long and winding road of sustainable development evaluation

Peter Hardi

Any way you'll never know
The many ways I've tried . . .
The Beatles

I.   INTERPRETING SUSTAINABILITY

The focus of this chapter is the need for a common interpretation of sustainable development (SD) in the context of evaluation. The starting assumption is that evaluation, its content, methods and results, will change with the differences in the definition of SD. In other words, the evaluation as a process is not independent of the content: it depends on and changes with the definition of SD. A capacity building project has the aim to influence decision-making in favour of SD, and its goal to make a consistent impact presupposes a common interpretation of SD. Or does it? The difficulty is that there is no standard and/or scientific definition of SD accepted across the board in science and in political/development practice. Unfortunately, there are several hundreds of different definitions and interpretations of SD world-wide. For better orientation, these definitions and interpretations can be grouped in a few clusters,[1] and the first objective is to present these clusters.

Four main clusters that cover the vast majority of SD definitions will be discussed. These clusters are the following:

- SD as a lifestyle (more narrowly, consumption) issue, rooted in the discussion of SD as a system boundary issue;
- SD as a process issue that is characteristic of every transition process, rooted either in the more general discussion of equilibrium or in a discussion of SD as a transition with a set of specific targets to be achieved;
- SD as an economic issue, related to the maintenance of capital assets;

- SD as a developmental issue, dealing with resource allocation in programmes.

Firstly, however, two of the boundary issues that provide context to SD will
be clarified: time and space.

System Boundary Issues

Any discussion of the boundary conditions of sustainability and/or SD[2]
must address two fundamental issues: time scale and spatial scale. Defining
the temporal and spatial scales is defining the *limits to sustainability*. This limitation is necessary in order to arrive at a practical, workable interpretation
of SD. If we leave these two boundaries too vague, i.e. infinite, then nothing
is sustainable (according to contemporary scientific knowledge, not even the
universe): on an infinite temporal scale, sooner or later all matter and every
energy-based component set will change.[3] Cosmological spatial boundaries
are not helpful, though astronomical boundaries, in particular boundaries
within the solar system seem to be appropriate already now. Yet most of the
definitions deal with spatial boundaries set within the Earth system (generally as a closed system, with two forms of openness: absorption of energy –
predominantly solar – and dissipation of heat into space). Within the spatial
scale of Earth, all variations are permitted, from the most local (from rural,
village to urban) to national, regional, sub- and full continental to global.

While spatial boundaries can be set with a useful degree of concreteness,
the temporal boundaries are more elusive and more arbitrary (though from
a systems perspective, political-administrative spatial boundaries are also
arbitrary), and very often they are not set explicitly. Even the most well known
temporal definition of SD, that of the Brundtland Report (Brundtland 1987),
speaks vaguely of 'future generations'; in most other cases the time frame of
SD is indefinite. We do not have more precise, let alone scientific, conditions
on the boundaries of the time scale for specific spatial units or processes that
should be sustained.

The most common implicit time frame within which SD is discussed is tied
to political processes and cycles. National SD strategies are discussed and set
in relationship to legislative cycles and political strategies of parties. Local
SD strategies, such as Local Agenda 21 plans, are set within the framework
of local politics. And even when these SD strategies are ambitious and
willing to discuss longer time frames, the strategies are agreed with a percep-
tible limitation of being subject to change with a change in political power.
International organizations offer the longest time frame for SD strategies,
whether as the programme of a UN agency (such as Agenda 21 of the
Commission on Sustainable Development, see CSD 1992) or an international

financial institution (such as the World Bank, see World Bank 1995) or a joint initiative (such as the Millennium Development Goals programme, see MDG 2000) – but even these time frames cover not more than a few decades.

The most limited and most explicit time frame is usually tied to a specific programme with approved budgets where the SD horizon is captive to the budgeting timeline. It goes without saying that the better defined the temporal and spatial scales the easier the evaluation. Unfortunately, there is no evidence that politically driven time frames have any relationship with time frames of SD.

II. INTERPRETING SUSTAINABILITY IN THE CONTEXT OF LIFESTYLES

The original discussion on SD had a strong connection to environmental degradation and the political desire to do something in order to stop that degradation, mitigate its impact and prevent further decline. According to the logic of the debate, the main causes of such degradation have been human activities and human lifestyles in a world of *finite resources*. A simultaneous process of political and scientific efforts has been unfolding since the 1980s: the *political process* is aiming at changing human lifestyles; the *scientific process* is aiming at better understanding the limitations set by finite resources. Both of these processes are based on a *macro-level* (global) approach to the definition of SD, and they are preoccupied with the concept of sustainability.[4]

The Political Process

The first culmination of the political debate and at the same time, the staging of a new international political agenda, was the 1987 publication of the report of the UN Commission on Environment and Development, commonly referred to as the Brundtland Report (named after its chair, the then Norwegian prime minister Gro Harlem Brundtland). The short 'classical' definition of SD according to the Brundtland Commission is the following, 'development that meets the needs of the present without compromising the ability of future generations to meet their own needs' (Brundtland 1987). The broader interpretation of sustainability by the commission relates economic growth, environmental protection and political equity, and makes an attempt to solve the apparent contradiction between environmental and socio-economic issues. The arguments focus on the contradiction between needs satisfaction and available environmental (natural) resources and call for a limitation of our needs satisfaction in order to preserve environmental resources and not to jeopardize their capacity to renew within the time frames of our actions. In other words, we need to change our lifestyles (particularly in the developed world) if we wish to avoid the irreversible depletion of environmental resources. The arguments address the human/political actors, and they formulate a kind of *moral* obligation, even in a weak format of mostly voluntary actions: we *need to* make changes. The moral character of the discussion is further emphasized by the introduction of the openly ethical concept of social and inter-generational *equity*. The underlying message is that it is *not fair* to compromise the need satisfaction ability of others (in the present and in the future) by maximizing our own need satisfaction in a world of finite natural resources.

The derivative political debate has been focusing on how this limitation can be achieved, and as the lifestyle changes are most closely related to limitations in consumption, they have been discussed mostly in economic terms. As one economist observed, 'the debate over various definitions of sustainability has for the most part been conducted within the framework of traditional welfare economics. Discussion has centered on technical issues imbedded within the functional forms of various optimization models' (Gowdy 2005). Political discussions and arguments based on welfare economics, however, have not been successful in triggering significant change.

The Scientific Process

While the UN and other political units have been trying to find a political solution to the clash between environmental (or broadly defined, *ecosystem*) and *human* (socio-economic) systemic characteristics, scientists have been trying to provide the political process with rational (scientific) arguments to prove why lifestyle changes would be important or even necessary. Science tried to provide an *unbiased* set of arguments for the definition of SD.

The starting point of the scientific discourse is a *thermodynamic systems* approach. It considers the Earth a closed system, with limited openness in the energy exchange (as mentioned before), but basically with a finite set of resources: some of them may be renewable (most of the raw materials, some sorts of energy – wind, solar, hydro, geo-thermal, etc., sink capacity), some of them partially renewable, depending on depletion rates (soil, forests, wetlands, sink capacity) and some of them not (fossil fuels, some raw materials, primary forests, biodiversity). The Earth system is analyzed in the terms of natural capital consumption as a function of time. The depletion of non-renewable natural capitals is progressing in time, in an irreversible process. The depletion of renewable natural capitals is progressing in time in a reversible process up to threshold limits, and beyond the thresholds the depletion of renewable natural capital reaches a turning point beyond which the depletion becomes irreversible. The underlying argument is that we should *limit the consumption* rate of natural capital, either to a minimum level in the case of non-renewable capitals, or to a rate that is slower than the rate of renewal of renewable natural capitals. Unfortunately, science does not quantify the exact minimum levels or the adequately slow rates: this is the task of the political process and ultimately is related to requirements for change in lifestyles.

This approach to SD is frequently called an ecological interpretation of SD. Central to this view is the notion that economic and social systems are sub-systems of the so called human system which, in turn, is a sub-system of the global environment, called the ecosystem. It follows that sustainability in the economic and social sub-systems is subordinate to sustainability of the ecosystem (NRTEE 1995). Sustainability, according to the ecological interpretation, is the resilience of the system: its maintained dynamic capacity to respond adaptively to changes and disturbance.

The scientific analysis of SD is further complicated by the concept of *substitutability*. Substitution is a practical concept based on human invention and technological progress; it means that natural capital can be substituted by human-made capital.[5]

Strong and Weak Sustainability

The basic difference between two subsets of the thermodynamic approach is the way they admit substitution. *Strong sustainability* does not allow substitution of natural capital: it considers human-made capital as complementary to natural capital. *Weak sustainability* does allow the substitution of some forms of natural capital with human-made capital. The two approaches may complement each other in cases when limits to substitution are considered. Sustaining critical ecosystem factors – i.e. vital, life-support services – may evoke the strong interpretation of sustainability: the definition of thresholds beyond (below) which substation is not permitted. Actions designed to prevent transcending these thresholds will also rely on the precautionary principle. In the case of non-critical factors the definition of thresholds for substitution may not be relevant, and for practical consideration, the weak sustainability approach can be accepted.

The practical consequences of the two different approaches are enormous (Neumayer 1999). Strong sustainability demands immediate actions and requires severe limitations in our present lifestyles (predominantly in the developed world) and in our future aspirations (predominantly in the developing world and of future generations). Weak sustainability requires significantly less limitations, and even those limitations and changes can occur at a slow pace, some of them being compatible with the rate of renewal of certain natural capitals. An extreme version of weak sustainability asserts that scientific and technological progress will (ultimately) find solutions to all problems related to the depletion of natural capital.[6]

Whether we speak about the political or the scientific process that defines SD, the emphasis is put on characteristics that need to be sustained through choices of lifestyles, hence *value judgments* are involved in the definition: we consider certain characteristics more important, more valuable than others. Consequently, the debate is not only political, but *ideological*. In other terms, 'sustainable development is a social construct, referring to the long-term evolution of a hugely complex system – the human population and economy embedded within the ecosystems and biogeochemical flows of the planet' (Meadows 1998).

An alternative solution to lifestyle changes is offered by another interpretation of sustainability. It breaks out of the ecosystem–economic system controversy and asserts that there are *ultimate ends* for our existence that humanity should seek to realize (Daly 1990; Meadows 1998). These ends can be happiness, respect and spiritual fulfilment. Nature, its assets like biodiversity, life-support capacity, etc. are *ultimate means* necessary to achieve the ultimate ends. Human lifestyles and consumption patterns cannot compromise these ultimate means without making it impossible to achieve the ultimate ends. The consequence is that our lifestyle based on material need satisfaction should be changed in order to achieve sustainability. In this interpretation, sustainability gains a teleological meaning, representing a stage to be achieved, and it is not a shorthand any more for the (process-oriented) concept of SD.

III.   INTERPRETING SUSTAINABILITY IN THE CONTEXT OF TRANSITION

SD is – as is all development – a process, a series of changes that can be interpreted as a set of *transitions*. When the emphasis is put on the transition, the definition is focusing on *intrinsic* characteristics of the process of SD, hence the discussion is not necessarily about values, and the analysis will be less ideological. This can be seen in some works (Rotmans et al 2000) that are preoccupied with the equilibrium state to be reached by a transition, while others continue to have an ideological, value based starting point, but try to provide a more scientific analysis of the process (Parris 2003).

Rotmans defines transition to a sustainable society as 'a *social transformation process*' with the following characteristics: the transition is a structural change in society (or in complex sub-systems of society); it is a long-term process that covers at least one generation; it is large-scale technological, economic, ecological, social–cultural and institutional developments that influence and strengthen each other; and it means interactions between developments at different scale levels (Rotmans et al 2000).

In the context of sustainability, we may speak about multi-scale, multi-domain, multi-temporal transitions that include social (population and structural), economic (globalized markets) and technological (accelerated innovation in all fields of science and technology) transitions that take place from local to global levels with different speed and different future impacts. Multiple transitions divide the stages of transition as follows:

- pre-development phase (dynamic equilibrium with no visible change)
- take-off phase (ignition phase where shift begins)
- acceleration phase (visible structural changes take place)
- stabilization phase when new dynamic equilibrium is reached.

This categorization of the stages of transition is valid for all transitions, even if they are not related to SD – hence the value-neutral character of the approach. For the present analysis, the last stage is the most important, because the stabilization phase can be interpreted as reaching sustainability (with the limitation that this new dynamic equilibrium can also change and become the pre-development phase of a new transition). Linking sustainable development to transitions, and sustainability to a stabilization phase or a new dynamic equilibrium has a great innovative power to promote new types of learning and management practices (networking, interactive governance), thus influencing the methods of evaluation (Rotmans et al 2001). This concept of transition can be practically relevant only when the scientific insights describe the exact mechanism and the approximate time frame of the changes from one stage to another.

While transitions do happen without intentional interventions, human action in the form of social choices (such as government programmes and social goals) can provide an orientation to the transition and can postulate its desirable goals. That is the case when we speak about value based and ideological approaches to transition, as the new equilibrium is not defined in value-neutral terms of quasi-independent outcomes, but as an outcome required by a set of targets. A good example for this is the definition of the National Research Council (US) according to which SD is meeting the needs of a stabilizing future world population while reducing hunger and poverty and maintaining the planet's life-support systems (National Research Council 1999). It is important to note that the interpretation of SD as a transition clearly emphasizes the process character of SD, and here the usage of the term 'sustainability' indicates that it is a shorthand for SD, indeed.

IV. INTERPRETING SUSTAINABILITY IN THE CONTEXT OF ECONOMIC THEORY

In the thermodynamic interpretation of SD, the Earth system has been analysed in the terms of natural capital consumption as function of time. Natural capital has been measured in physical units. A strictly economic interpretation of SD has been elusive for quite a long time, because economists were unable to develop a consistent theory to measure natural, human and social capitals in monetary terms. This was one of the main reasons why mainstream economists have considered SD at worst an ideological, at best a political concept rather than a concept with scientific or economic relevance. The first major breakthrough was achieved during the last six years when, through a reform of neo-classical economics, using accounting prices (i.e. substitution prices), it was possible to put a monetary value on key capital stocks in nature, human welfare and human knowledge, similarly to how such monetary values are placed on manufactured or human-made capitals (capitals in the classical economic sense) (Arrow et al 2004). The core idea is quite simple: if we (humankind, a nation, a group of actors) are able to manage all those stocks so that they don't decline over time, we would achieve sustainability. If we are able to increase them, we will achieve SD.

This economic interpretation of SD allows substitutions within the different forms of capitals, and it calculates the actual cost of replacement using accounting prices called 'substitution prices' (or, as an alternative, so called 'shadow prices' – prices people would be willing to pay for goods without a price or with an undervalued price) that do not vary with changes in valuation by the market. The economic interpretation of SD has generated a new definition of wealth, called *inclusive wealth*. 'It is an attempt to measure the change in value over time of all the critical capital stocks in an economic system, at constant prices . . . Inclusive Wealth is "inclusive" for two reasons: one, because it tries to include everything that actually matters in economic development (which is a first, even for economics); and two, because it includes the interests of future generation' (AtKisson 2005).

V. INTERPRETING SUSTAINABILITY IN THE CONTEXT OF DEVELOPMENT PROGRAMMES

A much more limited interpretation of SD is offered when SD is discussed in the context of strategies and development programmes. These strategies and programmes set specific targets to be achieved within a realistic time frame.[7] International institutions, and national and local governments can all use this approach. An example is the World Bank, that defines sustainability as the effectiveness of institutional development (WB 2005). Sustainability is linked to planning and implementation that needs to be monitored and evaluated. Successful implementation of the strategy or the development programme yields sustainability (see also USAID 2004). In this context sustainability is applied to 'clusters' of national programmes or similar initiatives in a number of countries (e.g. OECD 2002).

Strategy and programme-based interpretation of sustainability is a *meso* (institutional) or *micro* (community) level issue: an aspect of development programmes or projects. These are attempts to combine concerns with the environment and socio-economic issues (Hopwood et al 2005). Linking sustainability to strategy and programme implementation has created an emerging trend to evaluate sustainability at several levels at once, as the strategies and programmes usually define many simultaneous goals (economic, environmental, social, institutional, cultural, etc.).

On a meso level, sustainability is interpreted as maintaining long-term functioning, efficiency and accessibility of resources, services, infrastructures, income generation and community cohesiveness (CIDA 2002). Another interpretation defines sustainability as a long-term process with many different elements, including financial and economic sustainability and institutional and individual sustainability (CIDA 1997). On the micro level, the definition is related primarily to local communities. According to a community programme, sustainable communities are those 'in which people wish to live and can prosper' (University of Dundee 1997). There are numerous community programmes that frequently use the term 'sustainability' as the equivalent of sustaining the present lifestyle, community structure, traditions and physical environment for indefinite time, and it may be difficult to differentiate between conservation and sustainability.

VI.   LINKING EVALUATION TO SUSTAINABILITY[8]

'Evaluation is an organizational process that determines as systematically and as objectively as possible the relevance, sustainability, efficiency, effectiveness and impact of the organization's activities in relation to the objectives' (UNEP 2005). According to such a definition, evaluation measures results in the light of needs and objectives. It enables management to determine if needs are being met and objectives achieved. Evaluation provides management with empirical data on achievement or lack of it. Evaluation provides managers with evidence of whether activities are creating impact. The evaluation answers questions like, 'is the environment better and better managed as a result of our activities?' (UNEP op. cit.).

According to most practitioners, evaluation will provide clear answers to questions about change and sustainability, change in the environment, economy, society, etc. This is an *optimistic assumption* because they assume that evaluation will help explain how decisions and decision outcomes are linked. The corollary is that the right evaluation system will result in better decisions. This, however, is rarely the case. In reality, evaluation does not readily and automatically lead to changes in policy-making. Yet it does serve a useful purpose in the discourse on SD: it helps assimilate and better understand stakeholders' views, helps guide and make policy decisions, and helps make the process of governance more transparent. This is what we may consider a *realistic expectation*.

SD is a relatively new social goal, which has to become part of the mainstream of political and economic debate. Societies measure what they care about, and measures of SD contribute to the acceptance and legitimization of an important social goal. Evaluation as a measurement practice helps decision makers and the public to define a social goal, to link it to clear objectives and targets, and to assess progress toward meeting those targets. It provides an empirical and quantitative basis for evaluating performance and connecting past and present activities to the attainment of that future goal. Evaluating SD – just as we currently evaluate economic production – makes it possible for this complex social goal to become part of the mainstream of political and economic debate.

Linking sustainability and evaluation means to consider sustainability as a measurable target. 'Once sustainability is identified as an objective or a targeted result, it then becomes a criterion for measuring success. How this should be done, however, remains largely unclear' (CIDA 2002). This opaqueness has several reasons. First of all, targets are relative and grossly different. No standardized set of sustainability targets exists, and there is a long standing debate about both goals/targets and means by which they can be achieved. The most we can agree on is a set of requirements and guiding principles for sustainability evaluation.

Guiding Principles for Sustainability Evaluation

The most comprehensive set of guiding principles that may apply to all assessment efforts to assess SD is the Bellagio Principles for Assessment (Hardi and Zdan 1997). Such principles are a pragmatic expression of the most important notions that define the evaluation of SD. They serve as practical guidelines for the whole of the assessment process from system design and identification of evaluation tools such as indicators, from field measurement to compilation, to interpretation and communication of the result. They offer a framework that is able to link the evaluation process to the key characteristics of SD, so they should be applied as a complete set.

The Bellagio Principles link the evaluation process to SD in four areas:

1. The starting point of any assessment is to establish *clear goals* of SD that provide a practical definition in terms that are meaningful for the decision-making unit in question.
2. The content of assessment needs to merge a frame of the overall system with a *practical focus* on current priority issues.
3. Assessment as a *process* must be transparent, open for public participation and able to communicate the results to a wide audience.
4. Evaluation needs to be an ongoing process that requires a *continuing capacity* for evaluation and related institutional arrangements.

These principles are intended for use in starting and improving evaluation activities of community groups, non-government organizations, corporations, national governments and international institutions.

What to evaluate?

We have the guiding principles how to evaluate SD, but we still need to answer the question, 'What exactly to evaluate?'. The answer will depend on the actual interpretation of SD under consideration.

What do we evaluate in the case of lifestyle changes?

The Brundtland definition of SD is so vague that it cannot offer a framework within which evaluation could take place; we cannot evaluate progress toward (or away from) it. If the emphasis is on the political process, we should evaluate the success of decision makers in bringing the required changes about. That, in turn, requires a clarification of the changes. We need to agree first on the meaning of required changes. Is it the regulation of population growth? Is it a major shift in lifestyles such as consumption? Is it transportation or another dimension of our prevailing lifestyle? Is it the realization of better equity in society, between societies, between present and future? The general question of what to evaluate would be decomposed to many specific, concrete questions, almost all of them related to certain policy issues and collective as well as individual choices.

We will have a very similar outcome when we try to answer the 'what evaluate' question based on the thermodynamic systems interpretation of SD. We can evaluate the depletion rate of critical natural capital, the renewal rate of critical renewable resources, the rate of increase in human/social demands on these resources; we may try to determine the distance where we presently are in the consumption/depletion of these resources compared to critical threshold values. Based on the more science-oriented approach, the results of the evaluations will be more matter-of-fact in their character, leaving the choices and the decisions to the political processes.

A note is necessary here on the potential evaluation of strong and weak sustainability. Here again, the evaluation can focus on depletion rates and thresholds, plus the types and amount of substitutes. Strong sustainability is a very restrictive concept: in most cases it does not leave room for improvement, reforms and slow changes. The evaluation will frequently send the message, we must stop present practices. If, however, thresholds for vital ecosystem factors are established, even the evaluation of strong sustainability will provide practical information to decision makers. Take the example of the ecosystem approach to biodiversity conservation: for critical factors, the principle of no net loss is adopted, and decision makers have to achieve it. Weak sustainability offers many opportunities to evaluate achievements; a special area of evaluation could be the types and utility function of substitutes.

We encounter a different problem when we try to evaluate the sustainability of our lifestyle from the ultimate ends perspective. Issues such as happiness, satisfaction, fulfilment, etc. are much less tangible than material assets, and an objective, not to mention quantitative, evaluation of them is impossible. Instead, we may rely on the evaluation of the status of ultimate means, a process that may be quite similar to the one just described as the evaluation of SD within the thermodynamic systems approach.

What do we evaluate in the case of transitions?

Are we better off when we try to provide answers to the 'what evaluate' question in the context of transitions? If we follow the logic of the discussion in the first part of this chapter, we have to focus the evaluation on the outcome of the transition, i.e. the stabilization phase. Again, we will evaluate the social and political choices that facilitate the transition to the stabilized, new equilibrium. Will these choices differ from the ones we can evaluate in relationship to lifestyle changes? Most likely they will not, so concerning evaluation itself, the two approaches to the definition of sustainability do not yield significant differences in evaluation. The interpretation of SD as a transition in the context of implementing national SD strategies or strategic plans may become a rather restricted exercise, limiting the scope of the evaluation to the players and institutions of the policy process. One can evaluate how successful these actors are in meeting the goals set for themselves (e.g. whether ministries implement their own plans), without getting information on whether these goals or institutional strategic plans have any impact and bring about real changes in society. Interesting examples for such evaluation are the periodic reports published by the Commissioner of the Environment and Sustainable Development in Canada, a watchdog establishment within the Office of the Auditor General. The commissioner provides parliamentarians with independent performance analysis of and recommendations on the federal government's efforts to protect the environment and foster sustainable development, without evaluating the impacts of these efforts (for the latest report see, Commissioner 2005).

How about evaluating the transition as a process to achieve set targets? Obviously this offers the most practical framework for an evaluator. Performance would be evaluated against set targets, and policy impacts on population stabilization, hunger reduction, etc. are subject to quantitative measures as well as outcome and impact evaluation. Such a task is not much different from the ones that development programmes create for evaluation.

What do we evaluate in the case of economic interpretation?

The economic interpretation tries to make the valuation of the subject matter of SD more specific. It also starts from the concept of social welfare (in an intertemporal sense) by measuring a society's total asset base, but steps beyond the general statement the Brundtland definition implies, namely that social welfare should not decline over time. Inclusive wealth evaluates consumption levels as well as investments in capitals and whether the investments in several forms of capitals (e.g. in human and manufactured capitals) offset the depletion of other types of capitals (e.g. natural capital), doing all the evaluations in accounting terms and using monetary values (including so called substitution and/or shadow prices). The actual evaluations are refined by the inclusion of the impacts of population and technological changes. In other terms, evaluation of the changes in inclusive wealth allows for substitutability between individual assets over time, while at the same time incorporating adjustments for risk when critical thresholds maintaining a capital stock (e.g. ecological thresholds) are reached (CSIRO 2004).

What do we evaluate in the case of development programmes?

Where the task is to evaluate a meso- or micro-level programme, the declared intention usually is to evaluate outputs and outcomes against (well) defined strategies and programme goals. In these cases the framework and the boundaries of the evaluation are properly set, and the evaluation process becomes a sequence of technical issues. These may not differ much from programme to programme, because the evaluation will focus on the relationship between outputs/outcomes and strategies/goals, and it will be less independent on the character of the strategies and goals. Frequently, however, the evaluation becomes more limited in scope and focuses on the effectiveness and the efficiency of resource use in achieving the set targets. This is particularly clear in the case of evaluating the success of development programmes financed by major lender or grantor organizations, such as development banks.

VII. CONCLUSIONS

Evaluation is useful for decision makers particularly because it helps in understanding what SD means in operational terms. In this sense, evaluation is an *explanatory tool*, translating the concepts of SD into practical terms. It creates linkages between everyday activities and SD and provides a sense of direction for decision makers when they choose among policy alternatives; it is also a *planning tool*, connecting past and present activities to future goals. Evaluation helps decide the degree to which efforts are successful in meeting SD goals and objectives. In this sense, it is a *performance assessment tool*. Yet, it does not mean that we can agree on a common interpretation, let alone a definition of SD. The relevant questions are whether a common interpretation of SD is needed for evaluations, and whether such an interpretation is feasible. The variety of interpretations appears to signal that there is conceptual uncertainty with regard to the specific elements of sustainability and their connections. It also appears to signal that different interpretations appear to resonate with different regions, organizations or cultures. Evaluators need to take these differences into account and adjust their techniques according to the particular circumstances of the strategies, programmes and outcomes they need to evaluate. When strategies and programmes are explicitly stated, the framework and boundaries of evaluation are also well defined. When these boundaries are missing, and the evaluation process needs to define them, the task will be formidable. We have a long and winding road ahead of us to arrive at a broad acceptance of sustainability evaluation principles, and it is expected that even if a common foundation emerged, details of evaluation design and choice of tools would vary in any given application.

NOTES

1. There is always more than one way to group SD definitions, see several recent reviews by Faber et al 2005, Hardi 2001, Hopwood et al 2005, OECD 2000. The present grouping reflects the difference in broadness of the interpretations.
2. The issue whether the term 'sustainability' is only a shorthand for SD or has a different meaning will be discussed later.

3. We do not even know whether change itself is sustained indefinitely, as we do not have at hand the universal laws that determine change.
4. Some analysts apply the term 'absolute' sustainability to characterize macro-level interpretations of sustainable development, see Faber et al 2005.
5. Here we will not discuss the limitations arising from the fact that the production of human-made capital as substitute to natural capital is also dependent on some sorts of primary and non-renewable natural capital.
6. The most extreme interpretation would require a redefinition of our living space (Earth) as a closed system and would permit humans to leave Earth and create extra-terrestrial living space.
7. Using a different terminology, these strategies and programmes use a 'relative' definition of sustainability: We do not have to know what is 'absolute' sustainability, it is enough to compare different stages in the development process and assess them in relation to their progress towards the set goals. (Faber, op. cit.)
8. Here I will restrict the interpretation of evaluation to basics in order to make the link to sustainability understandable.

REFERENCES

Arrow, Kenneth J et al (2004), 'Are we consuming too much?', *Journal of Economic Perspectives*, 18(3), 147–72.

AtKisson, Alan (2005), 'Introducing "Inclusive Wealth": a new economic measure of sustainability', *Worldchanging*, 30 June 2005, http://www.worldchanging.com/archives/003004.html.

Brundtland, G H (1987), *Our Common Future*. Report of the UN Commission on Environment and Development, Oxford, Oxford University Press.

CIDA (1997), *Aga Khan Rural Development Programme Phase III (Pakistan)*, http://www.acdi-cida.gc.ca/cida_ind.nsf/0/49341db48f52ab8a85256cb90069f7b6?OpenDocument#toc (last update in 2003).

CIDA (2002), *Assessing Sustainability: What We're Learning About*, Ottawa, Canada, Canadian International Development Agency, Performance Review Branch Report No. 2.

Commissioner (2005), *Report of the Commissioner of the Environment and Sustainable Development*, Ottawa, Canada, Office of the Auditor General, also on-line, http://www.oag-bvg.gc.ca/domino/reports.nsf/html/c2005menu_e.html.

CSD (1992), *Report of the United Nations Conference on Environment and Development*, Rio de Janeiro, United Nations Commission on Sustainable Development, vol. 1–3.

CSIRO (2004), *Measuring and Modelling Sustainable Development in Australia using Inclusive Wealth*, Australian Commonwealth Scientific and Research Organization (CSIRO), Project Description, http://www.csiro.au/proprietary Documents/MMSDProjectDescription.pdf.

Daly, Herman (1990), 'Toward some operational principles of sustainable development', *Ecological Economics*, 2(1), 1–6.

Faber, Niels, Jorna, Rene and van Engelen, Jo (2005), 'The sustainability of "sustainability" – a study into the conceptual foundations of the notion of "sustainability"', *Environmental Assessment Policy and Management*, 7(1), 1–33.

Gowdy, John (2005), 'Toward a new welfare economics for sustainability', *Ecological Economics*, 53(2), 211–22.

Hardi, P and Zdan, T (eds) (1997), *Assessing Sustainable Development: Principles in Practice*, Winnipeg, Canada, IISD.

Hardi, Peter (2001), 'Trendsetters, followers and skeptics: the state of sustainable development indicators: a review essay', *Journal of Industrial Ecology*, 4(4), 149–61.

Hopwood, Bill, Mellor, Mary and O'Brien, Geoff (2005), 'Sustainable development: mapping different approaches', *Sustainable Development*, 13, 38–52.

MDG (2000), *United Nations Millennium Declaration*, New York, UN General Assembly.

Meadows, D (1998), *Indicators and Information Systems for Sustainable Development*, Four Corners, VT, The Sustainability Institute, http://sustainer.org/ pubs/Indicators&Information.pdf.

National Research Council (US National Academy of Sciences) (1999), *Our Common Journey: A Transition Toward Sustainability*, Washington DC, National Academy Press.

Neumayer, E (1999), *Weak vs. Strong Sustainability: Exploring the Limits of Two Opposing Paradigms*, Cheltenham, Edward Elgar (particularly Chapter 5 'Can sustainability be measured?', pp. 140–205).

NRTEE (1995), Hodge, T, Holtz, S, Smith, C and Hawke Baker, K (eds), *Pathways to Sustainability: Assessing Our Progress*, Ottawa, Canada, National Round Table on the Environment and the Economy.

OECD (2000), *Frameworks to Measure Sustainable Development: OECD Initiative on Sustainable Development*. OECD Expert Workshop, Paris, OECD.

OECD (2002), *Working Together Towards Sustainable Development: The OECD Experience*, Paris, OECD.

Parris, Thomas M and Kates, Robert W (2003), 'Characterizing a sustainability transition: goals, targets, trends, and driving forces', *PNAS*, 100(14), 8068–73.

Rotmans, J, Kemp, René and van Asselt, Marjolein (2001), 'More evolution than evolution: transition management in public policy', *Foresight*, 3(1).

Rotmans, Jan, Kemp, René, van Asselt, Marjolein, Geels, Frank, Verbong, Geert and Molendijk, Kirsten (2000), *Transitions and Transition Management*, Maastricht, ICIS, University of Maastricht (in Dutch: only summary is available in English).

UNEP (2005), *What is Evaluation?*, http://www.unep.org/eou/Evaluation/intro.asp.

University of Dundee (1997), *Dundee Partnership Community Regeneration Strategy: SIP Monitoring and Evaluation Manual*, Dundee, University of Dundee, http://www.trp.dundee.ac.uk/research/geddes/monitor/plan.htm.

USAID (2004), *FY 2004 Performance and Accountability Report*, Washington DC, US Agency for International Development, http://www.usaid.gov/policy/par 04/.

World Bank (2004), *Influential Evaluations*, Washington DC, World Bank Operations Evaluation Department, http://www.worldbank.org/oed/ecd/.

World Bank (2005), *Improving the World Bank's Development Effectiveness: What Does Evaluation Show?*, Washington DC, The World Bank Operations Evaluation Department.

3. Evaluation for sustainable development: the Rio model of governance

Martin Jänicke

I. INTRODUCTION

Evaluation – both ex post and ex ante – is part of the Rio model of governance, which emerged from the UN Earth Summit of 1992. This chapter provides a general overview of the Rio governance model that stands behind the strategic concept of sustainable development (SD) and of its implications for evaluation. This model of environmental governance has been remarkably successful as a knowledge-based model of steering – not based on power and legal obligation. However, it urgently needs further improvements, and the chapter makes a number of suggestions as to how the Rio model of governance may be strengthened, and discusses the role of evaluation in this undertaking. In particular, it looks at whether evaluation should use only a top-down perspective – the implementation of Agenda 21 or of national SD strategies – or should also adopt a bottom-up perspective relying on forces that are independent from, but supportive to, the strategy of SD (e.g. high energy prices or changing WTO rules).

II. THE EXPLOSION OF COMPLEXITY

The Agenda 21 (or Rio) model of multi-level, multi-sectoral and multi-stakeholder governance is important because it is the only governance model that takes into account the extremely high complexity of the field of action. There has been an 'explosion' of complexity in the configuration of actors of environmental governance since the early 1970s. Originally, the actor constellation of environmental policy was rather simple (Figure 3.1): government regulated (or at least tried to regulate) the environmental behaviour of polluters through one-sided action (command and control). While there may have occasionally been some pressure from NGOs or the media or bilateral

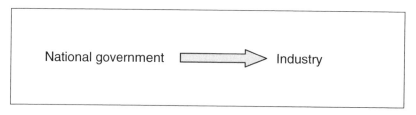

Figure 3.1   Original actor constellation of environmental policy

forms of co-operation between government and the target group, the actor constellation remained fairly simple compared with today. Now there is a new policy approach: instead of focusing on prescriptions regarding the environmental media – often limited to end-of-pipe treatment – environmental policy increasingly aims to internalize the solution of environmental problems into the polluting sectors. This is the core idea of 'ecological modernisation' (Jänicke 1985; Mol 2001). The polluting sectors have the best information about both the problems they cause and the innovation potential they have. But they themselves, as well as environmental policy, are part of a highly complex actor constellation that is being influenced from different levels – whether national, local or global. Also, civil society actors – NGOs, science organizations, the media – have increased the complexity of the actor constellation. They are not only local players but also influential at different levels. In addition, they do not only interact with government actors but often establish a direct relationship with the business community that takes the form of both criticism and cooperation (Figure 3.2).

The 'Rio model' of environmental governance can be seen as an answer to this increasingly complex constellation of actors. It is explicitly characterized by:

- long-term goals, time frames, monitoring and assessment (management by objectives)
- integration/sectoral strategies
- participation of stakeholders
- cooperation, activated self-regulation
- multi-level coordination.

The 'Agenda 21' (UNCED 1992) is the basic official document, and describes not only the main objectives of SD but also the main steering principles. The 'Rio process' of implementing Agenda 21 forms a body of rich experience that is a valuable resource for further strategic learning on how to change the behaviour of actors under the described conditions of complexity.

DIMENSIONS OF ENVIRONMENTAL GOVERNANCE

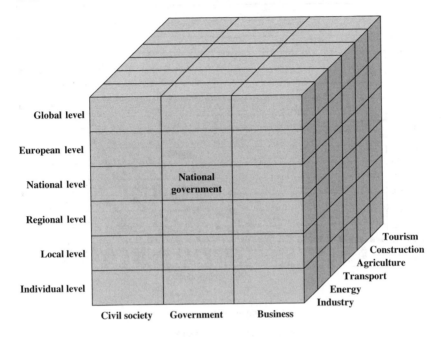

Global level

European level

National level — National government

Regional level

Local level — Tourism / Construction / Agriculture / Transport

Individual level — Energy / Industry

Civil society   Government   Business

Source: Jänicke (2003).

Figure 3.2   Dimensions of modern environmental governance

III.   ACHIEVEMENTS OF THE 'RIO MODEL'

The governance model of Agenda 21 and the subsequent 'Rio process' have achieved a certain degree of success. SD strategies now exist in most of the world's countries. In 2002, at least 6,400 local Agenda 21 processes in 113 countries had been initiated (OECD/UNDP 2002). There has also been a rapid diffusion of environmental policy innovations throughout the world since 1992 (see Figure 3.3). More than 100 environmental ministries have been established. Environmental NGOs have been strengthened at all policy levels. Some 'greening' of sectoral policies (e.g. energy) has taken place. In the European Community, institutional innovations have integrated environmental considerations into the general policy process. Broad environmental policy learning can be observed in companies, institutions and organizations. Some 90,500 companies world-wide have certified according to the ISO 14001 scheme, with an increase of 37% in 2004 (*Environment Daily*, 27 Oct. 2005). The knowledge base and the motivation

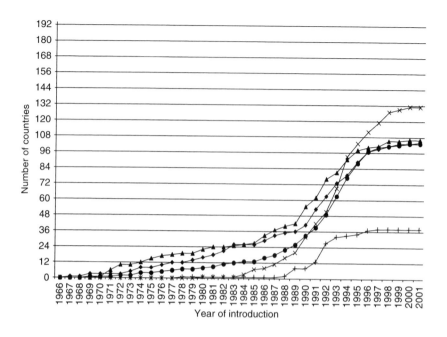

Source: Busch and Jörgens (2005).

*Figure 3.3   The global diffusion of environmental policy innovations: the
              example of five policy innovations*

of decentral actors have been strengthened. Multi-level environmental
governance has been significantly improved, especially within the EU.

IV. CRITICAL ISSUES OF THE 'RIO MODEL' OF GOVERNANCE

There are however, a number of critical issues related to the 'Rio model' of
governance that need to be evaluated too. The following shall be mentioned:

As the Rio Model is Essentially Knowledge-based, the Challenge is How to Deal With Power-based Resistance.

The 'Rio model' of governance has been successful not as a power-based mode of steering but as a knowledge-based strategy focusing on innovation and policy learning. The Rio model of governance is essentially a *voluntary* process of policy innovation, lesson-drawing and policy diffusion (Busch et al 2005). The most important implication was that small innovative countries like the Netherlands, Sweden or Denmark, rather than powerful countries like the US, have dominated the process. Never before have small countries played such an important role in the development of global policy (Jänicke 2005). However, a purely knowledge-based approach has also a number of weaknesses. Lack of clear responsibilities, for example, is a problem of an essentially voluntary mode of governance. Similarly, knowledge-based approaches often lack the institutional strength to guarantee successful implementation. The main challenge, however, is to effectively deal with powerful resistance.

The knowledge-based mode of governance has often been able to successfully compete with the power-based approach. Nonetheless, it has also been restricted by power constellations: national governments and powerful industries have often resisted knowledge-induced change, especially in cases where vested sectoral interests were affected. Power has always the privilege to ignore and *not* to learn (Deutsch 1963). Powerful actors *can* be highly innovative and ready to learn. But the pressure to do so is lower compared with actors that do not have much power at their disposal. Here, the lesson from evaluation may be to consider possible options of overcoming resistance by countervailing pressure for sustainable policy objectives.

Multi-level governance can provide several opportunities to exert pressure (to learn) against resistant polluters. The Brent Spar conflict has been a prominent example for a certain kind of pressure. But there are many other possibilities. Powerful actors may act as veto-players but they also act under different pressures for innovation. The pressure for environment-friendly innovation can be caused by a large variety of different factors that include price explosions, new technologies or new headlines. In the highly complex actor constellation of global environmental governance, this pressure can be exerted from below, or from above, or from different sides. It can originate from competitors as well as from pioneer countries setting regulatory trends (see Figure 3.2). Horizontal *pressure by political* and/or *technological competition* is especially interesting in this context. This is the mechanism where even powerful veto-players like the US government are in a weaker position.

There is a Need to Reinvent *Government* in the Context of *Governance* for SD.

Cooperative and self-regulatory approaches are indispensable especially if the solution of problems is to be internalized into the responsible sectors. But this mode of steering often needs the final responsibility, guarantee and capacity of governments, for the following reasons:

- First, elected constitutional governments have a higher institutional responsibility. Unlike private actors, they are not free to ignore the problem.
- Second, regulatory and legal approaches still dominate at least in environmental policy (RIVM 2004). And so far they have proven comparatively effective. They need however, more flexibility and goal orientation and should therefore be complemented by economic instruments.
- Third, there is currently much innovation in government intervention – innovation that consists mainly of new instruments combining regulation with high flexibility. While emission trading combines hard administrative caps with flexible responses, the Japanese 'top-runner' approach takes existing best practice of energy efficiency of 18 products as a basis for future standards. Obligatory feed-in tariffs for power from renewable energy are another example of this kind of flexible regulation.

There is a Need to Reinvent the Nation State in the Context of Multi-level Governance.

Compared with other actors, the nation state (at least the OECD-type) is best equipped to take the *final responsibility* within the complex structure of global multi-level governance, for the following reasons:

- First, it has the highest political visibility and, as a rule, it is the first redress in case of crises.
- Second, the media and public opinion are strongest at the national level. It is therefore at the national level where the pressure for political legitimation is highest.
- Third, the manpower of the nation state is high compared with the staff of international regimes.
- Fourth, the professional competence of the administration being comparably high, government administrations play an important role in international expert networks.

- Fifth, the national monopoly of coercion is still a very important political resource.
- Sixth, national regulatory innovation and its diffusion is an important determinant of global markets: policy-dependent national lead markets play an important role in the ecological modernization of global markets and international competition, not least the competition in markets for eco-efficient technologies (Jacob et al 2005).
- Finally, globalization has created a policy arena for pioneer countries (Jänicke 2005). Germany, the UK, Japan, Finland and Sweden claim to be 'pioneers' in environmental policy. This type of political competition and 'benchmarking' is a by-product of the Rio process.

Capacity Needs Assessment: Ambitious Strategies Need Adequate Capacities.

'Capacity' can be defined by the limit of possible action within a given political, economic and informational opportunity structure. Lack of institutional authority and manpower, and lack of knowledge or economic and technological resources have been the norm in the Rio process. There seems to be a contradiction between the ambitious objectives of sustainability and the general acknowledged objective of 'lean' government. However, capacity building (more manpower, larger institutions, more knowledge) is not the only possible answer to this challenge. There are also the possible options of:

- demand reduction: prioritization and focus on the main unsolved problems rather than holistic mega strategies;
- capacity saving strategies, e.g. through Internet consultations instead of real (physical) participation, or negotiation under the threat of regulation ('in the shadow of hierarchy');
- policy termination: more causal solutions, or where problems sometimes can be solved permanently, saving the capacity for other objectives.

A capacity-needs assessment should therefore be the first step of any strategy.

The Environmental Dimension of SD Should not be Restricted by the Three Pillar Approach.

The 'environmental dimension' – together with development – has originally been the most important dimension of SD. The triple bottom line has been invented after the Rio summit. The environmental dimension has its own goals, problems and interests, alongside those of the economic and social pillars. It has its own specific support structure (NGOs, etc.). The 'three pillar approach' as such has no societal support base. The environmental dimension as well as its economic counterpart needs its own expertise and specialization (holistic approaches that are too general create the danger of amateurism). It is weakest if there is conditionality between the three dimensions. The antagonisms between the three pillars are a reality and need pro-active, open conflict resolution by competent proponents in an inclusive network. The tendency of 'negative coordination' inherent in the three pillar approach (environment policy introduced only if economic or social interests are not negatively affected) should be overcome. Only positive coordination makes sense (win-win, search for synergies). Therefore, a minimum of autonomy and specialization of the environmental dimension is necessary.

NSD strategies Should be Both Problem-orientated and Innovation-oriented.

The Rio model of governance incorporates National Sustainable Development Strategies (NSDSs) as a key requirement of Agenda 21. However, it is necessary to note the main weaknesses and strengths of existing NSDSs. Only 12 percent of a total of 191 countries have strategies that are now being implemented. Another 24 percent have strategy documents that have been approved by governments (OECD 2005). There is a consensus among experts that lack of political leadership as well as insufficient institutionalization, capacity building, policy integration, target setting and monitoring is a generally observed weakness of national SD strategies (OECD/UNDP 2002). These factors help explain the low degree of effective implementation. The aforementioned restrictive and often confusing understanding of the 'three pillar approach' of SD may be added as a further explanation.

One further weakness of NSDSs, which has so far not been addressed, can be added. There is often a lack of problem-orientation on the one hand, and innovation-orientation on the other hand. Many NSDSs give too many answers without asking the right questions. And the answers often underestimate the market potential of innovative solutions. The environmental dimension is generally discussed with a focus on measures, i.e. on instruments, projects and best practice. The most urgent environmental problems, which should be at the core of such strategies, are often forgotten or substituted by 'visions' of all kinds. The initial step, therefore, should be a diagnosis of the most important unsolved problems. For example, if higher energy taxes or other additional costs are proposed, the underlying problems should be communicated to and accepted by those who are due to pay. In terms of the 'multiple-stream' theory (Zahariadis 1999), the *policy stream* of NSDS proposals should converge not only with the *political stream* (of political opportunities) but also with the *problem stream,* which has its own expertise and actor constellation.

The counter argument is that too much focus on problems ('alarmism') will deter the public. This, indeed, may also be true, even if we concede that political mobilization is an essentially problem-oriented process. The solution may be to 'balance' the bad news by good news about possible options and best practice. For instance, the general public must be familiar with the prognosis of climate change and the probable damage effects. But it will tend to suppress the bad news if there is no positive perspective of innovation (new markets for renewables, reduced costs by higher energy efficiency, etc.). The problem-oriented approach, therefore, should be systematically connected with an innovation-oriented perspective of eco-efficiency and ecological modernization (Jänicke 1985; Mol 2001).

This is a normative proposal but it is based on comparative evaluation. The most successful NSDSs are those that rely strongly on innovation. This is exactly the kind of solution that has been adopted by countries claiming to be pioneers in environmental policy – Sweden, Finland, Germany, the UK, the Netherlands, Japan and South Korea. The first steps to integrate the concept of eco-efficiency into the EU Lisbon strategy may also be mentioned in this context. The EU spring summit has explicitly declared that 'the development of eco-innovation and eco-technology as well as the sustainable management of natural resources' should be part of the EU strategy for growth and employment (European Council 2005: 5).

Marketable environmental innovations are characterized by two facts. They relate to global environmental needs and consequently to potential global markets. And they can lead to economic advantages like reduced costs (including the costs of environmental protection) through more sustainable low-impact technologies. This may be the most important explanation for the fact that national environmental policy (contrary to other policies) has not suffered so much from a regulatory downward competition ('race to the bottom'). On the contrary, the environmental issue has to a certain degree become a dimension of the competition for innovation between the highly developed countries. There is a high correlation between a stricter environmental policy and the competitiveness of a country (Jänicke 2005).

IV.   EX ANTE AND EX POST EVALUATION

Evaluation is an essential part of the Rio model of governance. It follows
the soft, knowledge-based mode of steering. Evaluation can take place
ex post and ex ante assessment (see Figure 3.4). There is also a distinction
to be made between the evaluation of policy outcomes and the policy
processes. Last but not least, ex post evaluation can be 'top down', starting
with the programme, and 'bottom up' (explaining the effects).

   Evaluation appears to be a primarily normative undertaking. But strictly
speaking, it is analytical work using generally accepted norms. The most
general criteria for policy outcomes are (with some connections regarding
the 'three pillars'):

- effectiveness, the achievement of objectives, measured improvements
- efficiency (the 'economic dimension'): adequate costs, but also win-
  win solutions
- equity, distributional justice (the 'social dimension') and – related –
  social acceptance.

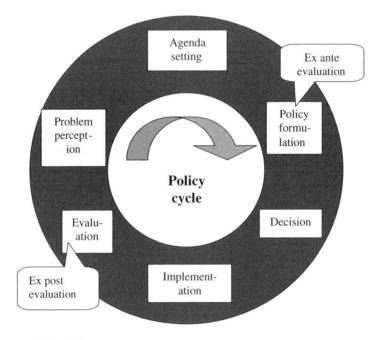

Source: Jänicke 2005.

Figure 3.4   Ex post and ex ante evaluation

While ex post evaluation, following the implementation phase of the 'policy cycle', has a very long tradition, there is also much evidence of ex ante assessment: the evaluation of the legal and constitutional implications of proposed laws, for instance, is a routine procedure in many countries across the world. In addition, there has always been a general public debate and quasi-evaluation of legal proposals. Also, the assessment of budgetary requirements and cost–benefit analyses of proposed policies are already well known tools (Howlett/Ramesh 2003).

Environmental impact assessment of laws, plans and policies, however, is a more recent approach. Here, integrated impact assessment is the most ambitious but also the most difficult policy innovation in this field. Environmental impact assessment should, indeed, be (and often already is) part of the routine of ex ante assessment. But its impact depends on certain conditions. Again, some autonomy must be secured.

There are different outcomes depending on the approach underlying the evaluation. Top-down and bottom-up approaches make a difference. In the first case, the evaluation starts with the formulated programme and its objectives, e.g. with a national SD strategy and its targets. Here the main question is in how far and at what cost the objectives have been achieved. The *bottom-up* approach starts with real changes regardless of whether the policy was the main cause or other factors. For example, oil prices may sometimes be a more important influencing factor than the formulated clean air or climate policy. Similarly, an improvement can be primarily due to a structural change in the economy. The greening of agriculture, for example, may not primarily be the result of an environmental sector strategy or the EU Cardiff process but rather the outcome of new WTO rules on subsidies.

This is the reason why the evaluation of SD strategies is different if it starts bottom up with 'outcomes'. There are more causal factors than the strategy itself, and many positive outcomes cannot be explained with SD strategies alone, which sometimes play only a marginal role, not really being integrated into the policy mainstream. One may feel more comfortable with bottom-up evaluation because the results often are more positive. Taking the Kyoto Protocol as an example, a top-down perspective will show slow implementation and heavy resistance of several countries, whereas a bottom-up perspective will reveal the booming market of renewables, the rapid diffusion of energy-efficiency policies, etc. (Tews and Jänicke 2005). At the same time, however, a top-down evaluation of target outcomes may reveal that despite these successes, the concentration of greenhouse gases in the atmosphere continues to rise. Therefore, both perspectives are necessary.

Top-down analysis is indispensable because we want to know what the outcomes of a special regulation are. But the causal factors that produce improvements free of charge should not be ignored. This is important for a number of reasons. One reason is the fact that the causal constellation that has led to the Rio process and its strategy for SD remains a causal factor also in the process of implementation: the underlying environmental problems have their own dynamics and can create special policy windows. The case of climate protection is an example whereby the problems together with the market success of new technological solutions can have a stronger influence than the existing national strategy of SD.

The actor constellation influencing environmental improvements is much more complex than the actor constellation underlying an SD strategy, which is too often the sole activity of a specifically designated and institutionalized 'epistemic community'. Here, we have to consider the effects of policy learning under the conditions of exploding complexity as just mentioned. These are fundamental issues in strategic level evaluation, which is rarely sufficiently precise to be able to measure the extent to which each of many possible causes can be ascribed to an observed effect. In such circumstances, the ex post and top-down evaluation of any particular strategic intervention may not be sufficient for a full understanding of policy learning. We may instead require broader research into the validity of the theoretical foundations on which the full set of policies is based. The main aim of ex post evaluation remains to identify whether the desired outcomes are being achieved, and if not, whatever the specific causes, to identify appropriate corrective actions.

V. SUMMARY AND CONCLUSIONS

Global environmental governance is necessarily multi-actor, multi-sectoral and multi-level. The Rio model of governance has so far provided an adequate answer. It is the only model that takes the highly complex actor configuration into account. A reform could therefore remain essentially 'path-dependent'. However, a general evaluation of this ambitious strategic concept and its critical issues leads to the following policy proposals:

- The role of government in the context of cooperative governance should be recognized and strengthened.
- The nation state is indispensable and has regained importance in the context of multi-level governance.
- The restrictive understanding of the 'three pillar approach' to sustainable development tends to dwarf the environmental dimension and should be overcome: a certain autonomy of the environmental dimension seems indispensable.

- Ambitious SD strategies, their implementation and evaluation generally need to solve capacity problems. There are, however, more options than the increase of capacity (which often contradicts policies for lean government).
- Strategies of SD should be problem-oriented, but not 'alarmist'. Instead the long-term problems should be related to the existing potential of innovation and ecological modernization.
- The tool of bottom-up evaluation draws our attention to the fact that there are more possible causes of environmental improvements than the SD strategy itself. The evaluation may do no more than reveal the need for corrective action, while the goal of policy learning may necessitate a wider research programme.
- The actor constellation influencing the outcomes of the strategy is not restricted to the actors responsible for its implementation. Therefore any SD strategy should be rooted as far as possible in the real policies of the relevant actors which for many reasons may act under pressures for environment-related innovation. In the highly complex actor constellation of global environmental governance, this pressure can be exerted from below, or from above, or – horizontally – from different sides. It can originate from competitors as well as from regulatory trendsetters.

Consequently, these points, particularly the latter show that there is a high potential for progress towards global environmental governance if these challenges and opportunities are taken up and lead to better-designed policy solutions.

REFERENCES

Busch, P O and Jörgens, H (2005), 'International patterns of environmental policy change and convergence', *European Environment*, 15, 80–101.

Busch, P O, Jörgens, H and Tews, K (2005), 'The global diffusion of regulatory instruments: the making of a new international environmental regime', *The Annals of the American Academy of Political and Social Sciences*, vol. 598, 146–67.

Deutsch, K (1963), *The Nerves of Government*, New York, Free Press.

European Council (2005), *Presidency Conclusions*, 23 March.

Howlett, M and Ramesh, M (2003), *Studying Public Policy: Policy Cycles and Policy Subsystems*, 2nd edition, Oxford, Oxford University Press.

Jacob, K, Beise, M, Blazejczak, J, Edler, D, Haum, R, Jänicke, M, Löw, T, Petschow, U and Rennings, K (2005), *Lead Markets for Environmental Innovations*, Heidelberg, Physica-Verlag.

Jänicke, M (1985), *Preventive Environmental Policy as Ecological Modernisation and Structural Policy*, Berlin, Wissenschaftszentrum Berlin (IIUG dp 85-2).

Jänicke, M (2003), 'The ambivalence of environmental governance', in Meuleman, L, Niestroy, I, and Hey, C (eds), *Environmental Governance in Europe*, RMNO, Den Haag.

Jänicke, M (2005), 'Trend-setters in environmental policy: the character and role of pioneer countries', *European Environment*, 15, 129–42.

Mol, A P J (2001), *Globalization and Environmental Reform: The Ecological Modernization of the Global Economy*, Cambridge, MA, MIT Press.

OECD (2005), *National Strategies for Sustainable Development: Good Practices in OECD Countries*, Paris, OECD, SG/SD(2005)6.

OECD/UNDP (2002), *Sustainable Development Strategies – A Resource Book*, compiled by B Dallal-Clayton and S Bass, London and Sterling, VA: Earthscan.

RIVM (2004), *Outstanding Environmental Issues: A Review of the EU's Environmental Agenda*, Bilthoven, RIVM (National Institute for Public Health and the Environment).

Swanson, D, Pinter, L, Bregha, F, Volkery, A and Jacob, B (2004), *National Strategies for Sustainable Development*, Winnipeg, International Institute for Sustainable Development.

Tews, K and Jänicke, M (eds) (2005), *Die Diffusion Umweltpolitischer Innovationen im Internationalem System*, Wiesbaden, VS Verlag.

UNCED (1992), *Agenda 21*, United Nations Conference on Environment and Development, United Nations General Assembly, New York.

Zahariadis, N (1999), 'Ambiguity, time, and multiple Streams', in Sabatier, P A (ed.), *Theory of the Policy Process*, Oxford, Westview Press.

4. Evaluation of regional network governance: capacity building for steering sustainable development

Wolfgang Meyer and Sebastian Elbe

I. INTRODUCTION

When discussing concepts like 'region', 'governance' and 'sustainable development' their normative characters must be taken into account. Regarding 'regions', their borderlines are the product of social processes, and they cannot be defined objectively. Even if enclosed by visible geographical landmarks like mountains or rivers, a 'region' is primarily defined by political occupations, cultural traditions and the subjective perceptions of its inhabitants. Concerning 'governance', a 'region' relies on its function as an administrative unit of the (nation) state with specific constitutional rights, regulative duties, tax resources and public tasks to ensure the welfare of the territory. However, this does not necessarily mean that people governed by this entity feel they belong to a single community and legitimize its authorities.

As the main administrative units of regions in Germany – the nation state focus of this chapter – federal states ('Bundesländer') were formed after the Second World War, and only some correspond with traditional political units. While the borders of the 'Bundesländer' have remained more or less stable since then, state definitions of smaller regional units (cities, villages, communes, districts, departments, etc.) are almost continuously varying. These on-going dynamics of government bodies are enlarging the responsibility of single regional decision makers through incorporation ('Eingemeindungen'), as well as reducing it as shared authorities are fused (e.g. 'regionale Verbünde'). Not only in Germany and not limited to administration, definitions of regions are far from constant over time.

Nevertheless, the key documents of the UN Conference on Environment and Development in Rio de Janeiro 1992 gave especial emphasis to the importance of regions for 'sustainable development'. Accordingly, 'regional governance' should not be limited to state administration but also includes the regional civil society, 'Each local authority should enter into a dialogue with its citizens, local organizations and private enterprises and adopt "a local Agenda 21". Through consultation and consensus-building, local authorities would learn from citizens and from local, civic, community, business and industrial organizations and acquire the information needed for formulating the best strategies' (Agenda 21, 28.3). Thus, building *local policy networks* for the *horizontal integration* of all stakeholder groups for developing and executing regional sustainability strategies became a task for all of the world's regions.

The reason why regions were viewed as carriers of hope was also formulated in Agenda 21, 'Because so many of the problems and solutions being addressed by Agenda 21 have their roots in local activities, the participation and cooperation of local authorities will be a determining factor in fulfilling its objectives. Local authorities construct, operate and maintain economic, social and environmental infrastructure, oversee planning processes, establish local environmental policies and regulations, and assist in implementing national and sub-national environmental policies. As the level of governance closest to the people, they play a vital role in educating, mobilizing and responding to the public to promote sustainable development' (Agenda 21, 28.1). By 'thinking globally', regions are supposed to transfer 'sustainable development' into 'acting locally'. Hence, a *multi-level governance structure* for *vertical integration* from the global to the local level was intended to synchronize the development and execution of policy strategies.

Implicitly, Agenda 21 assumes the superiority of 'regional network governance' compared to existing forms of regional steering. New participatory approaches seem to be indispensable for 'good regional governance', which itself is needed for establishing 'sustainable development' on the local level. But what do we really know about the impacts of 'regional network governance'? Are 'stakeholder networks' in all circumstances able to assure durably 'good governance' in each region of the world – and for all issues? How can we evaluate institutions and the impacts of 'regional network governance' in giving local people the information they need to steer 'sustainable development'?

This chapter presents some policy network research that provides a first step towards answering these questions. First, the normative approach of 'good governance' is transferred into an operational definition which is able to guide evaluation research. Second, the results of evaluation studies in Germany are presented for summarizing the knowledge on impacts of network governance. Finally, we present some conclusions on evaluation, to help improve our knowledge on steering sustainable development at the regional level.

II. WHAT IS 'GOOD REGIONAL GOVERNANCE'?

'Governance' is one of the 'buzz-words' of the last decade. It is used – and often abused – in several different contexts and has a large variety of meanings. Even if the focus is only set on the political system, the meaning of 'governance' strongly depends on the topic of scientific interest or political practice (see Meyer and Elbe 2006 for examples). 'Regional governance' is also not employed homogenously and there is no consensus on what regional governance really is (for discussions about Germany, see Benz 2004; Bogumil and Holtkamp 2004; Fürst 2004). However, there is broad agreement that regions are becoming increasingly important for political decision-making – not just due to the Rio process. Regional networks including state and non-state actors are supplying – maybe even replacing – political executives and their bureaucratic administration by transferring these decisions into actions (cf. Lawrence 2004).

In this chapter, 'regional governance' is defined as the *institutionalized process of making and executing political decisions within a commonly agreed geographic territory that is not identical with a nation state*. This emphasizes three core elements of governance: *political institutions, decision-making* and the *execution of decisions* – and combines it with an open territorial definition. 'Region' does not necessarily mean a legally delimited, bureaucratic established and commonly agreed unit, and it is not clear whether the process of making and executing decisions is run within the legal political system, a more or less legitimized policy network including state and non-state actors or a single authority. Accordingly, the definition is able to incorporate a broad variety of political institutions and processes.

By putting the normative aspect of '*good*' governance into focus, the generally legitimated and commonly shared goal of a region – '*how it should be governed in theory*' – must be assessed. This basic principle of political rule is in many regions far from a broadly agreed consensus, and many conflicts between social groups are based on discussions of this crude question of social order. The vast majority of existing 'governance structures' is the result of competing interests, social conflicts and power relations, and not a consensual agreement of regional stakeholders.

Moreover, arguing about 'good' and 'bad' ways of governing a region is – and will be – the key issue in any debate between parties within a democratic political system. The formation of civil society is primarily a result of dissatisfaction with political steering, leading citizens towards collective action to improve the quality of governance (cf. Meyer 2006). Therefore, any consensual agreement on 'good governance' within a 'region' will be limited to general – constitutional – aspects and highly aggregated strategies.

Following this definition of 'regional governance', four normative questions have to be answered for constructing a concept of 'good' governance:

- What kind of *political institutions* are required to fulfil the commonly shared expectations for steering regional development in a legal, legitimized and effective way? Do we need the 'guiding hand' of only one strong political leader or should we have complex participative structures including all stakeholders within and outside the political system into decision-making?[1]
- How should the *process of political decision-making* be run on a regional level? Is it necessary to find a general consensus acceptable for all stakeholders or do we have to follow simply the pressure of external dynamics (initiated by global or national authorities, markets, collective behaviour or requirements of the ecological system), leaving regional stakeholders little opportunity to decide?
- How can regional political decisions translate into *effective collective action*? Are 'proper solutions' the natural outcome of 'good decisions' or do we need additional efforts accompanying implementation processes and observing the impacts reached by the measures used?
- Finally, how should the affected *territory* be defined? Do we need common and identical definitions of all stakeholders or is it possible to run regional governance with respect for different traditions, historical developments and various regional emphases of each actor involved in decision-making and collective regional action?

In general, any attempt to change *political institutions* implies dissatisfaction with the *impacts of existing institutions*, in political decision-making and the execution of these decisions. As mentioned by Hanf and O'Toole (1992: 166), 'modern governance is characterized by decision systems in which territorial and functional differentiation desegregate effective problem-solving capacity into a collection of sub-systems of actors with specialized tasks and limited competence and resources'. While decision-making seems to be much easier in small, homogenous groups (cf. Ohtsubo and Masuchi 2004), the execution of these decisions needs the support of an increasing number of heterogeneous (and sometimes opposing) interest groups. Due to the required assistance in collective action, these actors are able to hinder or even block the execution of decisions.

Therefore, the most important task of political institutions is the *horizontal integration of decision makers and executers*, bringing their interests to a functional balance. In contemporary political research it is broadly agreed that such a balance can only be reached in multi-actor partnerships, including state and non-state actors in *policy networks* (cf. Sørensen 2002; Pierre

2000; Marsh 1998; Rhodes 1997; Marin and Mayntz 1991). Moreover, a transfer of *decision-making competencies* from national to local level, bringing decisions back to those people who are affected by its impacts, seems the most promising solution to significantly improve acceptance. Consequently, the *vertical integration of deciders and executers* through *multi-level governance* structures and processes becomes an essential coordination duty for newly designed political institutions (cf. Hooghe and Marks 2001).

While there seems to be a consensus about the importance of horizontal and vertical social integration and the role of policy networks, the positions on how to realize it practically are quite contrary. The debate concentrates on the questions of who should be *involved in decision-making* and what kind of *decision rules* should be used. In general, emphasizing the *process of making decisions* implies believing in the impact of a decision on social change. Hence, thinking about governance always means to believe in human ability to influence our own social, ecological and economical environment. Even if there are serious constraints and restrictions framing decision-making, steering measures are supposed to be effective – at least in theory.

By focusing on decision processes, the *input side of governance* (what people are doing to govern) is the key element of analysis. The *output side* (whereto the governed system is moving) will be addressed as a more or less determined result of human action. This implies there is a relationship with action theories, particularly rational-choice approaches (cf. Wiesenthal 1987).[2] Following the key idea of rational-choice theory, every decision is a subjective selection of the best opportunity (due to rational calculation of pros and cons) compared with other (perceived) opportunities. While analyzing real decision situations, this assumption can be criticized for 'over-rationalizing' decision-making (and therefore simplifying the process) – especially if group decisions are in focus. Here, this assumption has been taken as an *idealistic intention* for actors involved in decision-making processes and it is not used for explaining the *outcome of decision-making*. From a normative position, finding the best solution should be the goal of decision makers – but this is not necessarily the interest of actors involved in real decision-making processes.

Probably the most important social aspect of 'good governance' is its aim to *balance individual and common interests* in an optimized way. This kind of perfect outcome, reaching common goals with respect to all interests of all stakeholders, is only possible under certain and rare circumstances ('win-win situations'). Nevertheless, the trial to optimize the balance between individual interests and collective goals should be a remarkable element of 'good governance'. Moreover, 'good governance' is assumed to be effective in finding new pathways towards the aspired direction, transferring 'good decisions' to *adequate problem solving* by political action. Within the context of regional governance, the 'problems to be solved' are assumed to be commonly shared and perceived efforts of people living in the defined territory. These problems obviously distinguish them from people living in other regions (giving them social identity) and should be the driving force for building up a common governance structure.

To synthesize these normative assumptions, 'good regional governance' – and therefore the key criteria for evaluating regional governance – can be defined as followed:

> 'Good regional governance' is the durable implementation of social institutions including all stakeholders of a pre-given territory in a common decision-making process to assure rational decisions for those opportunities that are: (a) optimizing common goal-attainment (b) minimizing negative side-effects (c) perfectly reflecting all stakeholder interests, and (d) implementable in the most effective and efficient way.

This definition of 'good regional governance' postulates the existence of multi-actor networks. These lead us to another very important differentiation of governance. While concentrating on the *impacts of decisions for the region*, the successful steering process for achieving common goals by networks of regional partners is in the focus of interest (*governance through networks*). The main question is how far a regional partnership of governmental and non-governmental organizations is able to develop and to implement commonly shared policy strategies that are both innovative and effective. Assuming regional policy networks are *durable implemented institutions* for political steering and not only short-term measures with the limited task of strategy development, the governance of networks must be mentioned as well. The *governance of networks* is the self-regulation of participants' cooperation within a partnership, guaranteeing rational decision-making on behalf of the commonly shared goals. As far as network membership is voluntary, the most important task is to balance different interests by appropriate communication management and by generally accepted rules leading to common agreements and joint action (cf. Meyer and Baltes 2004). While governance through networks describes the *external effects* of network governance, governance of networks stresses the *internal coordination* of independent actors and the regulation problems associated with this. The same differentiation can also be made by discussing the role of single organizations in governance processes (cf. Meyer 2005).

Consequently, eight key fields for evaluation research targeting regional network governance can be identified (Table 4.1). The four dimensions – institutions, decisions, executions and territory – were mentioned as the

Table 4.1   Evaluation topic for regional network governance

Dimensions (Criteria)	Governance of networks (internal coordination)	Governance through networks (external effects)
Institutions (Functionality)	Membership rules	Social integration
Decisions (Rationality)	Interest balance	Need orientation
Executions (Efficacy)	Management capacities	Steering ability
Territory (Acceptance)	Satisfying performance	Regional relevance

core elements of 'regional governance' in the aforementioned generalized definition. Adding in the differentiation between internal coordination and external effects ('governance of networks' and 'governance through networks'), leads us to a framework for evaluation by using the mentioned criteria for 'good governance'.

Concerning the governance of networks, the main institution for internal coordination is *membership rules*, defining the entrance and exit conditions, the duties and rights of each member, and sanctions for those who do not obey these commonly agreed rules. At least implicitly (through a 'gentleman's agreement'), each group needs some kind of rules, for guaranteeing its existence, protecting itself against competitors or cheaters and ensuring collective action for common goal-attainment (cf. Heckelman and Olson 2003; Olson 2000). Making decisions in groups is a complex process of *balancing the interests* of group members that influences both the seeking and weighting of information available for single opportunities (cf. Schultz-Hardt et al 2002; Christensen and Westenholz 2000; Davis 1992). The execution of decisions is, from an internal coordination view, a question of *management capacities* and performances. Getting things done in the way the decision makers want it to be done is very difficult, even in a strictly hierarchical ordered organization, and several influencing factors have to be taken into account (cf. Cross 2004; Peterson et al 2000; Green and Knippen 1999; March and Olsen 1976). Finally, as a policy network implemented for the wealth of a specific territory, the organizations and people who invest their time (and money) in its governance must be *satisfied by the performance* of the network and believe in its positive outcomes.

This belief in outcomes is strongly related to the *relevance* of network decisions and their capability to influence regional development – the key dimension for evaluating the *governance through networks*. By executing their decisions, the policy network proves its *steering ability*, especially for those aspects most pressing for the territory. While depending not only on the cooperation of network members but also on (at least the majority of) the inhabitants, network decisions must meet the needs of the population.

Consequently, all network decisions should be *needs-orientated* for the whole region and not limited to particular interests of the policy network or single network members. Finally, governance through networks as a political institution for a region means to assure *social integration* of all relevant stakeholder groups in all decision situations concerning all kinds of problems the region may face. This also means delimitation against other territories and groups which are not interested in the wealth of the particular region.

The last point shows that 'good regional governance' does not necessarily mean 'good national' or 'good global governance'. In contrast, policy network governance may tend towards enclosure and separation which leads to new conflicts with higher aggregated administrative units like federal or national states. This has to be mentioned when focusing on 'sustainable development'. However, the recommended eight fields are able to guide evaluation studies for investigating 'regional network governance' and we will show its usability through use of an example in the next section.

III. WHAT DO WE KNOW ABOUT IMPACTS OF NETWORK GOVERNANCE?

Instead of giving a brief and systematic overview on research results, we will use an example to illustrate the effects of regional network governance. Our case is a huge political initiative of the German Federal Ministry of Consumer Protection, Food and Agriculture (BMVEL) called 'Regionen Aktiv' (cf. Federal Ministry of Consumer Protection, Food and Agriculture 2002; further information in the German language is available both on the website of the ministry www.verbraucherministerium.de and on the project website www.modellregionen.de).[3]

In 2001, a radical change of agrarian policy ('Agrarwende') occurred in Germany as a combined result of the FMD- and the BSE-crises and increasing political pressure caused by the WTO negotiations, EU-enlargement and the mid-term review of the Agenda 2000/CAP. The new policy is supposed to give the consumer perspective priority over producers' interests and intends to support not only agriculture but rural areas as a whole.[4] To support this policy, BMVEL initiated a nationwide competition, focusing on four main objectives: strengthening rural areas, creating additional sources of income, focusing on creating a consumer perspective and providing nature-friendly and environmentally compatible agriculture.

Eighteen model regions were chosen in a two-tier selection process. During the first stage, regions were encouraged to develop a joint vision for their own future. In December 2001, an independent jury comprising representatives of the key interest groups chose 33 regions out of a total of

206 submissions. In the second stage these regions were asked to formulate an integrated development plan (IDP), and finally 18 model regions were selected to receive funding to realize their IDPs between 2002 and 2005 (2.1 million euros per region on average).

The administrative and political definitions of these selected regions are diverse. For example, one of the 16 German federal states (Saarland) is participating, while another region (Schwäbische Alb) represents only one of the 323 German districts ('Landkreise'). Several participating regions are not administratively composed and some of them include parts not only from different districts but also from different federal states (Eichsfeld, Lübecker Bucht, Weserland). In sum, the structural diversity of the model regions is as large as possible in Germany. This is demonstrated by many other indicators such as the region's economic structure, labour market development, tourism and income (cf. Elbe and Meyer 2006).

The implementation process of IDPs followed three basic principles:

- *Programme-based instead of project-based funding.* The Federal Government's role is limited to setting the goals of the competition and to prescribing a set of minimum requirements as regards decision-making structures and self-assessment mechanisms. The aim is to improve funding for rural development without waiving control, using 'management by objectives' and not the bureaucratic approach of 'input controlling'. To assess their achievements and highlight the more detailed aspects of project management, the regions are required to set up a support and self-assessment system.

- *Network governance instead of top-down steering.* The regions are free to select and implement the measures they see as appropriate for achieving the goals of their IDP. But according to the basic agreements with the Federal Ministry, they have to ensure that stakeholder groups are included in planning, implementation and assessment of the regional development process and in the distribution of available funding. Partnership networks must be formed between the actors, municipalities, regions and non-state actors. These regional partnerships are the key actors for the implementation of the new steering approach.

- *Durable cooperation instead of temporal partnership.* 'Regionen Aktiv' should not be seen as a support programme in the classical sense, supporting projects whilst in operation, and ceasing to when the programme closes. The partnership structures initiated in the model regions should continue on a permanent basis so that they contribute to the development of the regions after 'Regionen Aktiv' has been discontinued.

These basic principles can be analysed by using the following three key determinants for durability and effectiveness of network governance, stated by Mayntz (2003) as a summary of her findings during approximately twenty years of research on this issue:

- *A strong state to ensure the functionality of self-regulation in policy networks.* Successful policy networks act 'in the shadow of hierarchy' with powerful political authorities serving as 'guardians of public welfare'. The threat of state intervention acts as a uniting force for co-operation and self-regulation.
- *A strong, functionally differentiated, and well organized civil society.* To balance the interests of different stakeholder groups, those interests must be organized autonomously and represented by corporate actors within negotiations. Without a well equipped and powerful civil society, multi-actor networks cannot work sufficiently.
- *A common identity of network members.* Any kind of collective action is in need of 'at least a minimal sense of identification with, and responsibility for, the greater whole, in short, a common identity' (Mayntz 2003: 5).

These determinants can be assigned to the aforementioned implementation principles of 'Regionen Aktiv', leading to specific conditions of governance that vary more or less between the eighteen model regions (Table 4.2). Due to the regularities of the competition, all participating regions have to respect the authority of the Federal Ministry – at least to get the funding to realize their IDP. Therefore, *the regional policy networks are acting in the shadow of the hierarchy*. But as soon as the funding stops, the nation state will lose control and the conditions of regional governance will change. As yet, there is little idea about what the future role of the Federal Ministry will be and how regional self-regulation and coordination between the regions can be assured without the driving force of the national state. The question of *sustainable vertical integration* therefore remains unanswered.

The competition rules set by the nation state fixed some formal issues according to the governance structure. For example, three core elements – the regional partnership (RP), a regional management (RM) and a public completion partner (AP) – had to be installed in all regions according to the will of the Federal Ministry. Within this framework, the regions were more or less free to create functional institutions for their own partnerships. Due to the *huge differences in capacity for organizing interests* both within a single region (e.g. the power distribution between ecological and economic interest groups) and between the regions (e.g. disparity in the organizational level of civil society between East and West Germany), the

Table 4.2   Conditions of governance in Regionen Aktiv

Determinants of network governance	Implementation principles Regionen Aktiv	Conditions of governance in Regionen Aktiv
A strong state to ensure the functionality of self-regulation in policy networks	Programme-based instead of project-based funding	Federal Ministry controls the framework of the competition (model regions act in the 'shadow of hierarchy')
A strong, functionally differentiated and well organized civil society	Network governance instead of top-down steering	Partnerships between state and non-state actors with huge differences between the eighteen regions (concerning the groups involved, their resources, the decisions for funding and the self-assessment measures)
A common identity of network members	Durable cooperation instead of temporal partnerships	Structures should be durable; IDPs are the common basis, not regional identity (at least in some regions)

problems and solutions for governance of networks should differ. This raises the question of whether all regions were able to solve the problem of *horizontal integration*, at least for the duration of 'Regionen Aktiv'.

Finally, the newly formed regional policy networks are supposed to develop a *common identity* that follows the IDP and assures the sustainability of this institution after the end of national funding. According to different traditions and experiences in cooperation (e.g. some policy networks were formed because of LEADER+ before 'Regionen Aktiv' started), the starting points for creating identity varied significantly. Without this identity, the *sustainability of horizontal integration* seems to be difficult.

We will not discuss all the findings according to the governance structure of 'Regionen Aktiv' and the variations between the eighteen regions here (for more details see Böcher 2004; Brandt 2004; Elbe et al 2004; Federal Ministry of Consumer Protection, Food and Agriculture 2004; Knickel et al 2004). However, some results concerning the eight fields for evaluating regional network governance should be mentioned.

The implementation of a functional *institutional framework for coopera-tion* was the first aspect of focus for the regional actors in 'Regionen Aktiv'. Due to LEADER+ and several other programmes, some regions had the opportunity to use existing partnership structures, but in most cases multi-actor policy networks and their central instruments for governance had to be developed at the beginning of the process. Institution building dominated the first two years, and in some cases it finished only just before the mid-term report in late 2003. However, none of the regions failed in this task.

The regional policy networks were formally established as associations following the German 'Vereinsrecht'. According to this law, managing committees, governing bodies and *several membership rules* within this organizational framework had to be built up. Due to this implementation, the regional partnerships are 'organizations' from a formal point of view and not 'networks' in the sense of policy network literature (cf. Scharpf 1993; Powell 1990). As a result, specific problems of network regulation did not occur (cf. Meyer and Baltes 2004).

The results of the mid-term evaluation showed that the overwhelming majority of participating regional actors were satisfied with the way deci-sions were made (cf. Brandt 2004; Knickel et al 2004). In particular the important impacts of RP meetings, bringing different regional interests and perspectives together, were emphasized. Most actors stress the learning aspect of their discussions on the development of network institutions, which increased the acceptance of project ideas and the engagement for joint action. Besides *balancing interests*, the decentralized concept of gov-ernance, the participatory process of institutional development and the transparent democratic decision-structures are widely seen as advantages of the 'Regionen Aktiv' process.

This positive feedback is largely an outcome of the work of the RM and its preparation of member meetings. Concerning the *management capaci-ties* of the RM, critics concentrate on the division of labour between different organizational parts of the management (especially between hon-orary working members of partnership organization and the employers of regional management) and the communication process in general. Most of these critiques can be interpreted as a direct outcome of the difficulties in coordinating heterogeneous networks. They are not addressing structural deficits or fundamental management failures. In general, the participating regional groups appear *satisfied with the performance* of the political insti-tutions established during the implementation of 'Regionen Aktiv'. The number of actors leaving regional partnerships remained small, and there-fore a selection bias cannot explain this positive feedback.

From the perspective of the *outcomes of regional network governance*, financial support for regional projects is still the most important result and it also links the network members together. In total, more than 600 projects have been realized and most of them with pronounced grassroots orientation. Hardly any data about the effects of these projects are available: the decision to leave the task for developing adequate methods of impact assessment to the regions overloaded the management capacities of the regional partnerships.[5] Instruments for monitoring project impacts were implemented only in some isolated cases (e.g. Weserland, Ostfriesland). This provoked a centralized mid-term evaluation by the BMVEL, in which the regions had to present a mid-term report based on so called 'Erfolgsfaktoren'[6] (factors of success). However, this report does not include a systematic investigation of project impacts.

The partnerships should implement *commonly shared policy strategies* for releasing competition between (for additional funding) and within the regions (for the best projects). While competition between the selected model regions was limited to the so called 'performance and quality reserve' (achievement-bound reserve), a small financial incentive competition for the best projects happened only in nine model regions. Most of the projects proceeded unrivalled because more funding was accessible than was demanded. Moreover, the division of money was also a political task in some cases, following the principle of justice between the network partners instead of competition.

Concerning the crucial principle of steering the regions towards the goals of their IDPs, till the mid-term review, the operationalization of these objectives has only been achieved to a very small extent. In consequence, the ministry set several incentives (stimulation and pressure) to qualify the goals. One reason for differences and problems in using the agreement on objectives within the framework of regional promotion is found in the structure of actors at the implementation level. Resources for implementation are primarily dependent on honorary work, and the outcome of continuously working on defining a mission statement, deriving objectives, defining products and so on does not result in direct benefits for single actors. According to this, the steering abilities of networks are limited and need time and external stimulus to develop common goals. A restriction is the limited management competences and capacities which hinder goal-oriented collective action of the regional partnerships.

It is also difficult to judge the '*needs orientation*' of the regional activities because no systematic information on the needs of the inhabitants has been collected. Nevertheless, representation of public needs is primarily bound to interest organisations and civil society groups. Due to the few visible impacts of network decisions for the region, no conflicts concerning these aspects occurred. But this is also a result of successful enclosure of a broad variety of regional groups and incorporation of the relevant stakeholders

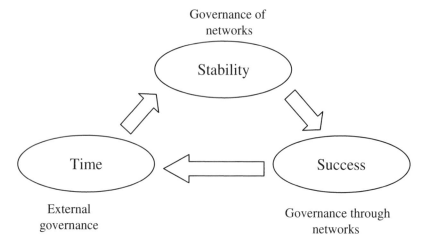

Figure 4.1   Lessons learnt from Regionen Aktiv

in each region. Obviously, this is also an indicator for successful social integration that was initiated by 'Regionen Aktiv'.

What are the general conclusions that can be drawn from these findings? First is the *possibility of establishing regional network governance* under a great variety of circumstances. Poor conditions do not seem to be principal barriers, although they do influence the time needed for implementation. Governance of the network can be handled within different social environments but it needs continuous input from external powers ('the shadow of the hierarchy') even if there are commonly developed goal systems like the IDPs. The regional networks were stabilized using well established formal implementation procedures (founding associations), and few problems occurred. The continuity and professionalism of network management (governance of networks) is a pre-condition for governance through networks, which significantly *needs much more time* to establish and to reach effective results. Without additional incentives from outside the networks, none of the regional partnerships seemed to be able to make their cooperation sustainable. This *lack of visible success*, at least in the first implementation phase, threatens the existence of regional policy networks and endangers the withdrawal of those interest groups which do not have the patience and resources to withstand a long period of establishing a regional governance system. Therefore, time becomes an important variable that cannot be treated adequately within regional network governance. During the 'Regionen Aktiv' competition, the national state took over the task to develop rules and resources to provide the time needed for implementation. The interrelationship of the three variables mentioned here is shown in Figure 4.1.

IV. HOW TO EVALUATE GOVERNANCE FOR SUSTAINABLE DEVELOPMENT?

Up to now, we have concentrated on regional network governance, and sustainable development has not yet been mentioned. Concerning a lot of discussion on what sustainable development is (cf. Hopwood et al 2005), at least a short introduction is needed. As outlined elsewhere (e.g. Meyer 2002, 2007), sustainable development can be understood as a *global utopian of total social integration* of three different dimensions.

According to the 'Brundtland Report' of the World Commission on Environment and Development, sustainable development is defined as development 'that meets the needs of the present without compromising the ability of future generations to meet their own needs' (World Commission 1987: 8). On an unlimited time dimension, social integration of different generations of human beings should be attempted. Following the aforementioned statements of the World Summit, a *vertical social integration* on a *territorial scale* should be realized by 'thinking globally and acting locally'. This implies that sufficient communication procedures are established for aggregating and disaggregating both 'thinking' (goal and agenda setting) and 'acting' (coordination and accumulation of impacts) between different levels of governance. Finally, the *horizontal social integration* of 'three pillars' comprising ecological, economical and social goals must be emphasized. Sustainable development needs the support of different social groups with diverse interests which should be integrated in a commonly agreed *target system* with respect to the ideals of 'good governance'.

When using this understanding of sustainable development, the German competition 'Regionen Aktiv' becomes a very interesting example of political steering that addresses all three dimensions. By building multi-actor policy networks, the horizontal social integration process at the regional level is obviously the main focus of the programme. Nevertheless, the structure of the whole competition also emphasizes the vertical (with financial incentives and some rules set by the Federal Ministry) and the time dimensions (with the durable implementation governance structures and IDPs). However, both vertical communication problems and the need for 'timing' to secure project and programme impacts and their 'micro-sustainability' have been totally underestimated. This caused some of the trouble described previously.

The implementation of a 'multi-level evaluation system' is one reason why at least some of these problems have been recognized relatively early on by the programme management. Hence, the planned monitoring and evaluation system was only partially implemented by 'top-down' steering. The regions experienced some significant problems in building up evaluation systems because of missing experiences, knowledge and traditions in running these kinds of information systems. Additionally, the experts and consultants who were involved conduct evaluations as 'a source of income'. They are not intending to be part of 'a regional learning system' with the aim to improve systematically the quality of monitoring. It goes against their financial interests to reduce the running costs of the system by transferring their knowledge to the programme management.

In conclusion, one can clearly recognize *the regional level as a problematic area for implementing suitable monitoring and evaluation institutions*. The additional challenges for advanced scientific methods and techniques for evaluating sustainable development are strengthening these difficulties. Each of the three dimensions of social integration implies the use of more sophisticated research methods:

- *Evaluation of the time dimension* is only possible if appropriate data (e.g. long and comparative time-series data), well established theoretical models for sound predictions (e.g. demographic models for estimation of population development) and well trained personnel (for handling difficult statistical analyses) are available. Besides the limited abilities of some sciences (e.g. economics is unable to forecast economic development for the next few years), the poor quality of local data is one of the most important barriers for implementing 'learning systems' in the regions. At the regional level, *developing adequate monitoring and evaluation systems* is an important precondition for better governance. In doing so, cultural specifics and regional identities have to be taken into account (cf. Ukaga and Maser 2004: 111).
- *Evaluation of the target dimension* requires integrative and interdisciplinary approaches which are still absent (cf. Brandon and Lombardi 2005: 74). However, the increasing complexity of this kind of evaluation needs larger evaluation teams with skills from different sciences which are not available in each region – even in a well-educated country like Germany. Therefore, *capacity building* for scientifically sound evaluations by using integrative and interdisciplinary research methods is very important on the regional level.
- *Evaluation of the territorial dimension* demands joint evaluations on different policy levels and the use of multi-level modelling as an analysis tool. There are several factors hindering the implementation of well developed impact assessment methods on each level (see, for instance, the problems for implementing environmental impact assessment mentioned by George 2002: 228). By conducting evaluations within a specific cultural framework, regional experts who are

familiar with the details are needed. These experts need to work together in *multi-level evaluation networks*. This represents a new challenge for coordinating scientific work and evaluation research.

Communicating the experiences gained in programmes like 'Regionen Aktiv' is vital for improving the standards for evaluation of sustainable development. If one is really interested in sustainable development, regional governance institutions with appropriate knowledge systems are strongly required all over the world. Hence, support programmes for building up international and interdisciplinary evaluation networks and for improving the evaluation capacities on the regional level are necessary to ensure an adequate standard of information for steering complex processes at the regional level.

NOTES

1. According to Dahl (1994), this polarization characterizes the democratic dilemma between system effectiveness and citizen participation.
2. For sure, the opposite viewpoint referring to system theory approaches can be taken, too (cf. Sydow and Windeler 2000).
3. 'Regionen Aktiv' also serves as a pilot project within the framework of the National Sustainability Strategy and was Germany's contribution to the World Summit on Sustainable Development ('Rio +10') in Johannesburg in Aug/Sept 2002.
4. In the meantime, the national government changed and so did the name of the ministry. By re-ordering the three issues 'consumer protection', 'food' and 'agriculture', putting 'consumer protection' from the first to the third place, the new government symbolized a change of priorities in November 2005.
5. This is not only a technical problem, it is also caused by the poor state of evaluation culture in most regions and in most partner organizations. Many people recognized the evaluation task as an annoying duty, not as a learning option.
6. These factors of success are: pressure of problems and will to find a solution; project design that supports win-win coalitions; short-term success; manageable structures and opportunities for linkage; powerful intercedes and partners; learning aptitude and exchange of information; transparency, process competence, and flexibility; participation; regional promoters as policy entrepreneurs; critical mass of labour time and money for the regional management; competent regional management (for details see Böcher 2004).

REFERENCES

Agenda 21 (1992), *United Nations Conference on Environment and Development*, Rio de Janeiro, Brazil, 3 to 14 June 1992, Agenda 21 (to be downloaded at, http://www. un.org/esa/sustdev/documents/agenda21/english/Agenda21.pdf).
Benz, A (2004), 'Einleitung: Governance – Modebegriff oder nützliches sozialwissenschaftliches Konzept?', in A Benz (ed.) *Governance – Regieren in Komplexen Regelsystemen* (Wiesbaden, VS Verlag), 11–28.

Böcher, M (2004), *Participatory Policy Evaluation as an Innovative Method for Achieving Sustainable Rural Development*. Paper presented at the XI World Congress of Rural Sociology 'Globalisation, risks and resistance' in Trondheim, Norway, 25–30 July.

Bogumil, J and Holtkamp, L (2004), 'Local Governance und gesellschaftliche Integration', in S Lange and U Schimank (eds) *Governance und Gesellschaftliche Integration* (Wiesbaden, VS Verlag), 147–66.

Brandon, P S and Lombardi, P (2005), *Evaluating Sustainable Development in the Built Environment* (Oxford, Blackwell).

Brandt, T (2004), 'Ergebnisbericht: Zwischenevaluierung des Regionalmanagements und der regionalen Partnerschaft, Vis à Vis e. V.' (Saarbrücken, Saarland University).

Christensen, S and Westenholz, A (2000), 'Collective decision making: toward a relational perspective', *American Behavioral Scientist*, 43/8, 1301–15.

Cross, R, Parker, A and Cross, R L (2004), *The Hidden Power of Social Networks: Understanding How Work Really Gets Done in Organisations* (Boston, Harvard Business School Press).

Dahl, R A (1994), 'A democratic dilemma: system effectiveness versus citizen participation', *Political Science Quarterly*, 10, 23–34.

Davis, J H (ed.) (1992), *Group Decision Making* (San Diego u.a., Academic Press).

Elbe, S, Kroës, G and Schubert, D (2004), *Sustainable Development in the EU Structural Funds Controlling Instruments for the Integration of Environmental Requirements into EU Structural Funds Aid in Germany* (Berlin, Federal Agency of Environment, Texte 31/04).

Elbe, S and Meyer, W (2006), *Competition and Regional Governance: New Approaches to Ecological Sustainable Development in Germany – Experiences from 18 Model Regions*. Paper prepared for the 7th Nordic Environmental Social Science Research Conference (NESS) at Gothenburg University, 15–17 June 2005 (to be published at http://scidok.sulb.uni-saarland.de/).

Federal Ministry of Consumer Protection, Food and Agriculture (2002), *Active Regions – Shaping Rural Futures: Competition Winners* (Bonn, BMELV, to be downloaded at, http://www.verbraucherministerium.de/data/000C223EE 46310 629CC36521C0A8D816.0.pdf).

Federal Ministry of Consumer Protection, Food and Agriculture (2004), *Regionen Aktiv – Land gestaltet Zukunft. Zwischenbericht zum Wettbewerb* (Bonn, BMELV, to be downloaded at, http://www.nova-institut.de/ra-attach/10883/ broschure_ 2004.pdf).

Fürst, D (2004), 'Regional governance', in A Benz (ed.) *Governance – Regieren in Komplexen Regelsystemen* (Wiesbaden, VS Verlag), 45–64.

George, C (2002), 'Environmental assessment and management', in C Kirkpatrick, R Clarke and C Polidano (eds) *Handbook on Development Policy and Management* (Cheltenham, Edward Elgar), 221–32.

Green, T B and Knippen, J T (1999), *Breaking the Barrier to Upward Communication: Strategies and Skills for Employees, Managers, and HR Specialists* (New York, Quorum Books).

Hanf, K and Toole Jr, L J (1992), 'Revisiting old friends: networks, implementation structures and the management of inter-organisational relations', in G Jordan and K Schubert (eds) 'Policy networks', *European Journal of Political Research*, Special Issue, 21/1–2, 163–80.

Heckelman, J C and Olson, M (eds, 2003), *Collective Choice: Essays in Honour of Mancur Olson* (Berlin/Heidelberg, Springer).

Hooghe, L and Marks, G (2001), 'Types of multi-level governance', *European Integration Online Papers*, vol. 5, no. 011, (http://eiop.or.at/eiop/ texte/2001-011a.htm).

Hopwood, B, Mellor, M and O'Brien, G (2005), 'Sustainable development: mapping different approaches', *Sustainable Development*, 13, 38–52.

Knickel, K, Siebert, R, Ganzert, C, Dosch, A, Peter, S and Derichs, S (2004), 'Wissenschaftliche Begleitforschung des Pilotprojektes, Regionen Aktiv – Land gestaltet Zukunft.' Ergebnisse der Begleitforschung 2002–2003 – Abschlussbericht (Frankfurt/München, Institut für Ländliche Strukturforschung IFLS an der Goethe-Universität Frankfurt; ZALF Müncheberg – Institut für Sozialökonomie; TUM-TECH GmbH München-Weihenstephan).

Lawrence, G (2004), *Promoting Sustainable Development: the Question of Governance*. Plenary address presented at the XI World Congress of Rural Sociology 'Globalisation, Risks and Resistance' in Trondheim, Norway, 25–30 July.

March, J G and Olsen, J P (1976), *Ambiguity and Choice in Organizations* (Bergen u.a., Universitetsforlaget).

Marin, B and Mayntz, R (eds, 1991), *Policy Network: Empirical Evidence and Theoretical Considerations* (Frankfurt/New York, Campus).

Marsh, D (1998), *Comparing Policy Networks* (Maidenhead, Open University Press).

Mayntz, R (2003), *From Government to Governance: Political Steering in Modern Societies*. Paper presented at the IOEW Summer Academy on IPP, Würzburg, 7–11 September, (http://www.ioew.de/governance/english/veranstaltungen/ Summer_Academies/SuA2Mayntz.pdf).

Meyer, W (2002), *Sociological Theory and Evaluation Research: An Application and its Usability for Evaluating Sustainable Development*, CEval-Working Paper no. 6 (Saarbrücken, Saarland University).

Meyer, W (2005), 'Regulation, responsibility and representation: challenges for intra-organisational communication', in I Demirag (ed.) *Corporate Social Responsibility, Accountability and Governance: Global Perspectives* (Sheffield, Greenleaf Publishing), 41–55.

Meyer, W (2006), *Wie Zukunftsfähig ist die Zivilgesellschaft? Zur Umsetzung der Anforderungen des Leitbildes 'nachhaltiger Entwicklung' im Dritten Sektor* (Saarland University, forthcoming).

Meyer, W (2007), 'Evaluation of sustainable development – a social science's approach', in U Schubert and E Störmer (eds) *Evaluating Sustainable Development in Europe: Concepts, Methods and Applications* (Cheltenham, Edward Elgar, Evaluating Sustainable Development series, vol. 1).

Meyer, W and Baltes, K (2004), 'Network failures: how realistic is durable cooperation in global governance?', in K Jacob, M Binder and A Wieczorek (eds) *Governance for Industrial Transformation: Proceedings of the 2003 Berlin Conference on the Human Dimension of Global Environmental Change* (Berlin, Environmental Policy Research Centre), 31–51 (to be downloaded from, http://www.fu-berlin.de/ffu/akumwelt/ bc2003/proceedings/032%20-%20051%20 meyer.pdf).

Meyer, W and Elbe, S (2006), 'Initiating network governance by competition: experiences from 18 German regions', in L Cheshire, V Higgins and G Lawrence (eds) *International Perspectives on Rural Governance: New Power Relations in Rural Economies and Societies* (Oxford, Routledge, forthcoming).

Ohtsubo, Y and Masuchi, A (2004), 'Effects of status difference and group size in group decision making', in *Group Processes and Intergroup Relations* 7/2, S., 161–72.

Olson, M (2000), *The Logic of Collective Action: Public Goods and the Theory of Groups* (Cambridge, USA, Harvard University Press, 18th print, first 1965).

Peterson, E, Mitchell, T R, Thompson, L and Burr, R (2000), 'Collective efficacy and aspects of shared mental models as predictors of performance over time in work groups', *Group Processes and Intergroup Relations*, 3/3, S., 296–316.

Pierre, J (ed., 2000), *Debating Governance: Authority, Steering, and Democracy* (Oxford, Oxford University Press).

Powell, W W (1990), 'Neither market nor hierarchy: network forms of organization', *Research in Organizational Behaviour*, vol. 12 (Greenwich, JAI Press), 295–336.

Rhodes, R A W (1997), *Understanding Governance: Policy Networks, Governance, Reflexivity and Accountability* (Maidenhead, Open University Press).

Scharpf, F W (1993), 'Coordination in hierarchies and networks', in F W Scharpf (ed.) *Games and Hierarchies and Networks: Analytical and Theoretical Approaches to the Study of Governance Institutions* (Frankfurt/New York, Campus), 125–65.

Schulz-Hardt, S, Jochims, M and Frey, D (2002), 'Productive conflict in group decision making: genuine and contrived dissent as strategies to counteract biased information seeking', *Organizational Behavior and Human Decision Processes*, 88, 563–86.

Sørensen, E (2002), *Democratic Theory and Network Governance*. Paper presented at workshop no. 12 'Demokrati og administrative reform i norden' at the NOPSA-conference 2002 in Ålborg, (http://www.socsci.auc.dk/institut2/nopsa/arbejds-gruppe12/eva.pdf).

Sydow, J and Windeler A (2000), 'Steuerung von und in Netzwerken. Perspektiven, Konzepte, vor allem aber offene Fragen', in J Sydow and A Windeler (eds) *Steuerung von Netzwerken. Konzepte und Praktiken* (Opladen/Wiesbaden, Westdeutscher Verlag), 1–25.

Ukaga, O and Maser, C (2004), *Evaluating Sustainable Development: Giving People a Voice in Their Destiny* (Sterling, Stylus).

UN ESCAP [United Nations Economic and Social Commission for Asia and the Pacific] (2004), *What is Good Governance?* (http://www.unescap.org/huset/gg/governance.htm).

Wiesenthal, H (1987), 'Rational Choice. Ein Überblick über Grundlinien, Theoriefelder und neuere Themenakquisition eines sozialwissenschaftlichen Paradigmas', *Zeitschrift für Soziologie*, 16/6, 434–49.

World Commission on Environment and Development (1987), *Our Common Future* (New York, Oxford University Press).

5. The role of evaluation in regional sustainable development

Joe Ravetz

I. INTRODUCTION

While evaluation is a central factor in regional development policy, it is evolving rapidly in theory and practice. The context is the widening of 'regional development' to 'regional sustainable development' ('RSD'), with a more integrated economic, social and environmental agenda. In parallel is the spread of 'rational management' and 'evidence based' policy at every level of public governance, with the pressure for participation making this task more challenging. There are procedural developments, such as the extension of impact assessment methods to sustainability appraisals, alongside technical developments, such as remote sensing and web-enabled databases. In addition, there are many experiments in communicative processes, community participation and organizational learning.

This chapter is based on the 'evaluation' strand of a project which aimed to bring together best practice in RSD across Europe, and point the way 'beyond' best practice.[1] It reviews two contrasting examples of evaluation methods in development. One concerns the modelling of 'tangibles' of environmental flows and impacts; and the other is focused on the 'intangibles' of evaluation of regional innovation strategy. Each example demonstrates the need for more integrated approaches, and the management of complexity and uncertainty in a practical process.

II. CONTEXT

Evaluation of regional development has accumulated a large body of theory and practice, since the emergence of European regional policy. Several underlying trends can be seen, which focus attention on new methods and tools for such evaluation.

The first is the widening of the scope of 'regional development' to 'regional sustainable development' (RSD), i.e. from a purely economic agenda to a more balanced economic, social and environmental agenda. Bringing these together and balancing the trade-offs, suggests the growing need for more integrated forms of evaluation, assessment and appraisal (Scrase and Sheate 2002; Eales et al 2005).

Another factor is the changing nature of EU regional development programmes, a key arena for the development of evaluation methods and tools. Evaluation in principle should be the final provider of feedback to policy development, but in reality it may be sidelined by political and institutional pressures, and a system of governance which is often weak and fragmented (Bertrand and Larrue 2004). With the forthcoming 2006+ regional policy and EU enlargement, there is a clear need to improve on current practice. This applies especially in the new accession states, where there is rapid change in the culture and practice of public administration, and often strong enthusiasm for new practices (Roberts 2003; EC 2001).

A third factor is the spread of 'rational management' and 'modernization' approaches at every level of public governance, and increasingly in various forms of corporate governance (EC 2001). The increasing scale and accountability of public interventions appears to require increasingly robust and transparent evidence and analysis at every level. At the same time the widening of the RSD agenda, and new pressures for participatory processes in multi-level governance, make this task increasingly challenging (Funtowicz et al 2002). Much of the administrative process for evaluation assumes distinct chains of cause and effect, i.e. clear and measurable links between policy inputs, outputs and outcomes. In practice while direct inputs and outputs may be measurable, there is little else that can be modelled or measured with confidence (Georghiou 2002).

In parallel there are also technical developments, particularly in digital information systems such as systems models, remote sensing, GIS and other databases. All of these are being rapidly transformed by the internet as the main access point. There are legal and procedural developments, such as the extension of EIA to strategic environmental assessment, and in some countries to sustainability appraisal. There is also a wide variety of experiments in procedural methods and approaches, to foster community participation, social inclusion, organizational learning and others (McEvoy and Ravetz 2001). Each of these points to the evaluation of RSD, as both a challenging theoretical question, and a fast growing industry in need of coordination, quality control and training capacity (Martinuzzi 2004).

So are the EU regions now moving towards RSD, and if not, what is wrong? Evaluation can in principle answer such questions. However, the REGIONET case studies show how the evaluation process is often misunderstood, misused and sometimes abused. In each example there are technical questions of boundaries, cumulative effects, risks and uncertainties. There are also process questions of accountability, transparency, participation, asymmetric information, and competition between technical and civil institutions.

III. EU POLICY CONTEXT

The background to the REGIONET project was the EU strategy for sustainable development, and the adoption of the Communication on Impact Assessment, which commits the EU to an impact assessment of all major policy proposals (EC 2002). The aim is to improve the quality and coherence of the policy development process, and to contribute to an effective and efficient regulatory environment, with 'reliable and applicable' indicators and tools (Tamborra 2002 and 2003).

The Communication on Impact Assessment brings together a range of assessments of the direct and indirect impacts of a proposed measure (i.e. business assessment, gender assessment, environmental assessment, impacts on small and medium enterprises, fiscal assessment, etc.). The impact assessment is also seen as an effective communication tool: consultations with interested parties generate useful discussion and bring in valuable information and analysis, as required by the communication on principles and minimum standards for consultation. It contains two stages: the first is a preliminary assessment or filtering exercise; the second is an extended impact assessment, including both qualitative and quantitative methods.

In parallel with this has been the refinement over many years of the evaluation and assessment methods for regional policy in the shape of the structural funds and community support frameworks. This has seen the recent transition in thinking from 'regional development' to RSD. One recent example of this was the major study for DG Regio, 'Thematic evaluation of the contribution of structural funds to sustainable development' (GHK et al 2003). This is a high level 'horizontal' evaluation with an innovative methodology based on four types of capital – natural, social, human and manufactured. The study also involved comparison between quantitative econometric modelling and the more qualitative 'four capitals' framework. The study used the approach of alternative 'development paths', a scenario method which helps to organize multiple and inter-dependent changes in economy, environment, society and institutions. This helps to highlight the trade-offs between the four capitals, at different scales, between social groups, and between levels of governance. One major conclusion is that investment in 'human resources' has the most positive balance of outcomes of any measures in the structural funds. While this study represents a certain state of the art and is now being carried further in the Framework Programme 6, the conclusions are quite open on their limitations, and raise many questions:

- Questions on social welfare: how this is defined and/or quantified, who defines it, and what indicators are appropriate?
- Questions on weighting: in the trade-off or balancing of competing objectives and criteria, how can priorities be assigned, and by whom?
- Questions on integration and common denominators: if economic cost-benefit analysis is not appropriate, then what other methods or units can be used?
- Questions on the management and priority of information: for the baseline or ex ante, mid-term and ex post evaluation stages?

Such questions are very topical for the DG Regio system of evaluation of structural funds, and for the wider field of evaluation of RSD.

IV. SCOPE OF 'REGIONAL SUSTAINABLE DEVELOPMENT'

While 'sustainable development' is discussed endlessly, the definition of RSD is still an open question. On the EU policy-research axis, a major public milestone was the 1998 conference, 'Regions – cornerstones of sustainable development', and the establishment of the ENSURE network (Gabriel and Narodoslawski 1998).[2] The current literature on RSD is reviewed in Ravetz et al (2004), and there is a venerable history to the concept of the ecological region, city region and so on (Hall and Ward 1998). In this paper we only point to the main features of the concept which has emerged in the last decade:

- A wider territorial perspective, both in formal administrative units, 'bio-region' and other units, with a particular focus on the interactions of urban and rural areas where possible;
- A wider scope than conventional economic development, including ecological, cultural, ethical, aesthetic and other dimensions;
- A wider cross section of society to be engaged through a participative process-based learning-style mode of governance;
- Implementing within the functional units of the regional or other territorial scale, the widely accepted 'Bruntland' goals – *inter*-generational equity and *intra*-generational equity (WCED 1987).

Within this broad field, the evaluation workshop threw up a crucial debate on wording, and the differences which this might hide or expose:

- *'Regional sustainable development' (RSD)*: this could be interpreted as – a goal-led model of structural transformation towards ecologically sustainable development, which is implemented at regional level, in parallel with local, national and global levels.
- *'Sustainable regional development'*: this could be interpreted as – a viable and self-financing process of regional economic development, which continues beyond the life of public subsidy, with adjustment for improved environmental performance and social responsibility.

The first appears to represent the ideals and paradigm shifts expressed in Agenda 21 and similar, while the second represents more of the present day reality of regional development. The principal challenge of the evaluation workshop was seen as developing methods and tools to link between them. In reality it is clear that many opportunities in RSD are not mobilized, while inter-regional and intra-regional disparities increase. One approach is to ask why regions are often NOT the 'cornerstones' of sustainability? (Ravetz 2002):

- Lack of definition: beyond administrative boundaries, many regional economic, political, social and environmental functional systems are often all complex, different and overlapping.
- Political and economic dependency: most EU member states retain ultimate legal and financial powers, and regional powers have to be negotiated with the centre.
- Urbanization and globalization: most regional economies now compete on a global scale, and the predominant role of urban centres as hubs and gateways can overtake the role of the region.

On the other hand, at the regional level there is often a strong correspondence and 'fit' between physical functions, social patterns, economic units and political territories. The environmental features of regional 'units' include water catchments, air dispersion bowls, soil types and agricultural markets. Economic features include urban hinterlands, travel patterns, housing markets, trade flows and industrial profiles. A further dimension is cultural identity, dependent on media and communications, rooted in language and customs, and overlaid with kinship and migration patterns (Moss and Fichter 2003).

In much of the EU the 'policy-scape' of agencies, programmes and objectives is intended to be integrated at the regional level, where chances for success may be better than at local or national levels. However the REGIONET experience of defining and evaluating RSD often shows that goals and objectives are fuzzy: data are scarce and unreliable, cause–effect linkages are uncertain, and social–cultural perspectives are many and different. This complexity and uncertainty puts the onus back on the process of participative deliberation and organizational learning. For this the regional level can potentially offer new linkages between the local and the national scale, where policy is often in a greater state of flux, and where the coherence of sectors and actors can be enhanced, as in Figure 5.1 (Mulgan 1997):

- horizontally, between different sectors or policy silos
- vertically, between top-down providers and bottom-up consumers
- laterally, between upstream causes and downstream effects
- culturally, between different worldviews, ethics and cultures.

EVALUATION FOR POLICY INTEGRATION

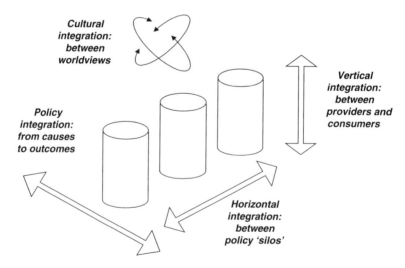

Source: Ravetz (2002).

Figure 5.1   Policy integration for regional sustainable development

In reality, policy at the regional level faces similar challenges as elsewhere, with typical conflicts between equity and efficiency, growth and decline, stability and change. Most current RSD strategies show tension between lower-risk adjustments to the status quo, and higher-risk aspirations for new policy models. The practical question is in the centre of this balance – what are the 'opportunities' for RSD and how can they be mobilized?

V. THE REGIONET THEMATIC NETWORK

The REGIONET Thematic Network project under the EU Framework Programme 5 aimed to bring together research on best practice in RSD, across the EU and the new accession states, and to point the way 'beyond best practice'.[3] The project partnership itself came from a decade of research networking, first drawn together at the aforementioned 'Cornerstones' conference, and continuing through the ENSURE (EU network for sustainable regional development research). The REGIONET project was structured in three key themes, each centred on an international workshop: structural funds and RSD, multi-level governance for RSD, and evaluation methods and tools.

This third 'evaluation' workshop, held in Manchester in June 2003, provided a review and synthesis of *existing* and *new* methods and tools in the evaluation of RSD. It covered a wide agenda, from *technical tools* to *social processes*, recognizing that combining these is essential in moving towards RSD. It focused on the *regional* dimension, recognizing that this involves both EU administrative regions, and other definitions between the national, urban and local levels. The workshop objectives included:

- Make links between evaluation methods and tools, and their processes and applications.
- Bridge the gaps between the evaluation of an *ideal model* for RSD, and the evaluation of the *realities* of current policies and programmes.
- Explore how *economic, environmental and social* evaluation methods can best be combined and integrated.

The workshop also aimed to provide practical guidance on extending EU methods and tools, such as the DG Regio 'Thematic evaluation on the contribution of the structural funds to sustainable development' (GHK et al 2003), and increasing the effectiveness of various 'integrated appraisal' toolkits at other levels of governance.[4]

Purposes of Evaluation

Appropriate tools and techniques will depend on the purpose of the evaluation. There may be a distinction between the stated or practical purpose
of an evaluation and its 'higher purpose', as expressed by Vanclay (2004).
One commentator sees three parallel strands in the higher purpose of evaluations (Chelimsky 1997):

- Evaluation for accountability: e.g. the measurement of results or
  efficiency, particularly where public funding is concerned;
- Evaluation for institutional development: e.g. the provision of eval-
  uative help to strengthen institutions;
- Evaluation for knowledge: e.g. the acquisition of a more profound
  understanding in some specific area or field.

Each of these alternatives raises questions on its underlying rationality.
The first and third purposes highlight the question of causality, i.e. the evidence and the theoretical basis which links causes and effects, which is
often problematic in many branches of social policy. In response, a systemic perspective is seen as one way to relate complexity and uncertainty
to a rational deliberative frame of action (Midgley 2000; Jiliberto 2004).
The second purpose, that of institutional development, highlights the
question of the legitimacy of governance and its evidence base, whether
this is external objective critique or internal subjective advocacy.

Each of these purposes also identifies the different roles of the 'evaluator' in relation to the 'evaluatee' (i.e. those whose actions are evaluated),
and the 'commissioner' (i.e. the agency for whom the evaluation is being
conducted). For the first and third purposes the evaluator is assumed to be
distant and critical, while for the second, the evaluator is often intended to
be more sympathetic to the organization. For all three purposes, the degree
of independence will depend on the objectives of the commisioning agency
and its relationships to the evaluatee and 'evaluatand' (i.e. the activity being
evaluated).

In practice many public organizations have little real interest in evaluation beyond the minimum legal requirements. However, they may have
stronger interest in performance benchmarking and 'change management',
both being in the wider frame of evaluation (Georghiou 2002). In practice
these purposes are often confused, and so then are the rationalities and
roles of the evaluators. In that case a 'lower purpose' may become the
default situation, i.e. where the evaluation is carried out simply to get or
justify the funding.

Scope of RSD Evaluation

There was intensive debate in REGIONET on definitions. Although terms such as evaluation, assessment and appraisal tend to apply to different types of evaluation for different purposes, there is considerable overlap in their usage. There were also questions on the definition of a 'region' – whether a formal administrative unit in the nomenclature of territorial units for statistics (NUTS) classification, or another type of functional economic, environmental, cultural or urban region. There was on-going comparison to the 'standard' administrative evaluation of regional development policies and programmes, both in terms of economic modelling, and in terms of public management, as exemplified by the MEANS collection (EC 1999).

Several definitions of 'evaluation for RSD' have been proposed, each of which is oriented towards a particular type of purpose:

- 'Applied science carrying out a systematic analysis of causal effects and relationships of an intervention, including criteria driven judgment, and/or recommendations in a transparent process, based on an integrated analysis of aspects of all three dimensions of sustainable development' (Martinuzzi 2004).
- Evaluation of regional sustainability is a dynamic decision-making tool for different levels of the European governance system, supporting implementation of EU anticipated policies and standards aiming at a 'sustainable Europe', and assessments based on quantitative criteria being part of evaluation framework (Goncz and Kistowski 2004).
- Evaluation is 'research to inform decision making' (Vanclay et al 2004).
- Evaluation of RSD 'refers to the integration of SD principles into regional development practice' (Clement 2004).
- Evaluation is an examination, as systematic and objective as possible, of a completed or on-going project/programme/strategy, to determine its efficiency, effectiveness, impact, sustainability and relevance (OECD 1997).

Various frameworks and concept maps were presented and discussed during the evaluation workshop. One overarching framework was discussed and refined through the workshop process (Figure 5.2). This maps out the scope and landscape of the evaluation agenda, in terms of several kinds of linkages:

- Formal evaluation of regional policy and programmes, as a legal requirement of the funding process. Surrounding this is a wider field of appraisal and intelligence building, on all aspects of regional development.

EVALUATION LANDSCAPE MAPPING

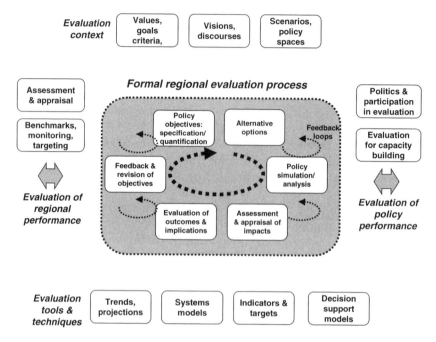

Source: Ravetz (2004).

Figure 5.2   Evaluation landscape mapping

- Upstream of the evaluation process are the origins of the goals, objectives and criteria for evaluation. Downstream of the evaluation process can be seen the outcomes of its application.
- Evaluation of 'regional performance', i.e. the *outcome and context* of policy: in contrast to evaluation of 'policy performance', i.e. the *inputs and outputs* of policy, and the efficiency of the project pipeline.
- Technical tools and information systems for evaluation, with a *quantitative* focus: in contrast to the social processes and policy debates with a more *qualitative* focus.
- Evaluation as a *product*, which aims to provide an objective input to apparently rational decision-making: in contrast to evaluation as a *process* of continuous learning and capacity building, of benefit to all involved.

Counter-Factual Questions

There is a tendency to assume that evaluation is a benign rational activity to assist public servants in their duties to society. To explore this further the REGIONET workshop focused on a range of 'counter-factual' questions which could not be answered from the available data:

- Did the evaluation make any difference to decision-making, apart from the necessary approval of funding?
- Would a counter-factual case of 'no evaluation' or no 'RSD' agenda show any difference?
- Did the evaluation take any account of alternative development models and cultural perspectives?
- How far did the evaluation use the 'RSD' rhetoric as public relations for a conventional development agenda?

REGIONET Policy Recommendations

The findings and recommendations resulting from these REGIONET debates can be summarized as follows:

Evaluation practice

- Identify clearly in the evaluation framework, which are project inputs, outputs, contingent factors contextual factors and policy outcomes.
- Analyse the critical pressures and 'pinch-points' for policy which are between economic, social and environmental domains, and therefore more difficult to focus with current methods.
- Identify a 'tree' of evaluations at different levels of a multi-level governance system; then identify a 'woodland' of evaluation trees which operate at different points in the policy and participation cycle; then identify a 'forest' or landscape which includes different cultural perspectives.
- Analyse more closely the social conflicts, distribution problems and cultural differences underlying the regional development agenda, then use these as the basis for the evaluation criteria.

Technical methods and tools

- Develop tools which link one domain to another: for example, economic activity to environmental pressures.

- Extend the modelling systems to information systems, and information systems to communications/data access systems.
- Identify clear sets of policy options: use scenarios and backcasting as a means to explore the options and the linkages; use trend analysis to identify cumulative effects; use 'story and simulation' approach to link scenarios and modelling.
- Identify social criteria and priorities and build them into a technical framework, using a multi-criteria or similar method.

Social processes and applications

The process focus is very much the new paradigm of evaluation, with much experimentation in progress:

- Evaluation process is a kind of mutual learning and organizational intelligence, and therefore has to be managed like other educational programmes: focused on learning needs; skilled with communications and human resources; student centred.
- Evaluation process should be organized around the communications process and deliberative democratic process, where possible at ex ante, mid-term and ex post stages.
- The evaluation process should extend beyond the formal appraisal of programmes to a more continuous reflexive and strategic deliberation, and evaluation criteria should be generated through a public/organizational discourse/vision process.

Integrated frameworks

The ideal 'integrated framework' is likely to remain out of reach – no one method or tool can deal with evaluations for different purposes at all levels in a large organization. However, it is possible to envisage an integrated framework which is like a connected set of tools:

- Integrating between sectors: from public policy to business strategy, identify how the needs for transparency and social accountability can transfer evaluation models between public and private.
- Focus on the inter-connections between different domains: *economic factors* including institutions, capacities, networks, innovations; *social factors* including multiple worldviews, cohesion, citizenship, capacity; *environmental factors* including resource flow, life-cycle, footprint analysis, socio-environmental values.
- Develop integrated frameworks which combine technical integration and process integration, identifying where this is not directly possible, in conflicts, trade-offs, social and cultural divergence and dissonance.

● Identify where improved evaluation practice is directly part of improved strategic planning, management or monitoring practices: e.g. so that the evaluation is embedded in the organization.

The next section examines two contrasting types of evaluation tool under development, following on from the REGIONET programme. The first is focused on quantitative technical modelling, and the second based on a more qualitative approach to mapping of complex problems.

VI. TYPES OF EVALUATION TOOLS

Evaluation via Technical Modelling

The use of environment–economic modelling in the UK holds out great potential for improved sustainability appraisal and assessment. However, our experience so far shows that the models are only as effective as the learning process which takes place around them, i.e. the extent to which they are incorporated into decision-making.

The UK sustainable development strategy focuses on 'Sustainable consumption and production', a framework for future policy development (HMG 2005). On the 'production' side, the agenda can be framed in terms of 'resource productivity', with eco-efficiency as a driver for business competitiveness (PIU 2001). This suggests analysis of the material flows in industrial sectors, clusters and supply chains; new approaches to innovation and environmental regulation; and the 'eco-modernization' of local and regional economies (Ravetz 1999).

On the 'consumption' side, there is emerging thinking on the sociocultural dynamics of consumption, and the environmental implications of global trade (Jackson and Michaelis 2003). An example of combining the production and consumption sides is the 'factor four' approach, which proposes action on both supply and demand sides to double resource efficiency and halve resource use, as a way of meeting global sustainability targets (von Weizsacker et al. 1997).

Meanwhile the emerging agenda for regional governance has identified a growing demand for tools which can help with enhanced policy integration, evaluation and appraisal (Ravetz et al 2004). Key strands of the RDA economic strategies include industrial clusters, market development and innovation strategies. In parallel, the regional spatial strategies attempt to integrate environmental with spatial planning (Haughton and Counsell 2004). These strands are now converging to form a new policy-technical agenda for RSD, which in its 'stronger green' form, aims to connect global long-term targets with regional policy. This then raises expectations that the technical models can support policy development, and in turn, that the policy development will be stimulated by new technical tools.

The REWARD programme

The conventional economic approach to regional analysis has now been extended to include environmental issues, by the REWARD programme ('Regional and Welsh appraisal of resource productivity and development'). This provides an information base for regional resource productivity, and the beginning of a longer-term programme, 'SCP-net'.[5] The first of its technical tools was the 'REEIO' ('regional economy–environment input–output') model: this provides quantitative analysis of regional strategy and policy appraisal, based on the econometric 'Local economy forecasting model' (Brettell 2003). The REEIO contains a 49-sector input-output structure, and links economic changes with environmental pressures:

- Waste sector: arisings from household, industrial/commercial, construction and agriculture
- Energy sector: demand from households, transport, industrial/commercial; supply by 13 sectors and 6 fuels
- Air emissions: including greenhouse gases and acid precursors
- Water sector: demand related to households/economic activity.

To identify the policy applications, the 'Linking-up' study looked at the use of the model in future studies, strategic planning, and evaluation and appraisal (CURE 2003, see Figure 5.3). The main conclusions were that while such models could play a valuable role in the training and capacity building of policy and other stakeholders, the complex processes involved were not understood well enough to be modelled sufficiently to be of direct use in decision-making. In other words, the model did not quite fit either the technical problem definition or the policy user requirements, and was not suitable for public use at all. However, the mere existence of the model, and the effect of involving different organizations in gathering its data, has some significant effect. So far the REEIO model has been applied in the Northwest, to commercial/industrial waste minimization (CURE 2004), and by other regional development agencies, to assess the types of environmental pressures that may arise under alternative economic scenarios.

Regional material flow analysis

In parallel to the economy–environment approach, there is a variety of complementary modelling techniques which can examine regional material

TOOLKITS FOR REGIONAL SUSTAINABLE DEVELOPMENT

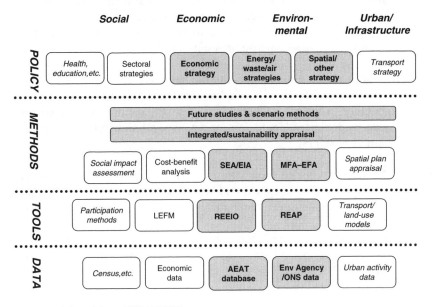

Source: Adapted from CURE (2003).

Figure 5.3 *REWARD methods and tools for regional sustainable development*

and energy flows. Material flow analysis (MFA) looks at inputs in terms of raw materials and products, and outputs in terms of waste and emissions, and stock changes, in terms of key physical indicators (Brunner and Rechberger 2004; Wackernagel and Rees 1996):

- *Direct material consumption* (DMC): the total materials directly used in the regional economy and consumed in the region, i.e. excluding exports.
- *Total material consumption* (TMC): total material use, including DMC and the indirect or 'hidden' material flows associated with it.
- *Carbon dioxide emissions* (CO_2): may be modelled specifically, as the largest component of climate change emissions.
- *Ecological footprint analysis* (EFA) measures material and energy flows in 'global hectares per person'. This may, for example, be calculated from the CO_2 emissions, land use changes and material flows throughout the entire planning period, as a simplified form of life-cycle analysis. The EF is analysed on a 'consumer responsibility'

basis, measuring impacts from all material flows involved in meeting the final demand from households and government. While there are technical questions concerning the comprehensiveness of the analysis, the EFA has great communicative power, and is very popular with regional and local environmental initiatives.

Since 1996, a major research programme has been sponsored by the Biffa plc waste company, via the UK Landfill Tax Credit Scheme funding.[6] These 'mass balance' projects have focused on industrial sectors – substances and products – and selected UK regions or devolved administrations. There are two main approaches:

● Production centred focus: this includes raw materials and manufacturing within the region, and includes exports plus regional final demand. This is more compatible with the aforementioned REEIO model.
● Consumption centred focus: the products and services delivered to final consumers, both direct and indirect, with impacts both local and global. This is based on a life-cycle analysis approach and the EFA as a simplified version.

In principle a combined system could include both production and consumption, as follows, although this is limited by available data (Figure 5.4):

● There is a five-stage breakdown, corresponding to the primary, secondary, tertiary, demand and 'externalities' economic sectors: each shows a different relationship between material flow and economic value added.
● Various waste streams are shown by the shaded boxes on the right hand side, coming off each of the stages.
● Mass balances of production and consumption are shown at each stage in the production–consumption chain, including for exports and imports.
● The 'products in use' circle shows the operation of infrastructure such as vehicles or buildings.
● Resource efficiency or productivity, i.e. the useful outputs per unit of input, can be measured at various stages along the chain.

The REAP model

The resource and energy analysis programme (REAP) model is an adaptation of the 'Long-range energy analysis programme' by the Stockholm Environment Institute at York, with CURE in Manchester.[7] It is organized

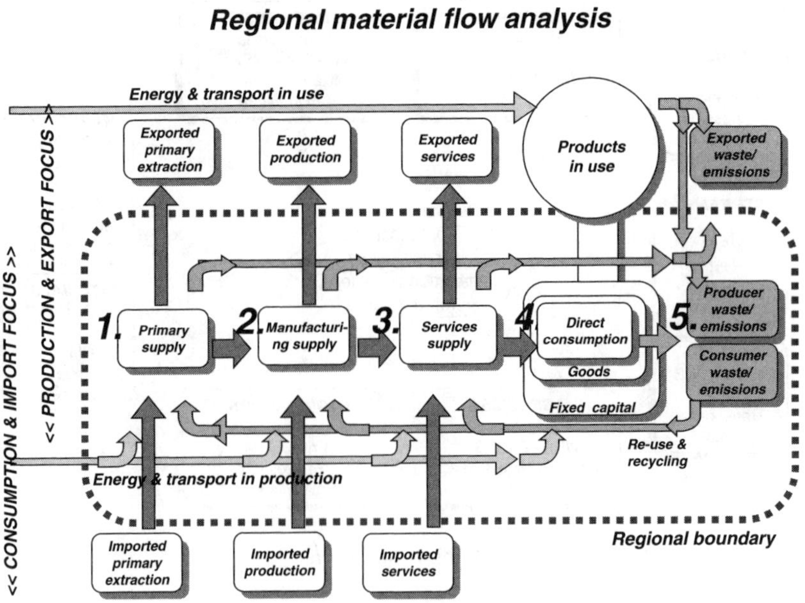

Regional material flow analysis

Source: CURE (2005).

Figure 5.4 Regional material flow analysis framework

around the MFA framework mentioned previously, to provide an advanced data and modelling toolkit, mainly focused on climate emissions, MFA and EFA. In this it provides some unique features:

- analysis of inter-dependencies between sectors and supply chains, via physical input-output tables and database for the UK regions. These are organized in 76 sectors corresponding to the Office of National Statistics Environmental Accounts, and over 300 product types from the PRODCOM database (Vaze and Balchin 1996; Ekins 2004);
- analysis of total impacts of consumption to meet final demand, through a detailed model of international trade and UK imports;
- analysis of material flow at regional and local authority level. The local level is calculated through applying physical throughput to household expenditure data and then to the local area Acorn classification.

Applications of the models

Experience shows that modelling and benchmarking tools have to be situated within policy and business practices, if they are to be used and useful. It is also clear that few modelling or benchmarking tools are well equipped

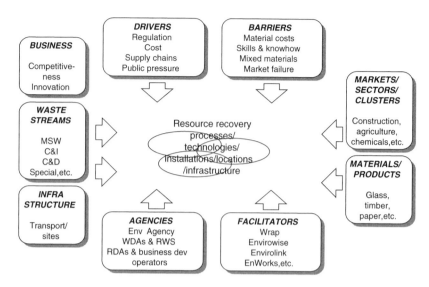

Figure 5.5   Waste sector mapping round table

to deal with the complexities of supply chains, actors and networks, let alone the challenge of evolutionary and structural change. However, there are growing aspirations and rapid learning from regional policy makers on the issues of RSD and resource productivity. This tends to force the development and application of such tools, even in the absence of a full understanding of causal relationships and the availability of accurate data. In waste management policy, for instance, few conventional models are able to deal with the new policy agenda for global effects, supply chain analysis, and extended responsibilities for different actors. A 'sector mapping' round table process may be able to facilitate the kind of partnership working which is needed. As far as technical models can enable and inform more qualitative processes of this nature, then their contribution is very real (Figure 5.5).

Evaluation via Problem Mapping

Some of the REGIONET partners are now engaged in a follow-on project, which aims to apply these lessons to a very topical theme in RSD – regional innovation policy. In the last decade, some 120 EU regions have used the RIS/RITTS (regional innovation strategy/technology transfer scheme) approach to develop their innovation policies. Their project evaluation reports have looked at the immediate outputs and impacts, but not so much at the longer-term outcomes, indirect effects, or any benchmarking between nations and sectors. With the very large funds now being targeted on innovation activities, there is a clear need to push the state of the art further, and this is the aim of the current FP6 project 'EUROCOOP' (2005–08).

The EUROCOOP starts with the perceived limits and challenges from the current experience of evaluation:

- Evaluation of qualitative processes which are arguably more significant than quantitative 'output' indicators. For instance, the output indicators include 'number of patents', which may be a significant measure in western EU capitals, but not in many other regions, where the quality of interaction between firms and agencies is more important.
- Evaluation of interventions in complex systems undergoing rapid and uncertain change. There are no deterministic models which can begin to represent the complexity of a regional economy, and therefore the estimation of longer-term outcomes and impacts from intervention is more intuition than science.
- Evaluation of multi-level interventions where the question of 'agency' by the evaluators/'evaluatees' is an essential part of the picture.

One recurring question in the evaluation of any public policy intervention is that of additionality – the extent to which the outcomes would have occurred without intervention. Here the former mechanistic view on additionality is now shifting towards a 'systems of innovation' framework, where temporary financial interventions may be less important than efforts to change the whole pattern of interactions between organizations, networks, supply chains and technologies (Cooke et al. 2003). If it is accepted that RIS-type actions are correcting an inherent tendency for short-term horizons and fragmented networks, then an RIS may be best evaluated in terms of its ability to change values and behaviour in these directions (Georghiou 2002).

This perspective on 'behavioural additionality' changes the focus of the evaluation towards the more qualitative, embedded, socio-cultural and process-based interactions. A more extended evaluation process will look at the interactions of RIS-type interventions with the strategies and cultures of participating organizations, and involve more complex judgments on organizational change, multi-level governance and socio-technical diffusion. In dealing with such complexity and uncertainty the onus then shifts towards the evaluation of process rather than product, and evaluation itself as part of the process. This then tends towards other process-oriented activities such as regional foresight (PREST 2003), which are not strictly evaluation as such, but which can contribute greatly.

A further question is how 'innovation' may be defined and constructed as a goal in itself, or for larger goals (competitiveness, quality of life, sustainability, etc.). There is a general policy assumption that innovation is concerned with new technology. In response the EUROCOOP project also looks at other types of innovation in other sectors:

- innovation in institutions/governance to handle technology networks and partnerships
- innovation in financial models, inter-mediation, trading schemes and social markets
- innovation in consumer and public services on the demand/consumption side
- innovation in social enterprise and citizen responsibility to enhance social capital.

In response to such challenges, the REGIONET approach to evaluation points towards an alternative mode. In EUROCOOP this has been defined as 'policy opportunity evaluation' – a more entrepreneurial and dynamic approach to exploring opportunities and risks, rather than a mechanistic assessment method which assumes simple cause and effect. In the EURO-COOP project this is now emerging as a twin track approach:

- 'Complex problem mapping': for instance, when technology, supply chains, markets, investment, labour skills, capacity building, infrastructure do not magically all coincide, what can be done? Going beyond the official EC model of policy impact assessment, the EUROCOOP toolkit combines elements of strategic choice, soft systems analysis, AIDA (analysis of inter-connected decision areas), priority choice, and visioning/foresight techniques, etc.
- 'Component level evaluation': this runs in parallel to the complex approach as a practical benchmarking method. It focuses on the components or precursors of innovation systems activity, in all its complexity. This includes not only formal qualities of patents, R&D, etc., but soft/informal factors of ICT access, global networks, and the informal/grey/black economies as indicators of latent entrepreneurial capacity.

VII.   ROAD MAPPING FOR SUSTAINABLE ECONOMIC DEVELOPMENT

Clearly there is potential for the *quantitative modelling* approach to facilitate and inform the *qualitative mapping* approach, and this points towards future developments for the next decade. For instance, the policy agenda for 'sustainable economic development' clearly needs the best available tools for evaluation, appraisal and capacity building, for example, an extended evaluation process would identify the dynamics of industrial supply chains, and explore the potential for partnership policy development, with the aim of enabling more integrated supply chain management, all within the macro-level environmental targets (Ravetz 2006). The 'road map' of the SCP-net, now under development in the UK as an interactive website, shows the potential opportunities for sustainable economic development in the near to medium future, and this then acts as the 'base case' for project appraisal and evaluation within that framework (Figure 5.6).

The 'policy opportunity evaluation' process can then take this moving picture as the context, rather than any 'default' based deterministic assessment. It then explores current trends and possible interventions in terms of this enlarged field of opportunities, and in so doing becomes part of the enabling and learning among the actors involved.

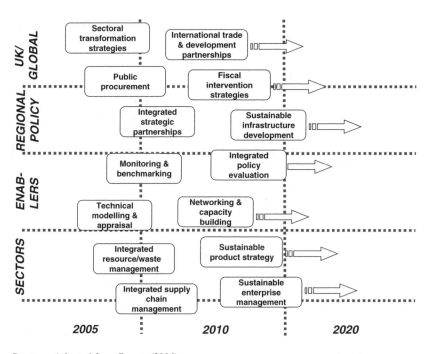

Source: Adapted from Ravetz (2006).

Figure 5.6 'Road mapping' for regional sustainable economic strategy

VIII.   CONCLUSIONS

Just as public policy is undergoing rapid transition, so is the practice of evaluation and appraisal. Such transitions are seen in emerging techniques of appraisal, in new possibilities for information and communications, and in changing modes of management and governance. Many such innovations are centred on the integration between environmental, social and economic agendas; between different sectors and actors; and between different levels of government. These are some of the dimensions of this field:

- Institutional-oriented evaluation – a closer fit to stages of the policy/management cycle, via characterization of policy discourse, policy spaces, sectoral linkages and institutional context;
- Social/cultural-oriented evaluation – a deeper and more active engagement with stakeholders, aiming to identify underlying needs/values, and hence objectives and criteria;
- Economic and sectoral-oriented evaluation – comparing different economic perspectives from producers and consumers, to help quantify and rank differing values and criteria;
- Environment and resource-oriented evaluation – focusing on externalities in time and space; whole systems of production and consumption; cross-media and cross-sectoral effects; communications and awareness-raising;
- Future studies and vision-oriented evaluation – this uses trend analysis and participative scenario studies, to enable a wider whole-systems perspective as a context for policy evaluation and impact assessment;
- Agent-based evaluation – aims at deeper understanding of constraints and opportunities of actors, and hence better analysis and communication of actual policy spaces.

While the future is clearly exciting, the current state of the art is often not well advanced. There is tension between policy applications which need simple and robust methods, and technical applications which call for increasingly sophisticated data management. The optimum balance depends on the purpose, the organizations and the learning potential of the actors involved, each of which is a moving factor.

Finally, the counter-factual questions from the REGIONET experience lead to several concerns about the usefulness of RSD evaluations. Are the current efforts on counting indicators akin to those of medieval theologians, evaluating how many angels might dance on a pinhead? Are the evaluation reports another kind of media product, blending objective and subjective information, to provide little but in-group therapy for policy makers? In the interests of evaluation as both an art and a science, we may propose three provocative hypotheses for further testing. First, the practical purposes of evaluation are generally the distribution of money, the exercise of power, therapy (mitigation of contradictions) and hegemonic reproduction of society (and generally in that order). Second, one 'higher purpose' of evaluation is to generate learning on the internal contradictions of societies and cultures at the regional scale, otherwise known as regional sustainable development (RSD). And third, any public strategy which fully adopts the results of an independent evaluation will be flexible enough for this higher purpose to be politically acceptable. Each of these has been demonstrated in some way by the REGIONET results, and each suggests further avenues for future research.

NOTES

1. The REGIONET Thematic Network.
2. European Network for Sustainable Urban and Regional Development research: current papers are available on *www.iccr-international/ensure* (October 2005).
3. REGIONET: strategies for regional sustainable development: an integrated approach beyond best practices: contract EVG1-CT-2001-2003. All project papers on *www.iccrinternational.org/regionet*.
4. The results of the conference are reported in Ravetz et al (2004). The full set of conference papers, slides, briefing papers, proceedings and EC policy reports can also be found on the project website *www.iccr-international.org/regionet* and *www.art.man.ac.uk/PLANNING/cure/regionet*.
5. Details on *www.reward-uk.org* or *www.scpnet.org.uk*.
6. Details on *www.massbalance.org*.
7. Details on *www.ecologicalbudget.org.uk* and *www.regionalsustainability.org* (October 2005).

REFERENCES

Bertrand, F and Larrue, C (2004), 'Integration of the sustainable development evaluation process in regional planning in France', *Journal of Environmental Assessment Policy and Management*, 6 (4).

Brettell, S and Gardiner, B (2003), 'Application of econometric models to evaluation', in European Commission (ed.) *Methods for Evaluation of Structural Programmes* (MEANS) Handbook, Luxembourg.

Brunner, P and Rechberger, C (2004), *A Practical Handbook of Material Flow Analysis*, London, Lewis Publishers.

Chelimsky, E (1997), 'The coming transformations in evaluation', in Chelimsky, E and Shadish, W R (eds) *Evaluation for the 21st Century*, London, Sage Publications.

Clement, K (2004), 'A holarchical model for regional sustainability assessment', *Journal of Environmental Assessment Policy and Management*, 6 (4).

Cooke, P. Roper, S and Wylie, P (2003), 'The golden thread of innovation and Northern Ireland's evolving regional innovation system', *Regional Studies*, 37 (4), 365–80.

CURE (Centre for Urban & Regional Ecology) (2003), *Linking Environmental-Economic Modeling into Sustainable Planning in Wales and the Regions*, Bristol, Environment Agency. Available as of January 2007 on www.scpnet.org.uk.

CURE (Centre for Urban & Regional Ecology) (2004), *REWARD NW: Building*

Evidence to Inform Regional Commercial & Industrial Waste Policy, Bristol, Environment Agency. Available as of January 2007 on www.scpnet.org.uk.

Eales, R, Smith, S, Twigger-Ross, C, Sheate, W, Özdemiroglu, E, Fry, C, Tomlinson, P and Foan, C (2005), 'Emerging approaches to integrated appraisal in the UK', *Impact Assessment and Project Appraisal*, 23 (2), 113–23.

European Commission (1999), *The MEANS Collection: Evaluating Socio-economic Programmes, vol.1, Evaluation Design and Management*, Luxembourg, Office for Official Publications of the European Communities.

European Commission (2001), *European Governance: A White Paper*, from http://europa.eu.int/eur-lex/en/com/cne/2001/com2001_0428en01.pdf on 10/9/2003.

European Commission (2002), *Communication from the Commission on Impact Assessment*, COM(2002) 276, Brussels 5.6.2002.

European Commission (2005), *Impact Assessment Guidelines*, SEC(2005) 791, Luxembourg.

Funtowicz, S, Martinez-Alier, J, Munda, G and Ravetz, J (2002), 'Multicriteria-based environmental policy', in Hussein, A and Baranzini, A (eds) *Implementing Sustainable Development: Integrated Assessment and Participatory Decision-Making Processes*, Cheltenham, Edward Elgar, pp. 53–77.

Gabriel, I and Narodoslawski, M (eds) (1998), *Regions: Cornerstones of Sustainable Development*, Technical University of Graz.

Georghiou, L, 'Impact and additionality of innovation policy', in Boekholt, P (ed.) (2002) *Innovation Policy and Sustainable Development: Can Innovation Incentives make a Difference?*, Brussels, IWT-Observatory.

GHK, Policy Studies Institute, Institute for European Environmental Policy, Cambridge Econometrics (2003), *The Contribution of the Structural Funds to Sustainable Development: A Synthesis Report* (volume 1) to DG Regio, EC. Available on (accessed October 2004), http://europa.eu.int/comm/regional_policy/sources/docgener/evaluation/rado_en.htm.

Goncz, E and Kistowski, M (2004), 'A method for environmental sustainability assessment: the case of the Polish regions', *Journal of Environmental Assessment Policy and Management*, 6 (4).

Hall, P and Ward, C (1998), *Sociable Cities: The Legacy of Ebenezer Howard*, Chichester, Wiley.

Haughton, G and Counsell, C (2004), *Regions, Spatial Strategies and Sustainable Development*, London, Routledge.

HMG (2005), *Securing the Future: A National Strategy for Sustainable Development*, London, TSO.

Jackson, T and Michaelis, L (2003), *Policies for Sustainable Consumption*, London, Sustainable Development Commission.

Jiliberto, Herrera R (2004), 'A holarchical model for regional sustainability assessment', *Journal of Environmental Assessment Policy and Management*, 6 (4).

Lafferty, W and Narodoslawski, M (2003), 'Editorial introduction', in Lafferty, W and Narodoslawski, M (eds) *Regional Sustainable Development in Europe: The Challenge of Multi-level Governance*, Oslo, Prosus.

Martinuzzi, A (2004), 'Evaluating sustainable development in 11 countries', *Journal of Environmental Assessment Policy and Management*, 6 (4).

McEvoy, D and Ravetz, J (2001), 'Toolkits for regional sustainable development', (introduction to guest-edited special issue), *Impact Assessment and Project Appraisal*, 19 (2), 90–3.

Midgley, G (2000), *Systemic Intervention: Philosophy, Methodology and Practice*, New York, Kluwer Academic/Plenum Publishers.

Moss, T and Fichter, H (2003), 'Lessons in promoting sustainable development in EU Structural Funds Programmes', *Sustainable Development*, 11, 56–65.

Mulgan, G (1997), *Connexity*, London, Calder & Boyars.

OECD (1997), *Sustainable Development: OECD Policy Approaches for the 21st Century*, Paris, OECD.

Performance & Innovation Unit (2001), *Resource Productivity: Making More with Less*, London, TSO.

PREST (2003), *Practical Guide to Regional Foresight in the United Kingdom*, Luxembourg, European Commission. Available as of January 2007 on http://cordis.europa.eu/foresight/cgrf.htm.

Ravetz, J (1999), 'Citizen participation for integrated assessment: new pathways in complex systems', *International Journal of Environment and Pollution*, 11 (3), 331–50.

Ravetz, J (1999), 'Economy, environment & the sustainable city: notes from Greater Manchester', in Roberts, P and Gouldson, A (eds) *Integrating Environment and Economy: Local and Regional Strategies*, London, Routledge.

Ravetz, J (2000a), *City-Region 2020: Integrated Planning for a Sustainable Environment*, London, Earthscan (with the TCPA).

Ravetz, J (2002), 'New toolkits for regional sustainable development: information and communications systems for integrated policy and action', *Okologisches Wirtschaften*, 1, 12–16 (ISSN 1430 8800).

Ravetz, J (2004), 'Evaluation of regional sustainable development – mapping the landscape' (introduction to guest-edited issue), *Journal of Environmental Assessment Planning and Management*, 6 (4), v–xxi.

Ravetz, J (2006), 'Regional innovation & resource productivity – new approaches to analysis and communication', in Randles, S and Green, K (eds) *Industrial Ecology & Spaces of Innovation*, Cheltenham, Edward Elgar.

Ravetz, J, Coccossis, H, Schleicher-Tappeser, R and Steele, P (2004), 'Evaluation of regional sustainable development – transitions and prospects', *Journal of Environmental Assessment Planning & Management*, 6 (4), 585–619.

Roberts, P (2003), 'Partnerships, programmes and the promotion of regional development: an evaluation of the operation of the Structural Funds regional programmes', *Progress in Planning*, 59 (1), 1–69.

Scrase, J I and Sheate, W R (2002), 'Integration and integrated approaches – what do they mean for the environment?', *Journal of Environmental Policy and Planning*, 4 (4), 275–94.

Tamborra, M (2002), *Socio-economic Tools for Sustainability Impact Assessment: The Contribution of EU Research to Sustainable Development*, European Commission, EUR 20437.

Tamborra, M (2003), *Socio-economic Tools for Sustainability Impact Assessment*, European Commission, DG Research, in proceedings of REGIONET Workshop 3, www.iccr-international.org/regionet.

Vanclay, F (2004), ' "Committing To Place" and evaluating the higher purpose', *Journal of Environmental Assessment Policy and Management*, 6 (4).

Vaze, P and Balchin, S (1996), 'The pilot UK environment accounts', *Econ. Trends*, 514, 41–67.

von Weizsacker, E, Lovins, A and Lovins, L H (1997), *Factor Four: Doubling Wealth, Halving Resource Use*, London, Earthscan.

Wackernagel, M and Rees, W (1996), *Our Ecological Footprint: Reducing Human Impact on the Earth*, British Columbia, Gabriola Island, New Society Publishers.

WCED (World Commission on Environment and Development) (1987), *Our Common Future*, (The Bruntland Report), Oxford, Oxford University Press.

6. Considering environmental aspects in integrated impact assessment: lessons learned and challenges ahead

Klaus Jacob, Julia Hertin and Axel Volkery[1]

I. INTRODUCTION

The tool of impact assessments (IAs) has steadily gained attention throughout the last years.[2] Whereas in the 1980s only a few countries had introduced procedures for regulatory impact assessment, it diffused more rapidly throughout the 1990s amongst OECD countries (Radaelli 2004, 2005). Initially, the main concern was to minimize costs for business actors and to increase transparency of rule making (OECD 1997). Over the last five years or so, there have been efforts to integrate several sectoral assessments into one overall integrated procedure (European Commission 2002). This development is driven on the one hand by the concern for implementing the 'better regulation' agenda. On the other hand, IA is also promoted to address the requirements of sustainable development. Both agendas require a better integration and coherence of policies, and IA is considered as a key tool to accomplish this task. The new impetus for integrated IA has been met with great interest and expectations from the environmental side since integrated IA appears to offer a new way of strengthening environmental policy integration. However, there are also many critics who fear a sidelining of the environmental agenda due to the obvious tensions with the better regulation agenda (Volkery and Jacob 2005).

This chapter compares IA systems in Canada, the EU, the Netherlands, the UK, Australia, Italy and the US, exploring how the different systems work, which functions they have, how they are situated within the political process and whether they achieve the different aims of IA. The analysis of 1A systems was performed in 2004 and early 2005. We are particularly concerned with the question of how IA relates to environmental policy integration: does IA promote environmental policy integration and are there tensions between the better regulation agenda and the sustainability goal?

Does IA offer an opportunity for rationalizing the decision-making process or does it open up a new forum for bargaining and political conflict? This chapter argues that a constructive and balanced approach to IA is dependent on a number of procedural and institutional requirements.

The chapter is organized as follows: in the next section, we discuss the overall rationale of IA, describing the objectives and goals, highlighting the challenges and pointing to obstacles in the practical routines of modern bureaucracy. In the third section, we analyse the procedures for IA in the seven jurisdictions. We then draw conclusions from our comparative research and propose a preliminary list of requirements for ensuring an adequate consideration of environmental concerns in integrated IA. The final section concludes the chapter.

II. AIMS AND OBJECTIVES OF INTEGRATED IMPACT ASSESSMENT

Typically, an assessment describes a policy problem, identifies potential measures, assesses possible effects and describes options to achieve the policy objectives efficiently. Rationalizing the process of policy-making in this way aims to enable decision makers to choose the policy option with the greatest benefits at lowest costs. Consequently, the overall regulatory quality is supposed to increase whereas the overall regulatory and administrative burden for business and society should be reduced, resulting in a net benefit for all sides. The quest for the most efficient and effective solution should be supported by early stimulation of interdisciplinary cooperation and early consultation between administrations and stakeholders.

This traditional understanding of IA as regulatory impact assessment (RIA) has been broadened in many countries over the last decade. There is a trend to include aspects other than costs of regulation, for example environmental issues, economic competitiveness, concerns of small and medium enterprises, gender aspects, or, more broadly conceptualized, the implementation of sustainable development. IA is now a common device for the consideration of cross-cutting, generic objectives within government.

Recently, the European Commission and several member states have launched initiatives aiming to integrate the various assessment procedures in one single assessment framework. The idea is to undertake a comprehensive assessment of all possible impacts of new legislation, including unintended side-effects and the assessment of inter-linkages between different issues of concern. Such an integrated perspective aims to reveal conflicts between objectives or identify win-win solutions at an early stage of decision-making.

Thus, integrated IA is based on the assumption that policies can be (at least to a certain extent) designed according to principles of rational and linear decision-making. However, such a stringent order of policy steps – defined problems, probing of alternative solutions and decision-making by unitary actors (OECD 1997) – does not usually reflect the reality of the policy-making process. The reality of decision-making is better described as a process where solutions, actors and problems are largely independent and constantly modified. Policy-making is strongly influenced by politics and thus follows a logic which is different from linear problem solving (see the contributions in Sabatier 1999). For example, Richardson (1996) argued convincingly that EU policy-making is closer to a model of a garbage can (Cohen et al 1972) than to rational-synoptic policy process: interest bargaining against the background of changing situative framework conditions leads to policy outputs that reflect what was possible rather than what was the best regulatory option. Following this perspective, we would expect different actors to try to use IA for their own goals, depending on their preferences (Bernauer and Caduff 2004): bureaucrats, for example, may use IA to legitimate the activities of the civil service, while companies and business associations would seek protection against regulations that negatively affect their competitiveness.

Hence, IA procedures will not only vary according to the main purpose of the assessment. It depends also on the group of actors involved in the decision-making process and the function within the political process. Four functions can, in principle, be associated with IA:

- Analysis function: IA can help provide information, data and analysis to support the assessment of intended and unintended impacts of planned policies.
- Transparency function: through the definition of decision criteria and procedural steps IA can enhance the transparency of the policy process.
- Participation: through consultation during the IA process, a range of social groups can contribute to the analysing and weighing up of the potential costs and benefits of a policy.
- Integration: a structured process of IA can support the consideration and integration of generic objectives such as enhancement of competitiveness, gender mainstreaming or sustainability within the decision-making process.

Within these functions tensions may arise. A dispute about objectives, methods and tools can easily undermine the overall legitimacy of IA. Legitimacy is, however, crucial for the success of any IA. A lack of legitimacy might either degrade an IA into a meaningless exercise or lead to highly contested assessments that delay the process of rule making. IA may also have undesirable effects on the regulatory process, for example by enabling early lobbying activities, delaying decisions or legitimizing decisions that were not open to a public debate. This may lead to a sidelining of weaker interests, such as those representing social or environmental concerns. On this background of different issues, actors and functions of IA, it remains a question open to investigation whether the balance between different objectives can be secured through certain institutional provisions.

III. COMPARISON OF IA SYSTEMS: SIMILARITIES, DIFFERENCES AND TRENDS

IA in Practice – Convergence of Approaches?

The analysis of IA procedures and practice covers the EU and six OECD countries (most of which are regarded as forerunners in ex ante appraisal of generic national-level policies): Australia, Canada, Italy, Netherlands, the UK and US. In the following, key results from detailed case studies (cf. Bartolomeo et al 2005) are summarized. We focus on the basic orientation of the IA procedure and on the features and differences in the practical operation.

Four countries (US, AUS, UK, IT) have IA systems that are focused on reducing regulatory burden and promoting alternative policy measures by subjecting new legislation to an analysis of costs and benefits. In two of those countries (AUS, UK) there have recently been attempts to broaden the scope of analysis to include environmental and other sustainability issues. In both cases this was prompted by pressure from political institutions (departments and/or advisory bodies for environment and sustainable development). The effect of these changes on the practice of IA has so far been limited. This broadening has usually involved qualitative rather than quantitative analysis due to methodological difficulties, the inherent complexities of sustainability issues and a lack of data. Three of the seven regulatory systems (EU, UK, NL) have in the past experimented with specific environmental assessment procedures for national-level policies. However, only the Netherlands has integrated an explicitly environmental procedure into the mainstream IA system. The assessment procedures in Canada and in the European Commission combine the aim of improving the quality of regulation with efforts to use IA as an instrument to promote policy integration and sustainable development.

Overall, it appears that in most countries, requirements to consider environmental aspects during the development of new regulatory proposals have been strengthened in recent years. Although a certain degree of convergence is notable, the ways in which this has occurred and the extent to which it has affected policy-making in practice vary considerably. Variation is not only apparent in the basic orientation of the IA system, but also with regard to formal procedures, institutional context and assessment practice (Table 6.1).

Key Features and Differences of Integrated IA Procedures

The key similarities and differences can be summarized as follows:

1. **Trigger**: an IA is usually mandatory when expected impacts are large. In countries with emphasis on cost-benefit analysis (US, UK and AUS), a monetary threshold is sometimes given, while others use the proportionality principle in a less formal way (EU).
2. **Coordinating body and evaluation**: in countries with strong IA procedures, coordination is often in the responsibility of the president's or prime minister's office, although the Italian case shows that central coordination is not a guarantee for implementation. The coordinating body is usually (but not always) in charge of guidance, support, evaluation and review. In some of the countries considered (UK, CAN) the coordination is perceived as a political role, while in others (EU, NL), coordination is limited mainly to technical assistance of IA procedures.
3. **Consultation**: the role of stakeholders in the assessment process varies strongly. No consultation is foreseen in either the US (where emphasis is on transparency rather than participation), or in the Netherlands, where the focus is on information provision. Consultation plays an important role in several other systems (EU, UK, AUS) where the contribution of stakeholders to scoping, data gathering and analysis is seen as central for the officers.
4. **Implementation**: the rate of implementation varies from almost 0% (IT) to close to 100% (UK). High implementation rates (UK, US and AUS) were found in countries with a long tradition of conducting IA and have been achieved through strong political commitment at high political levels as well as tight quality assurance procedures.
5. **Impacts considered**: in principle, most IA systems aim to consider all relevant impacts, whether economic, social or environmental. In practice, however, most procedures focus on direct, short-term and financial costs. The scope of assessments was significantly broader in several countries (AUS, UK, CAN).
6. **Level of detail and quantification**: the comprehensiveness of analysis in practice is very different. The US system is the most rigorous, detailed and quantitative, at least with regard to economic costs and benefits.

Table 6.1 Comparison of procedures for integrated and regulatory impact assessment

	Australia	Canada	EU	Italy	Netherlands	UK	US
Name of main IA procedure	Regulatory impact statements	Regulatory impact assessment statements	Impact assessment	Regulatory impact assessment	Business-test and environment test	Regulatory impact assessment	Regulatory impact analysis
Date of first introduction	Federal: 1985 Inter-govern-mental: 1995	1999: current RIA 1977: previous system	2002	1999	1995	1985	1981
Primary focus	Reducing negative impacts of regulation on business and competition	Maximizing benefits from regulation	Improving quality of policy and promoting sustainability	Simplifying and improving regulation	Improving quality of regulation, reducing effects on business and implementing environmental policy	Reducing regulatory burden and improving quality of policy	Reducing regulatory burden and maximizing benefits from regulation
Trigger for assessment procedure	Federal: direct or indirect impacts on business or competition Inter-governmental: impact on	All, proposals, quantitative CBA if direct costs exceed $10 million	Current: proposals selected by Commission From 2005: all proposals in Commission's Work	Preliminarily: all Full: if costs are likely to exceed a certain threshold	Preliminary: all	Proposals expected to have an impact on business, charities or the voluntary sector	All eco-nomically significant regulations (effects on economy > $ 100 million)

95

Table 6.1 (continued)

	Australia	Canada	EU	Italy	Netherlands	UK	US
	business or individuals		Programme				
Legal basis	Federal: Cabinet decision Inter-governmental: COAG guidelines	Cabinet directive	Commission communication	Law	Government decision	Regulatory Reform Bill, decision by prime minister	President's order
Coordinating body	Office of Regulation Review	Treasury Board	Secretariat-General	Prime Minister's Office	Proposed Legislation Desk (Ministries of Economic Affairs and of Justice)	Prime Minister's Cabinet Office	President's Office of Management and Budget
Evaluation and quality control	Strong advice, evaluation and review mechanisms by ORR	Strong advice, evaluation and review mechanisms by RAOIC, TB and General Auditor	Weak advice and evaluation role by Secretariat-General	Some review by Prime Minister's Office foreseen	Quality control left to responsible ministry	Strong advice, evaluation and review mechanisms by Cabinet Office; each minister can challenge RIA	Strong advice, evaluation and review mechanisms by OMB
Support	Guidance documents, ORR staff assist RIS preparation	Guidance and training provided by RAOIC and privy council	Some advice provided by Secretariat-General	Prime Minister's Office and expert committee provide advice	Proposed Legislation Desk	Cabinet Office provides advice and support	

Involvement of stakeholders in the assessment	Consultation with affected groups, consultation statement forms part of RIS	Not foreseen	Consultation with affected groups, consultation process to be described in IA report	Extensive involvement foreseen, but few practice examples	Not foreseen	Formal consultation with stakeholders, especially small firms, government departments and enforcers	Not foreseen
Impact areas formally included	Direct and indirect, short and long-term economic, social and environmental impacts on all affected groups	All costs and benefits; SEA to be conducted if environmental effects are expected	Economic, social and environmental impacts	Impacts on citizens, firms and public administration	Environmental and business impacts	All direct and indirect costs and benefits, including unintended and distributional effects	All types of costs and benefits

Source: Jacob et al (2005).

The Dutch system on the other side of the spectrum is very selective and pragmatic. Those looking at a broader range of impacts tend to be more qualitative in nature.

IV. SAFEGUARDING THE ENVIRONMENTAL DIMENSION IN INTEGRATED ASSESSMENT PROCEDURES

In most countries, environmental policy appraisal was initially conceived as a separate procedure. The approach and methodology drew on established assessment methodologies for site-specific projects such as environmental impact assessment and strategic environmental assessment. As the experience in several of the cases shows, there is a recent trend to integrate environmental appraisal into existing regulatory appraisal schemes. This is both a response to the integrative character of the sustainability agenda and to the proliferation of appraisal procedures.

The cases of the EU and the UK suggest that integrating environmental aspects in widely used systems of regulatory analysis may be more promising than introducing specific environmental appraisals which are little used despite formal requirements. However, simply adding environmental criteria to the existing procedures and guidance documents does not guarantee that these are considered in practice. To address this – particularly given the potentially wide range environmental effects and the propensity of desk officers in sectoral ministries to minimize effort devoted to IA – the procedure has to set out how it should be decided which environmental impact areas should be considered by an IA. Some of the studied IA procedures have attempted to address this issue, for example by integrating into the IA guidelines a comprehensive list of impact areas to be considered (EU) or through a short set of generic questions (NL, UK). Another more rigorous, but also more time-consuming option would be to charge an interdepartmental working group with the task of drawing up a list of relevant impact areas on a case-by-case basis.

Addressing Environmental Concerns at Each Stage

To ensure adequate treatment, environmental concerns have to be considered at each step of the IA. Environmental concerns may be included either as a formal requirement or by empowering environmental actors (most often the Ministry of the Environment) to take part in the decision-making process in order to safeguard the consideration of environmental concerns. In some countries (UK, Canada), the final responsibility is shifted to the prime minister's office. Furthermore, in Canada, the Commissioner for Sustainable Development is entitled to review the process of IA. There is no other example for a systematic external review. In principle, it would also be possible to ensure a balanced approach by making IA subject to a legal review, but we have not found an example of this practice. The examples of the EU, UK and Canada underline the need for a high level political commitment: in all of these countries the special environmental impact assessment procedures have not been systematically applied for several years until the prime minister's office or other central parts of government took over the lead for the process. In Italy, there is clearly a lack of commitment for the conduct of IA, and hence the tool is hardly applied at all.

Occasionally, the selection of proposals for IA creates a dispute among involved departments (e.g. in the EU). Again, this can be solved by drawing up a list of formal criteria. However, where formal thresholds have been introduced, these usually refer to economic impacts. Regarding environmental impacts, most country guidelines call for an IA if 'substantial' impacts can be expected without providing a more precise definition. Therefore, the selection of proposals for IA is often based on political bargaining between the different departments.

Typically, in the first step of an IA, the policy problem is defined. A balanced consideration of impacts is crucial in the framing of the problem (to ensure that the policy choice is not pre-determined by the process of problem formulation) and the definition of the baseline ('no policy') scenario against which options are assessed. Environmental concerns should be given equal weight to economic and social concerns.

Supporting the Analysis of Unintended Effects

Even in the forerunner countries a full implementation of quality standards in ex ante assessment has proven difficult. Although IA is designed to cover all areas of sustainability, many current reports focus on the conventional aspects of regulatory analysis. Typically, the assessment covers only the direct and intended effects of a planned policy. However, to improve the appraisal procedure it is important to understand and acknowledge both political and technical difficulties associated with the assessment of unintended consequences.

The perceived role and mission of sectoral ministries has traditionally not included environmental concerns. Therefore, assessing policies on environmental criteria can be perceived as a marginal requirement. Moreover, as the identification of significant unintended effects may open the door to political challenges, departments can be expected to embark on the analysis of these effects cautiously and sometimes reluctantly.

Anticipating environmental effects in detail is frequently very difficult, especially in areas with uncertainty, a lack of data, external effects and complex causal chains. Desk officers will not always have the expertise to identify and assess potential environmental impacts. They may also be unwilling to engage with what appears to be speculative and normative analysis. Accessing expertise in other parts of the administration involves transaction costs and institutional barriers. Even where knowledge is made available, substantial resources are needed to carry out the analysis.

Although these barriers are difficult to overcome, certain measures can help address them. Sectoral departments need to be strongly encouraged to provide the time and resources that would allow desk officers to gather evidence, undertake further analysis and consult internal and external stakeholders if required. At the same time, the analysis must focus on the most relevant impacts to avoid overloading the process. A central support unit (such as the Dutch Proposed Legislation Desk) can play a very positive role in providing expertise and quality assurance as well as intermediating between departments. In other jurisdictions this function is provided only to a certain degree. Surprisingly, in none of the IA systems studied, do environmental agencies below the ministerial level play an important role within the procedures. To facilitate constructive engagement of these agencies, this should be done in a way that acknowledges the priorities and sensitivities of sectoral departments. Desk officers could also be given support tools that help identify links between common drivers of environmental degradation (for example transport demand, green site development, increased packaging) and their impacts (air pollution, waste, biodiversity loss and so on). Guidance needs to emphasize that IA is not only about accepting or rejecting a policy, but also that it aims to identify adjustments or accompanying measures that can improve the outcome and exploit win-win potentials.

Using Methodologies that Capture Environmental Impacts Appropriately

Assessment reports usually describe the problem to be addressed, propose options and discuss a range of impacts. Data are often provided to back up the specific points of the essentially qualitative analysis. Many appraisal procedures, for example in the US, the UK and the EU, aim to encourage quantification and monetization of both market and non-market effects to improve the evidence base of decisions. The methodologies most widely used for this purpose are cost-benefit analysis (CBA), cost-effectiveness analysis (CEA) and multi-criteria analysis (MCA). More selectively applied are economic modelling (econometric, equilibrium, sectoral and biosphere models), and risk analysis. They tend to contribute specific knowledge on individual impact areas, rather than to serve as a framework (that is, providing an overall result of the assessment).

The opportunities and risks associated with different methodologies have been discussed extensively in areas such as technology assessment, risk assessment and policy analysis. Without re-iterating this debate, a number of key points can be made drawing on recent work in this area as well as practical experiences with IA. From an environmental perspective, using quantitative methodologies can have the benefit of facilitating the integration of previously neglected ecological impacts into decision-making, for example the future costs of climate change. On the other hand, some methodologies tend to bias against environmental measures by:

- giving less consideration to those environmental and health effects that are difficult to quantify or monetize (although cost-benefit analysis can principally be used to assess any impact, economic valuation of non-market effects poses large difficulties);
- failing to reflect specific characteristics of impacts that are often particularly relevant in the environment, for example their long-term character, irreversibility and uneven distribution of costs across regions and social groups;
- over-estimating the economic cost of environmental policies. While technological development has shown in the past to substantially reduce implementation costs (the so called 'innovation offsets' of environmental regulation), the forecasting of such learning effects is difficult and they are not usually considered in IA.

In principle, any scientifically valid methodology can contribute evidence to IA. It is, however, crucial that the use of CBA and CEA does not narrow down the analysis towards intended impacts and market effects, and that impact areas less amenable to quantitative or monetary analysis are given appropriate weight in the decision. The experience in the US, and to some extent in the UK, shows that the inclusion of wider social, economic and environmental effects in RIA is difficult to achieve in practice if CBA or CEA serves as the *overall framework* of analysis. Multi-criteria techniques appear more suitable to structuring the assessment of a wide range of diverse and uncertain impacts. Quantitative and monetary methodologies can then be used within this framework to address the more tangible effects for which sufficient data are available. Where quantitative methodologies are used to analyse uncertain or external effects and where monetization and other forms of aggregation are employed, any underlying assumptions need to be made transparent and possibly negotiated with the stakeholders. Where basic assumptions remain contested, sensitivity analysis should be undertaken. Aggregation should not obscure key trade-offs and distributive effects.

Finally, better guidance should be provided on the selection of methodologies to use for different impact areas and on how to address any uncertain and controversial impacts. This should draw on the significant body of literature on the balanced use of methods for IA (with Arrow et al 1996 as probably the most prominent example) and on indicator systems, and data sources have been developed for this purpose.

Harmonizing and Improving Process Standards

The balance between the objective of increasing transparency and justification of decisions on the one side and the improvement of analysis and evidence based policy-making on the other side varies between countries (for example the US system is more geared towards transparency) but also between individual policy cases. For IA to work as environmental appraisal of sectoral policies, it is crucial that it does inform the decision-making process and that it also broadens decision criteria. To achieve this, process standards have to be met in relation to the timing of IA, openness and consultation, and in quality assurance and evaluation. Each of these is now discussed.

Timing of IA

Ideally, IA should be conceived of as an on-going process throughout the policy formulation process (see Wilkinson, Fergusson et al 2004). In practice, most IA procedures are based on a main assessment carried out over a fairly short period of months or even weeks. Where this is the case (as, for example, in the EU), it is important to ensure that it is carried out at the right point in time. If it is undertaken before policy options are formulated, the assessment will be necessarily vague, risking the potential to undermine the external credibility of the procedure. It is also more likely to focus on direct costs and benefits. If it is undertaken after the basic design of the policy had been decided, it will not have a significant impact, and policy decisions may take the form of a defensive and selective presentation of evidence. Although EU IA is integrated into the Commission's Strategic Planning and Programming cycle, it does not appear that the assessment has always been carried out at the appropriate moment in time.

Openness and Consultation

The results of analysis of environmental impacts will usually depend on potentially controversial assumptions (for example the value of environmental goods, the importance of future impacts such as discount rates in CBA, and the willingness of society to take environmental and health risks), as well as the boundaries of the assessment (for example whether or not it includes impacts in third countries and how far into the future it looks). Answers to these questions are made on the basis of value judgments as well as expertise and practical constraints. Therefore, both boundary decisions and key assumptions need to be discussed with external and internal stake-holders. From an environmental perspective, consultation should ensure transparency of the assessment process, including the publication of all IA reports on a central website. It should also include the early and constructive involvement of environmental departments or agencies (in both the scoping and the assessment phase), as well as timely consultation with external stake-holders (including environmental NGOs), not just on the substance of the policy but also on the methods and assumptions of the assessment.

Quality Assurance and Evaluation

Given the need to allow individual departments to flexibly apply IA to their specific policies, it is crucial that there is a functioning process of quality assurance. It appears to be most effective where it is supported with a well resourced coordinating unit; an influential quality assurance process, either by a respected outside body or by a powerful government department (such as the UK Cabinet Office); and the possibility for the coordinating department (and perhaps other departments) to delay or reject an initiative if the assessment falls seriously short of quality stan-dards (as, for example, in the UK).

V. CONCLUSIONS

One condition for the successful development of integrated regulatory and sustainability assessments is an understanding of the relationship between the better regulation agenda and sustainable development. The review of relevant procedures highlights that there are commonalities as well as the tensions. Both aim to increase accountability and transparency in policy-making; to promote dialogue and participation in decision-processes; to improve coherence between different policy areas; and to enhance the evi-dence base and quality of regulation.

Tension arises mainly from the aim of regulatory reform to demand higher standards for the justification of policy intervention with a view to reducing the burden of regulation on business and society. In contrast, addressing the common sustainability challenges (such as poverty, climate change and biodiversity loss) may require more rather than less policy intervention. Similarly, some see a conflict between the 'soft' and cooperative instruments favoured by new governance approaches and the short-term effectiveness of environmental policy.

The assessment of the potential ecological, economic and social effects is a complex and difficult task, especially where the policy proposes changes to a complex system of rules. Most observers agree that integrated policy appraisal procedures are an important opportunity for sustainable development. However, to realize the potential benefits, the assessment process needs to be genuinely open, have the support from key internal and external stakeholders and avoid capture by one specific set of interests.

Early experiences suggest, therefore, that for IA to achieve its ambitious aims, current procedures must be improved, and the consideration of sustainability issues should be strengthened. The six key starting points to ensure a well functioning and balanced ex ante policy appraisal system emerging from the country studies underlying this chapter are: (1) a high level political commitment to the assessment procedure and its role in promoting sustainable development (2) the provision of guidelines and positive criteria for the selection of proposals and relevant impact areas for assessment (3) the empowerment of actors and departments within governments to effectively coordinate and cooperate in inter-departmental decision-making on IA procedures (4) to provide data, methods and training on their application that allow an integration of quantitative and qualitative data (5) an iterative and reflexive assessment process that is adapted to the different stages of decision-making, and finally (6) a well resourced formal evaluation process that is independent from the agency in charge for the IA and which has an effective sanctioning mechanism.

A central question is how much the comprehensiveness, openness and analytical rigour of the IA procedure can be improved without over-burdening and alienating the administrations implementing it. The experience in several countries shows that over-ambitious and insufficiently resourced appraisal processes will be poorly implemented. Therefore, the potential for improving the standards of IA is closely linked to the willingness to provide the political mandate and resources to support it.

NOTES

1. The opinions expressed here do not reflect any opinion of the European Environment Agency. They reflect the personal opinions of the author and have been developed when the author was affiliated with the EPRC, Freie Universität, Berlin.
2. This paper draws on previous publications: Jacob et al (2004) and Hertin (2004).

REFERENCES

Arrow, K J, Cropper, M L, Eads, G C, Hahn, R W, Lave, L B, Noll, R G, Portney, P R, Russell, M, Schmalensee, R, Smith, V K and Stavins, V R (1996), 'Is there a role for benefit–cost analysis in environmental, health and safety regulation?', *Science*, 272 (5268), 1571–3.

Bartolomeo, M, Giugni, P, Hertin, J, Jacob, K, Rennings, K, Volkery, A, Wilkinson, D and Zanoni, D (2005), 'Approaches to impact assessment in six OECD countries and at the European Commission. Findings and recommendations for the European Commission, Unpublished Report', Milano, Avanzi.

Bernauer, T and Caduff, L (2004), 'In whose interests? Pressure group politics, economic competition and environmental regulation', *Journal of Public Policy*, 24 (1), 99–126.

Cohen, M D, March, J G and Olsen, J P (1972), 'A garbage can model of organizational choice', *Administrative Science Quarterly*, 17 (1), 1–25.

European Commission (2002), 'Communication from the Commission on Impact Assessment', European Commission, Brussels.

Hertin, J (2004), 'The environmental dimension of impact assessment – learning from experiences', SPRU, Brighton.

Jacob, K, Hertin, J, Bartolomeo, M, Volkery, A, Cirillo, M and Wilkinson, D (2004), 'Ex ante sustainability appraisal of national-level policies: a comparative study of assessment practice in seven countries'. Paper presented at the 2004 Berlin Conference *Greening of Policies? Interlinkages and Policy Integration*.

OECD (1997), 'Regulatory impact analysis: best practices in OECD countries', Paris, OECD.

Radaelli, C (2004), 'The diffusion of regulatory impact analysis: best-practice or lesson drawing?', *European Journal of Political Research*, 43 (5), 723–47.

Radaelli, C (2005), 'Diffusion without convergence: how political context shapes the adoption of regulatory impact assessment', *Journal of European Public Policy*, 12 (5), 924–43.

Richardson, J (1996), 'Actor-based models of national and EU policy-making', in Kassim, H and Menon, A (eds) *The European Union and National Industrial Policy*, London, Routledge, pp. 26–51.

Sabatier, P A (ed.) (1999), *Theories of the Policy Process*, Davis, Westview Press.

Volkery, A and Jacob, K (2005), 'The environmental dimension of impact assessment'. Documentation of a workshop organized together with the Federal Ministry for the Environment, Nature Conservation and Nuclear Safety, 17–18 June 2004, Berlin, Environmental Policy Research Centre.

Wilkinson, D, Fergusson, M, Bowyer, C, Brown, J, Ladefoged, A, Monkhouse, C and Zdanowicz, A (2004), 'Sustainable development in the European Commission's integrated impact assessments for 2003', London, IEEP.

7. The contribution of environmental assessment to sustainable development: toward a richer conceptual understanding

Matthew Cashmore

I. INTRODUCTION

It is increasingly recognized that environmental assessment – a collective term for forms of appraisal that address the environmental consequences of policies, programmes, plans and projects – is at a defining point in its development. Institutionalized within an ever-expanding range of policy arenas and encompassing a broadening scope of concerns, expectations about its contribution to sustainable development appear to be at a zenith. Yet despite the relentless 'colonization' of decision-making by environmental assessment (Holder 2004, p. 10), fundamental concerns about its operational effectiveness persist (Benson 2003; Flyvbjerg 1998).

The majority of criticisms levelled at environmental assessment relate to internationally recognized problematic practices, such as a limited consideration of alternatives, scientifically inadequate impact predictions, and the difficulties associated with involving stakeholders in a meaningful and productive manner (Petts 2003; Sadler 1996; Wood 2003). It is suggested, however, that there is a more fundamental problem that, to a large degree, underlies such criticisms. The problem is that the relationship between environmental assessment and sustainable development – at all levels of the policy hierarchy – is inadequately understood, there having been remarkably little consideration of what sustainable development actually means for its theory and practice (Cashmore et al 2004; Gibson 2001). Thus, most criticisms are based on conventional (and mainly rationalist and positivist) assumptions about how environmental assessment should operate, which largely pre-date contemporary concern for, and understanding of, sustainability. Given the changing nature of environmental assessment (in particular, the increasing institutionalization of strategic environmental assessment (SEA)) and of the societal context in which it operates, it is imperative that the implications of sustainable development are given concerted consideration.

This chapter thus aims to advance the debate on environmental assessment, not by concentrating on tangible solutions to problematic practices, but by contributing to a richer conceptual understanding of its relationship to sustainable development. The unpacking of this relationship commences with a critical examination of the implications of the lack of a consensual interpretation of sustainable development. The discussion then focuses on the development of a richer conceptualization of the mechanisms by which environmental assessment can contribute to sustainable development, drawing in part on new empirical research. Finally, it is suggested that the environmental assessment literature has been blighted by unrealistic expectations about what can be achieved in practice. It is important that these assumptions are counteracted if effectiveness is to be accurately measured. On the basis of these three strands of the analysis, it is concluded that, as certain authors have previously suggested (e.g. Sadler 1996; Sadler and Jacobs 1989), environmental assessment has the potential to make a significant contribution to sustainable development, but it does so in a markedly different manner from conventional expectations.

II. DEFINING CONDITIONS FOR SUSTAINABILITY: THE IMPLICATIONS OF MULTIPLE AND CONFLICTING DEFINITIONS

Precisely what sustainable development means, both in theory and practice, is a vexed question, for its broad appeal has not led to coherent interpretations. It is generally accepted that sustainable development involves reconciling social, economic and environmental imperatives in development planning, coupled with the application of precaution. It also incorporates issues of distributional and generational equity (Adger et al 2003). However, the detailed principles required to implement these concepts are profoundly contested (Gibson 2001; O'Riordan 2001).[1]

The lack of singularity of definition has resulted in two polar approaches to implementing sustainability, the implications of which are of considerable relevance when understanding environmental assessment's contribution. The first approach involves expounding rigorous and comprehensive principles or decision rules for sustainable development (for example the environmental economics capital model (Turner 1993)). An inescapable conclusion of such approaches, however, is that there can be no objective, technical method of establishing sustainability principles, because their development is inevitably a value-laden process (Bosshard 2000; Owens and Cowell 2002).

Nowhere is this more evident than in decisions concerning distributional and generational equity.

The alternative approach attempts to circumvent the complexities of defining a comprehensive set of sustainability principles by implementing only the core concepts of sustainable development (George 1999). This may appear to constitute a pragmatic solution to divergent interpretations of sustainable development. Whilst the core concept approach can focus attention on existing international or national commitments (such as the principles contained in the Rio Declaration on Environment and Development (George 1999)), such an approach risks merely concealing the values inherent in sustainability principles unless there is sufficient opportunity for stakeholder engagement. This is because there is invariably an element of interpretation required in the implementation of core concepts. Furthermore, this approach also entails difficult questions about boundary setting in determining what constitutes a core concept and what it encompasses.

Thus, Owens and Cowell (2002, p. 70) conclude, '. . . that to conceive of these [environmental appraisal] approaches as instruments in promoting some preformed, consensual concept of sustainability is profoundly misleading. In practice, all are bound into power struggles in which conceptions of what is sustainable are actively constructed and negotiated' (original emphasis). That there can be no straightforward answer to conceptualizing what sustainability means in the context of environmental assessment is an inescapable, if uncomfortable, conclusion. Sustainable development is a concept that varies over time and space.

This does not mean that sustainability-influenced environmental assessment practices are unproductive. It is suggested, however, that their main contribution, even under conditions of limited stakeholder engagement, is to provide a forum in which the meaning of, and visions for, sustainability can be debated, rather than implemented *per se* (Owens and Cowell 2002). The importance of this contribution should not be underestimated, for if it is accepted that operationalizing sustainable development involves values, then it is logical that democratic processes are employed to debate which values take precedence. The institutionalization of SEA thus provides a potentially significant opportunity for increasing community engagement in debates concerning sustainable development. Surmounting barriers to public participation in environmental assessment (Petts 1999, 2003) becomes a key priority under this conception of environmental assessment's role and contribution.

III. THE CONTRIBUTION OF ENVIRONMENTAL ASSESSMENT: UNDERSTANDING OUTCOMES

It has been suggested that defining a universal set of sustainability principles is neither feasible nor desirable and that environmental assessment's predominant contribution to sustainable development to date has been in providing fora for visioning, but this does not preclude the development of a richer conceptualization. The conceptual model merely focuses on the outcomes by which environmental assessment can contribute to sustainable development, rather than defining *a priori* sustainability conditions to guide environmental assessment practices.

The accepted theoretical position is that environmental assessment is a predictive and participatory process with two principal outcomes: its contribution to design and consent decisions (Glasson 1999; Sadler 1996).[2] In respect to sustainable development, environmental assessment tends to be viewed either as a tool to determine whether or not a development is sustainable or to promote integrated consideration of environmental, economic and social concerns (George 1999; Pope et al 2004). The architect of the US National Environmental Policy Act (the legislation which introduced the first mandatory system of environmental assessment) and his colleague have, for many years, argued that these interpretations of environmental assessment substantially underestimate its sophistication and subtlety (e.g. Bartlett 1986, 1988; Caldwell 1995). In relation to its practical outcomes, Bartlett (1989, p. 2) asserts that, 'I can think of no other initiative in our history that . . . had such a fundamental impact on the way government does business . . . I am qualified to characterise that process as truly a revolution in government policy and decision-making'. Such claims have been viewed with some scepticism (Holder 2004), not least given their source, but it is increasingly acknowledged that environmental assessment might have broader sustainability potentialities than has hitherto been recognized. It is also important to remember that outcomes and decisions are not necessarily one and the same (Adger et al 2003).

Nevertheless, where additional outcomes to influencing consent and design decisions have been considered, they have typically been presented singularly or as discrete models (e.g. Bartlett and Kurian 1999; Culhane et al 1987). There is, however, no logical reason why multiple outcomes should not be expected to occur in individual cases. Furthermore, the greatest contribution to sustainable development is likely to be achieved if multiple outcomes are realized routinely (Cashmore et al 2004). An integrated model of the plurality of outcomes by which environmental assessment may contribute to sustainable development is presented in this chapter.

The outcomes are delineated into four categories: learning, governance and developmental outcomes, and attitudinal and value changes. The conceptual model draws on the literature, but is grounded in new empirical research, involving the in-depth analysis of three case-study environmental assessment processes using data obtained from interviews, questionnaires and document analysis. The cases concerned were a mines stabilization programme, an offshore windfarm, and the remediation of land used to dispose of waste from the demolition of a former chemical weapons establishment.[3] Aspects of the empirical work are essentially exploratory, and the precise focus of the discussion therefore varies depending on the research attention that specific outcomes have previously received.

Learning Outcomes

A potentially significant form of causation in the context of environmental assessment's contribution to sustainable development – which although widely acknowledged, has received limited consideration – is the fostering of multiple types of learning in various policy actors (Diduck and Sinclair 1997; McDonald and Brown 1995; Owens et al 2004). Interest in learning outcomes reflects, in part, increased emphasis on early, participatory and inclusive stakeholder involvement in environmental decision-making; revised forms of governance create opportunities for additional outcomes. It is also increasingly recognized that impact analysis and passive information provision might have outcomes above and beyond those traditionally ascribed to them under rationalist theory (Hills 2005). Regardless of the origin of a learning outcome, the ramifications are potentially wide ranging (Sabatier 1988). For example, a member of the public who has learnt about the ways in which their actions affect the environment may conceivably alter the criteria on which they base everyday decisions. The significance of learning outcomes thus lies in their societal consequences beyond an individual environmental assessment.

Despite broad recognition of the potential for environmental assessment to result in learning outcomes, the subject has, with few exceptions, received only cursory attention. This is starting to change as SEA implementation fosters greater input from the policy sciences, where learning has long been an important research focus. Nevertheless, contemporary deliberations about the learning outcomes of environmental assessment remain based primarily on intuition, as there is a dearth of empirical data. The research on outcomes thus provides a valuable empirical insight into the types of learning that can occur in practice.

Four categories of learning outcomes were identified based on the research data. The first category of learning observed was an increase in environmental awareness. This was defined as a change in stakeholders' general understanding of environmental conditions and concerns, and was most evident in, but not limited to, public understanding of local environments. In the case of the mines stabilization programme, for example, protracted debate on the need for, cost and insurance implications of bat habitat conservation raised community awareness about the existence of internationally important bat populations. This does not mean the bats were valued as a result, for they were widely viewed as an unwelcome impediment to mines stabilization, but people were aware that a trade-off had to be made between biological conservation and social objectives.

Second, several forms of what was classified as technical learning were discerned, and in a range of stakeholders. This type of learning was defined as knowledge acquired through applied scientific, engineering and management practices. It thus included, amongst other things, new knowledge about baseline environmental conditions, experiential learning of project management skills, and development of an enhanced understanding of procedural provisions for environmental governance. An example of technical learning is that in order to be taken seriously, and thereby potentially exert an influence on decision-making, a member of the public and a representative of a non-governmental organization believed that they needed to be proficient in standard environmental assessment methods. They had thus learnt to use certain technical methodologies. This could be interpreted as evidence of environmental assessment contributing to increased rationality in decision-making.

Scientific learning was the third category of learning recorded, but it was primarily the potential for, rather than actual, scientific learning that was observed. The potential for scientific learning tended to be linked to data collection activities (e.g. the baseline study or post-decision monitoring); sometimes such data had wider scientific application, particularly where the environment concerned had not previously been studied in-depth. No examples were observed of scientific learning about the response of environmental variables to human perturbations as part of impact prediction. This might partly reflect limited resource allocation to impact prediction, a widely recognized problem in environmental assessment (Wood 2003). Feedback provided as a consequence of the impact monitoring provision of the EU SEA Directive (European Commission 2001) might increase scientific learning in the future, but this is only likely to occur in jurisdictions where there is strong political support for sustainable development. The only form of actual scientific learning observed in the empirical research related to the development of new scientific survey methods. This was a direct result of the unprecedented demand for bird surveys created by the surge in environmental assessment activity for proposed offshore windfarms around the UK.

The final form of learning discerned from the research data was catego-
rized as social learning. This was interpreted to constitute learning derived
from social interactions over solutions to shared problems (Bandura 1986;
Webler et al 1995). Forms of social learning included learning about
ways to communicate effectively, to influence others, and in individuals'
understanding of other stakeholders' values. This form of learning was
associated primarily with the more participatory case studies.

Governance Outcomes

The second category of outcomes elaborated in this conceptual model is
the contribution of environmental assessment to governance. Many components of environment assessment that have typically been viewed as procedural means to an end (such as stakeholder involvement or provisions for
judicial review) also constitute governance outcomes in their own rights.
This is important in the context of sustainable development for as Gibson
(2001, p. 19) states, '[b]etter governance is a prerequisite and probably also
a product of steps towards sustainability'. It is also a category that takes on
particular significance for proponents of decision theories that encompass
notions of power and agency.

Most conceptions of governance are complex and multi-faceted, but it is
evident that environmental assessment has the potential to contribute in a
variety of ways. The most obvious governance outcome is the generation of
information (and the characteristics of that information) for use in decision-
making, but this can also contribute to a number of additional outcomes. It
may serve to raise the profile of environmental issues (Stinchcombe and
Gibson 2001). It can increase transparency and accountability in decision-
making: by placing data in the public domain, the information on which
decisions are made – and the trade-offs therein – should be evident. If supported by provisions for judicial review, information disclosure also provides stakeholders with an opportunity to review and challenge the
adequacy of data used in decision-making, as has frequently been the case
in environmental assessment-related litigation in the US (Wathern 1988).

Public participation, and stakeholder involvement more generally, in
decision-making are integral to modern conceptions of good governance.
The opportunities environmental assessment provides for stakeholder
involvement (in terms of nature (e.g. consultation versus participation),
timing, frequency and inclusivity) thus constitute a potentially important
governance outcome. Stakeholder involvement can also contribute to local
autonomy and local democracy in a variety of ways: for example, by facilitating the incorporation of local identity into decisions and in providing
fora for the honing of democratic skills at the local level (Pratchett 2004).

Governance models also invariably emphasize the importance of horizontal networks in a world of 'governance without government' (Schout and Jordan 2005, p. 206), and environmental assessment can contribute to the formation and dynamics of such networks. The contribution may be active and purposeful: for example, in the case of the empirical research on outcomes the establishment of working groups promoted greater interaction within a fragmented government bureaucracy, and led to the development of relationships potentially acquiescent to joint problem solving in the future. The contribution could also be passive: networks may develop as a consequence of opposition to policy proposals and the opportunities environmental assessment provides to voice disapproval. Opposition to individual onshore windfarms in England and Wales, for instance, has resulted in the development of a loose alliance of like-minded individuals (ostentatiously titled 'Country Guardian') who exchange information and share expertise on an ad-hoc basis. The precise degree to which environmental assessment is responsible for the development of this amorphous network is uncertain, but the strategy employed by some of its constituents to oppose windfarm developments relies extensively on the improved access to information and decision-making that environmental assessment produces. Information disclosure is used to identify weaknesses in the developer's analyses, and stakeholder involvement provides an opportunity for the veracity of these analyses to be questioned publicly.

Research on the effectiveness of environmental assessment indicates that there is considerable scope for improving the contribution it makes to governance. Voluminous technical reports that cost large sums of money and are only available to view at certain times (Clark 1993; Holder 2004) make a questionable contribution to public access to information; high levels of stakeholder involvement remain atypical in many jurisdictions (Petts 1999); and a combination of resources, power and agency empower some stakeholders to participate more than others (Wandesforde-Smith and Kerbavaz 1988). Furthermore, the empirical research on outcomes indicates that the contribution to governance directly attributable to environmental assessment was considerably more limited than superficially appeared to be the case. Of the three environmental assessments investigated, two were associated with high levels of stakeholder involvement, including elements of delegated power in one instance (see Table 7.1 end of chapter). The stakeholder involvement programmes were attributed to the environmental assessment process in documentation and by research participants in both instances, but a detailed analysis indicates that it was contextual factors other than environmental assessment ideology that exerted the greatest influence on stakeholder involvement. In the case of the mines stabilization scheme, it was a combination of overwhelming public opposition to an earlier stabilization proposal, the need to obtain the agreement of all landowners above the mine, and the requirement to gain planning consent within a short funding-window that were the primary determinants of the high level of involvement. Extensive stakeholder involvement in the remediation of land containing demolition waste from a former chemical weapons establishment appears to be a result of a sea-change in the attitude of parts of the military bureaucracy and the influence of an individual local politician. Media coverage of Iraq's claimed 'weapons of mass destruction' capability and the subsequent war, were also probably influential factors. Nevertheless, recognition that environmental assessment's contribution to governance represents an important end-result in its own right, not merely from a procedural perspective, might provide additional impetus to enhance governance outcomes.

Attitudinal and Value Changes

The third category of outcomes in this conceptualization of environmental assessment's contribution to sustainable development is attitudinal and value changes. This category incorporates theories that environmental assessment can produce institutional reform in the government bureaucracy and the private sector (Bartlett and Kurian 1999; Taylor 1984; Tonn et al 2000), for this is achieved – directly or indirectly – through value transformation (Bartlett 1990). The conceptualization goes further than models of institutional and organization reform, from the perspective of outcomes, in that value changes are deemed relevant to the full breadth of environmental assessment stakeholders. It is also broader in that it includes less profound (and hence potentially more transient) changes in attitudes, such as confidence, trust, and community spirit and cohesion. This category of outcomes is intuitively linked to learning (i.e. the first category of outcomes in this conceptualization), and the value changes discussed in this section are analogous in many instances to the concept of policy learning (see Sabatier 1988).[4] However, attitudinal and value changes might also result from variables such as alterations in procedural norms and organizational culture (Bartlett 1986).

Given the magnitude of the human impact on natural systems, societal transformation is interpreted as a prerequisite to achieving more sustainable forms of development (O'Riordan 1993), at least under all but extremely weak interpretations of the concept. It has been speculated that the institutionalization of values inherent in environmental assessment ideology could make a profound contribution to societal reform. Bartlett (1990, p. 82) talks of its potential to 'transmogrify the administrative state from within – gradually and not entirely predictably'. Empirical validation of value changes is problematic for they are likely to be subtle for the most

part, long term and multi-factorial. Nevertheless, based on an approxima-
tion of the exposure of UK stakeholders to environmental assessment ideology, Bond (2003) concludes there is potential for value changes to be
widespread (see Table 7.2 end of chapter). Similarly, it has been estimated
that operationalizing SEA in China will require 100 000 trained practitioners (Dalal-Clayton and Sadler 2005).

The research on outcomes indicated that the impact of environmental
assessment on attitudes and values in UK government institutions was
limited. Whilst bureaucrats may be routinely involved in environmental
assessments, this had not influenced recruitment or professional development strategies. Staff involved with environmental assessment had received
little formal training in its theory: they had, by default, been expected to
learn through experience (see Table 7.3 end of chapter). Where attitudinal
and value changes occurred, they were thus linked to an individual's experiences of particular environmental assessments. There was no evidence of
changes in values resulting from the environmental capacity gains some
individuals (e.g. Cashmore et al 2004) believe are necessary for effective
implementation of environmental assessment legislation. Staff turnover in
government institutions and the isolation of experience in individuals also
limited the potential for environmental capacity gains to exert a sizeable
influence on the value systems of government institutions.

The paucity of evidence of attitudinal and value change in government
institutions is arguably primarily attributable to the minimalist approach to
environmental assessment adopted by successive UK governments. It also
reflects agendas within the government bureaucracy. An employee of
English Nature, who had been contracted specifically to address ecological
issues arising from the development of offshore windfarms, acknowledged
the organization had limited engagement with environmental assessment
procedures. Given their focus on designated sites, other legislation was
interpreted as providing the organization with the necessary powers to fulfil
their legal responsibilities. Thus, as Clemente-Fenández (2005) concludes,
based on an analysis of environmental capacity in the Spanish bureaucracy,
whilst value transformation is in theory highly germane to environmental
assessment's contribution to sustainable development, in practice a causal
mechanism above and beyond the introduction of legislation and process-
ing of reports is required if its potential is to be realized.

There was considerably more evidence in the research on outcomes that
environmental assessment influenced the attitudes and values of stakeholders outside of the government bureaucracy, at least in the short term. For
example, institutional reform of the type envisaged by Taylor (1984) was
observed, but in the so called third sector. A non-governmental organization decided that in order to be taken seriously in decision-making they had

to adopt the rationalist philosophy upon which environmental assessment is predicated. This had discernable consequences for recruitment and organizational culture, in a transformation described as the 'professionalisation' of the organization.

There was evidence in all three cases that environmental assessment influenced trust between stakeholders, both positively and negatively. In the land remediation case, for example, the apparently open and transparent approach adopted by the developer resulted in a measurable increase in the trust placed in it by an outspoken non-governmental organization. A local politician also noted that whereas the public had at first completely distrusted the military bureaucracy, they now generally believed they were being told the truth by its representatives. This might appear to constitute modest progress, but it is a quite remarkable outcome, given the history of secrecy surrounding the former chemical weapons establishment (and of military activities in the region more generally), and the resentment this generated.

The overwhelmingly positive experience of stakeholders in the mines stabilization case affected the attitudes of some individuals to environmental assessment. Two local politicians remarked that they would be considerably more likely to advocate the use of environmental assessment in the future, irrespective of whether it was legally required. It was also reported that environmental assessment reassured the local population. There was a perception that an exhaustive assessment had been undertaken and that the relevant issues had received due consideration.

It is important to note that the methodology employed in the research on outcomes was not designed to elucidate medium- or long-term (i.e. 10 years plus) trends in values. The focus on individual cases and a short-term time horizon (five years or less) provide a potential explanation for the observation of many attitudinal, but few value, changes. This is clearly an area where further research is warranted.

Developmental Outcomes

The final category in this conceptualization is labelled developmental outcomes. This category encompasses conventional theory on the purposes of environmental assessment in that it includes its contribution to design and consent decisions. It also recognizes that environmental assessment has the potential to influence social, economic and environmental outcomes during the full life-cycle of a development. The World Bank, for instance, has tried to reinforce such outcomes by explicitly linking environmental assessment to development implementation through the production of environmental management plans (World Bank 1999).

Precisely what is meant by statements that environmental assessment contributes to design and consent decisions, and what form might the implied outcomes take? The manner in which environmental assessment can and should contribute is contested. Nevertheless, from the perspective of outcomes, it is theorized that environmental assessment could influence the choice of alternatives, mitigation measures and design specifications; alter the consent decision; facilitate informed decision-making; and contribute to the establishment of consent conditions (Glasson 1999; Jones 1999; Morgan 1998). Research indicates, however, that in practice the contribution of environmental assessment to such outcomes is extremely limited.

Indeed, based on the empirical evidence it is reasonable to question whether environmental assessment, as currently practised, really can influence developmental outcomes in the complex maelstrom of real world decision-making. Firstly, in relation to design outcomes, the limited influence of environmental assessment is extensively documented (Frost 1997; Kobus and Lee 1993; Sadler 1996). This was also evident in the research on outcomes. Extensive documentation on the selection of alternatives was produced in each of the case studies, indicating that a broad array of alternative options had been considered (see Table 7.4 end of chapter). However, some of the comparative assessments were essentially documented justifications of decisions that had already been made. For instance, the environmental assessment manager in the mines stabilization case acknowledged that they had identified their preferred stabilization method prior to tendering for the work.[5] The inclusion of a detailed section on alternative stabilization techniques in the environmental assessment documentation, it was implied, was necessary to publicly justify the experts' choice and satisfy quality criteria set by the Institute of Environmental Management and Assessment. Furthermore, some of the alternatives considered in this case were unrealistic. A broad array of what are termed strategic solutions in Table 7.4 (end of chapter) was evaluated, but in reality, the choice had been substantially curtailed by the influential Mines Inspectorate, of the Health and Safety Executive, who had decreed the mines must be infilled. It is also highly improbable that the option of abandoning the settlement above the mines, although covered in the documentation, would ever have been politically acceptable, regardless of stabilization costs.

In contrast to this post-hoc justification of technical specialists' judgments, comparative assessments did not always result in the selection of a preferred design option. This was an issue with the offshore windfarm, as many of the design decisions (e.g. the choice of the turbine foundation and turbine installation method) were left to the discretion of the engineering company subsequently contracted to build the development. The iterative nature of development planning, and the potential limitations of applying environmental assessment at one discrete decision point, were also evident in the land remediation case. A representative of the Environment Agency expressed a belief that planning, and hence environmental assessment in this case, was about establishing the broad principles of a development. It was at a later stage of permitting (Integrated Pollution Prevention and Control permitting in this instance) that they believed precise technical details are established.

This does not mean that environmental assessment caused no design outcomes, but those that occurred tended to represent 'fine-tuning' of developments rather than selection between strategic alternatives. For example, whilst the choice of engineering solutions appears to have been curtailed in the mines stabilization case, the design and environmental assessment teams met regularly to discuss detailed design considerations, such as which cultural resources should be protected, habitat replacement for the bats, and engineering protocols for reducing environmental impacts. This arguably represents an important outcome, albeit one which is discordant with mainstream environmental assessment theory.

Secondly, whilst there is a surprising paucity of research on the contribution of environmental assessment to consent decisions, the research that has been undertaken indicates its influence, once again, is limited. Wood and Jones (1997), in the most detailed empirical investigation of decision outcomes that has been undertaken, report that of a sample of 40 consent decisions, in only one case (3%) was the environmental assessment perceived to substantively alter the outcome of a consent decision. In a substantial number of cases (47%) planning officers felt environmental assessment made no difference at all to the consent decision, whilst in the remaining cases (50%) it was indicated that, although the decision would not have changed, environmental assessment produced other benefits. These benefits were the provision of additional information for consideration in decision-making and for use in establishing consent conditions.

It was difficult in the research on outcomes to identify a clear role in consent decisions for the information generated by environmental assessment. Planning officers and other stakeholders freely acknowledged, as other studies have reported (e.g. Gwilliam 2002), that they did not have the time to read all the environmental assessment documentation. Considerable reliance is placed instead on the statutory consultees to highlight potential technical and environmental problems (Wood and Jones 1997). Local politicians, where they were involved as decision makers, emphasized that, as community representatives, public opinion was their primary concern. Thus, as one local politician stated, 'I can read it [the environmental assessment documentation] and I can make my own assessment. That's fine. But if it comes out that this is absolutely fine for the community, but they don't want it or don't like it, that's what I'm there for'.

Environmental assessment also appears to have played a limited role in informing the establishment of consent conditions in the research on outcomes. A number of research participants believed that statutory consultees and planning officers would have proposed the same types of consent conditions, irrespective of an environmental assessment being conducted. The information the environmental assessment provided might have enabled the consent conditions to be more site-specific in some instances, but that was perceived to be the limit of its contribution. The environmental assessment project manager for the offshore windfarm had to actively engage the decision maker after the consent decision had been taken to encourage greater use of the results of the environmental assessment in setting the consent conditions.

It is concluded that, rather than contributing to informed consent decisions, the developmental outcomes of environmental assessment in practice appear often to be linked more to the creation of a perception of due diligence. Nevertheless, it is evident that environmental assessment has the potential to significantly influence consent decisions, albeit in a manner which may be unacceptable to many theoreticians. In the land remediation case, an effective participation programme overcame virtually all stakeholder opposition to the development. The same is true of public opinion (but not, initially, those of statutory consultees) in the mines stabilization case. In the absence of significant opposition, local politicians had no mandate to object to the developments. Yet as was noted in the section on governance, stakeholder involvement in both these cases was concluded to be a result of contextual factors other than environmental assessment ideology.

Theory on the developmental outcomes of environmental assessment is clearly detached from the realities of its practice. This does not mean that environmental assessment cannot play a greater role in shaping developmental outcomes. As the example of its role in abating public opposition illustrates, its contribution could be highly cogent in the political context of development planning. Rather, what the empirical evidence highlights is the gross inadequacies of much writing on environmental assessment and the limitations of the procedural models of environmental assessment enshrined in legislation (see also Cashmore et al 2004). It has long been argued that the introduction of SEA will enhance environmental assessment's contribution to design outcomes, but without more careful consideration being given to design processes this is unlikely to occur. Similarly, in the absence of a model of causation for environmental assessment's contribution to consent decisions, it appears improbable that its influence will be anything other than limited in the majority of cases. Enhancing environmental assessment's developmental outcomes remains a truly inordinate challenge.

IV. UNREALISTIC EXPECTATIONS

Whilst it is suggested that the breadth of outcomes environmental assessment contributes to has been under-appreciated and under-researched, it can also be argued that some expectations of what this policy appraisal tool can achieve are unrealistic. One important source of unrealistic expectations that has been the subject of extensive debate in recent times is the divergence between normative theory concerning the operation of environmental assessment and decision-making practices in the real world. The influence of behavioural variables on decisions, most importantly the interplay of power relationships, has been repeatedly demonstrated in empirical contexts (Flyvbjerg 1998; Flyvbjerg et al 2003; Phillips 2002). Most procedural models of environmental assessment, however, remain based on a false presumption of rationality in decision-making. This is not a criticism of rational theory. But given the influence of behavioural variables, it is, at minimum, misleading to evaluate the contribution of environmental assessment to sustainable development based on such premises. Expecting there to be, for instance, a direct relationship between the quality of environment assessment and its influence upon, and the quality of, a decision is thus unreasonable. Whether practices should be reformed, given the existence of behavioural variables, is a more complicated issue, and one which is being played out concurrently in a number of disciplines, notably in the field of economics.

Environmental assessment has also been criticized for failing to satisfy demands for more deliberative systems of governance (Benson 2003), yet this is not because participatory mechanisms are unavailable or that environmental assessment is inherently incompatible with principles of deliberative democracy. The failure to achieve the ideals of deliberative democracy is ultimately attributable to the reluctance of governments to impose such requirements on the public and private sectors. The same logic applies to criticism of other technical aspects of environmental assessment, such as the consideration of alternatives or social impacts. Experience from the Netherlands indicates technical problems are largely surmountable (Deelstra et al 2003), but political will is critical if this is to be achieved (Caldwell 1995).

An important source of unrealistic expectations of particular relevance to contemporary developments in SEA arises from uncritical presentations of the benefits of environmental assessment. There has been a tendency amongst both academics and practitioners to emphasize the benefits of SEA in order to promote it to policy makers (see Feldmann et al 2001; Partidário 2000). The danger is that if the theoretical benefits are ill-considered and do not materialize in practice, disillusionment may result.

There are obviously legitimate constraints to the effectiveness of environmental assessment in practice, but some claims concerning SEA's benefits appear circumspect, particularly in light of the theoretical and practical advances made in recent years. The omnipresent assertion that SEA can strengthen or streamline project appraisals (Fischer 2003; Stinchcombe and Gibson 2001; Thérivel and Partidário 1996; Wood and Djeddour 1992) is, at best, improbable in many contexts. Petts (2003), for example, labels as naive the notion of tiered decisions in the context of waste management in the UK. Differences in data resolution between decision tiers also brings into question whether SEA is likely to provide valuable data for the analysis of project-specific impacts. Furthermore, it is increasingly recognized that the model for SEA enshrined in pan-European legislative instruments is based on out-dated theoretical premises (Dalal-Clayton and Sadler 2005; Dalkmann et al 2004; Nitz and Brown 2001). This is likely to inhibit achievement of its proclaimed aims.

This discussion on unrealistic expectations is not intended to be comprehensive, merely illustrative. The issue is raised to highlight the importance of giving due consideration to the theoretical premises underlying debates on environmental assessment's contribution to sustainable development. This is important if effectiveness is to be accurately measured.

V. CONCLUSIONS

The difficulties associated with producing an authoritative operational definition of sustainable development represent a significant barrier to making sustainability more than just a rhetorical vision of almost universal appeal (George 1999; O'Riordan 1993, 2001). The most intractable problem in defining sustainability principles is that they involve fundamental moral and political choices, and are, therefore, context dependent (Owens and Cowell 2002). This means that the use of environmental assessment to assess whether a development proposal is sustainable will always be a complex and contestable endeavour, regardless of improvements in scientific understanding of environmental responses to human perturbations or technical improvements in environmental assessment procedures.

This chapter has sought to develop a more detailed and empirically grounded conceptualization of the contribution of environmental assessment to sustainable development. The analysis indicates that contemporary theory, in focusing primarily on environmental assessment's role in consent and design decisions, substantially undervalues the breadth of its sustainability potentialities. Four discrete categories of sustainability outcomes were identified in this conceptualization: learning, governance and developmental outcomes, and attitudinal and value changes. Based on this analysis, it is concluded that, as Sadler (1996) envisaged, environmental assessment has the potential to operate as a 'frontline' tool in facilitating the transition towards sustainability. However, it does so in a markedly different manner to that traditionally (and, it could be argued, naively) expected. The analysis also underlines the considerable theoretical and practical challenges to enhancing the effectiveness of environmental assessment in contributing to sustainable development.

It should be noted that the conceptualization presented in this chapter is based on exploratory research, and further work will be needed to validate the occurrence, and investigate the operation, of many of the outcomes highlighted. The conceptualization is also based almost entirely on Western literature and ideology. The four principal categories of the conceptualization are probably equally relevant to all nations (although this is an assumption that requires empirical validation), but the precise outcomes and their perceived significance will vary in different geopolitical contexts.

NOTES

1. Meadowcroft (2000) implies that varying interpretations occur because sustainable development was intentionally formulated as a unifying political meta-objective, with only a suggestive normative core. In attempting to bridge the divide between North and South, East and West, environment and development, efficiency and effectiveness, it is inevitable that the precise principles needed to operationalize this concept will be disputed. A more sceptical perspective is that a counter-hegemonic concept has been subjugated to support the mainstream neoliberal agenda (Carruthers 2001).

2. The ambiguous term 'contribute' is used purposefully, for the form this contribution should take is disputed. For some, the contribution involves the passive provision of objective analyses (e.g. Rosenberg et al 1981), while others believe environmental assessment should seek to influence, rather than just inform, decision-making (e.g. Beattie 1995; Dryzek 1993).

3. The locations of the developments are not described in order to protect the identity of research participants. Anonymity was a prerequisite to their involvement in many instances.

4. Whereas certain authors have taken learning to constitute a change in attitudes, values or actions resulting from knowledge acquisition (e.g. Argyris and Schön 1978; Hall 1993), a distinction is maintained in this conceptualization between cognition and any attitudinal or value changes which may result. Learning may represent an important cause of attitudinal and value changes, but these need not occur when learning takes place (Fitzpatrick and Sinclair 2003; Huber 1990). The empirical difficulties in differentiating rhetoric from learning do not warrant conflating the distinction.

5. This is an unremarkable finding. What would be more surprising was if an engineering company bid for design work, which they had no idea how to achieve.

REFERENCES

Adger, W N, Brown, K, Fairbrass, J, Jordan, A, Paavola, J, Rosendo, S and Seyfang, G (2003), 'Governance for sustainability: towards a "thick" analysis of environmental decisionmaking', *Environment and Planning A*, 35, 1095–110.

Argyris, S and Schön, D (1978), *Organizational Learning: A Theory of Action Perspective*, Addison-Wesley, Reading, MA.

Arnstein, S R (1969), 'A ladder of citizen participation', *Journal of the American Institute of Planners*, 35, 216–44.

Bandura, A (1986), *Social Foundations of Thoughts and Action: A Social Cognitive Theory*, Prentice-Hall, Englewood Cliffs, NJ.

Bartlett, R V (1986), 'Rationality and the logic of the National Environmental Policy Act', *The Environmental Professional*, 8, 105–11.

Bartlett, R V (1988), 'Policy and impact assessment: an introduction', *Impact Assessment Bulletin*, 6, 73–4.

Bartlett, R V (1989), *Policy Through Impact Assessment: Institutionalized Analysis as a Policy Strategy*, Greenwood Press, Westport, CT.

Bartlett, R V (1990), 'Ecological reason in administration: environmental impact assessment and administrative theory', in R Paehlke and D Torgerson (eds) *Managing the Leviathan: Environmental Politics and the Administrative State*, Belhaven, London, pp. 81–96.

Bartlett, R V and Kurian, P A (1999), 'The theory of environmental impact assessment: implicit models of policy making', *Policy and Politics*, 27, 415–34.

Beattie, R B (1995), 'Everything you already know about EIA (but don't often admit)', *Environmental Impact Assessment Review*, 15, 109–14.

Benson, J F (2003), 'Round table: what is the alternative? Impact assessment tools and sustainable planning', *Impact Assessment and Project Appraisal*, 21, 261–80.

Bond, A J (2003), 'Let's not be rational about this', *Impact Assessment and Project Appraisal*, 21, 266–69.

Bosshard, A (2000), 'A methodology and terminology of sustainability assessment and its perspectives for rural planning', *Agriculture, Ecosystems and Environment*, 77, 29–41.

Caldwell, L K (1995), 'The National Environmental Policy Act', in R V Bartlett and J N Gladden (eds) *Environment as a Focus for Public Policy*, Texas A&M University Press, College Station, pp. 167–79.

Carruthers, D (2001), 'From opposition to orthodoxy: the remaking of sustainable development', *Journal of Third World Studies*, 18, 93–112.

Cashmore, M, Gwilliam, R, Morgan, R, Cobb, D and Bond, A (2004), 'The interminable issue of effectiveness: substantive purposes, outcomes and research challenges in the advancement of EIA theory', *Impact Assessment and Project Appraisal*, 22, 295–310.

Clark, R (1993), 'The National Environmental Policy Act and the role of the President's Council on Environmental Quality', *The Environmental Professional*, 15, 4–6.

Clemente-Fenández, P C (2005), 'Capacity development for environmental impact assessment – the Spanish public institutions as a case study', School of Environmental Sciences, University of East Anglia, Norwich.

Culhane, P J, Friesema, H P and Beecher, J A (1987), *Forecasts and Environmental Decisionmaking: The Content and Predictive Accuracy of Environmental Impact Statements*, Westview Press, London.

Dalal-Clayton, B and Sadler, B (2005), *Strategic Environmental Assessment: A Sourcebook and Reference Guide to International Experience*, Earthscan, London.

Dalkmann, H, Jiliberto, R and Bongardt, D (2004), 'Analytical strategic environmental assessment (ANSEA) developing a new approach to SEA', *Environmental Impact Assessment Review*, 24, 385–402.

Deelstra, Y, Nooteboom, S G, Kohlmann, H R, van den Berg, J and Innanen, S (2003), 'Using knowledge for decision-making purposes in the context of large projects in the Netherlands', *Environmental Impact Assessment Review*, 23, 517–41.

Diduck, A and Sinclair, A J (1997), 'The concept of critical environmental assessment education', *The Canadian Geographer*, 41, 294–307.

Dryzek, J S (1993), 'Policy analysis and planning: from science to argument', in F Fischer and J Forrester (eds) *The Argumentative Turn in Policy Analysis and Planning*, Duke University Press, Durham, NC, pp. 213–32.

European Commission (2001), 'Directive 2001/42/EC of the European Parliament and of the Council of 27 June 2001 on the assessment of the effects of certain plans and programmes on the environment', *Official Journal of the European Communities* L197/30, 30–37.

Feldmann, L, Vanderhaegen, M and Pirotte, C (2001), 'The EU's SEA Directive: status and links to integration and sustainable development', *Environmental Impact Assessment Review*, 21, 203–22.

Fischer, T B (2003), 'Strategic environmental assessment in post-modern times', *Environmental Impact Assessment Review*, 23, 155–70.

Fitzpatrick, P and Sinclair, A J (2003), 'Learning through public involvement in environmental assessment hearings', *Journal of Environmental Management*, 67, 161–74.

Flyvbjerg, B (1998), *Rationality and Power: Democracy in Practice*, University of Chicago Press, London.

Flyvbjerg, B, Bruzelius, N and Rothengatter, W (2003), *Megaprojects and Risk: An Anatomy of Ambition*, Cambridge University Press, Cambridge.

Frost, R (1997), 'EIA monitoring and audit', in J Weston (ed) *Planning and Environmental Impact Assessment in Practice*, Addison Wesley Longman, Harlow, pp. 141–64.

George, C (1999), 'Testing for sustainable development through environmental assessment', *Environmental Impact Assessment Review*, 19, 175–200.

Gibson, R (2001), 'Specification of sustainability-based environmental assessment decision criteria and implications for determining "significance" in environmental assessment'. Monograph prepared under a contribution agreement with the Canadian Environmental Assessment Agency Research and Development Programme.

Glasson, J (1999), 'Environmental impact assessment – impact on decisions', in J Petts (ed) *Handbook of Environmental Impact Assessment. Volume 1. Environmental Impact Assessment: Process, Methods and Potential*, Blackwell Science, Oxford, pp. 121–44.

Gwilliam, R S (2002), 'The integration of environmental impact assessment into development control and planning decisions: the perception of English planning officers', School of Environmental Sciences, University of East Anglia, Norwich.

Hall, P A (1993), 'Policy paradigms, social learning and the state: the case of economic policymaking in Britain', *Comparative Politics*, 25, 275–96.

Hills, S (2005), 'Falling through the cracks: limits to an instrumental rational role for environmental information in planning', *Environment and Planning A*, 37, 1263–76.

Holder, J (2004), *Environmental Assessment: The Regulation of Decision Making*, Oxford University Press, Oxford.

Huber, G P (1990), 'Organizational learning: the contributing processes and the literatures', *Organization Science*, 2, 88–115.

Jones, C E (1999), 'Screening, scoping and consideration of alternatives' in J Petts (ed) *Handbook of Environmental Impact Assessment. Volume 1. Environmental Impact Assessment: Process, Methods and Potential*, Blackwell Science, Oxford.

Kobus, D and Lee, N (1993), 'The role of environmental assessment in the planning and authorisation of extractive industry projects', *Project Appraisal*, 8, 147–56.

McDonald, G T and Brown, L A (1995), 'Going beyond environmental impact assessment: environmental input to planning and design', *Environmental Impact Assessment Review*, 15, 34–45.

Meadowcroft, J (2000), 'Sustainable development: a new(ish) idea for a new century?', *Political Studies*, 48, 370–87.

Morgan, R (1998), *Environmental Impact Assessment: A Methodological Perspective*, Kluwer Academic Publishing, London.

Nitz, T and Brown, A L (2001), 'SEA must learn how policy making works', *Journal of Environmental Assessment Policy and Management*, 3, 329–42.

O'Riordan, T (1993), 'The politics of sustainability', in R K Turner (ed) *Sustainable Environmental Economics and Management: Principles and Practice*, John Wiley and Sons, Chichester, pp. 37–69.

O'Riordan, T (2001), 'The sustainability debate', in T O'Riordan (ed) *Environmental Science for Environmental Management*, Prentice-Hall, Harlow, pp. 29–62.

Owens, S and Cowell, R (2002), *Land and Limits: Interpreting Sustainability in the Planning Process*, Routledge, London.

Owens, S, Rayner, T and Bina, O (2004), 'New agendas for appraisal: reflections on theory, practice and research', *Environment and Planning A*, 36, 1943–59.

Partidário, M R (2000), 'Elements of an SEA framework – improving the added-value of SEA', *Environmental Impact Assessment Review*, 20, 647–63.

Petts, J (1999), 'Public participation and environmental impact assessment', in J Petts (ed) *Handbook of Environmental Impact Assessment. Volume 1. Environmental Impact Assessment: Process, Methods and Potential*, Blackwell Science, Oxford, pp. 145–77.

Petts, J (2003), 'Barriers to deliberative participation in EIA: learning from waste policies, plans and projects', *Journal of Environmental Assessment Policy and Management*, 5, 269–93.

Phillips, F (2002), 'The distortion of criteria after decision-making', *Organisational Behavior and Human Decision Processes*, 88, 769–84.

Pope, J, Annandale, D and Morrison-Saunders, A (2004), 'Conceptualising sustainability assessment', *Environmental Impact Assessment Review*, 24, 595–615.

Pratchett, L (2004), 'Local autonomy, local democracy and the "new localism"', *Political Studies*, 52, 358–75.

Rosenberg, D et al (1981), 'Recent trends in environmental impact assessment', *Canadian Journal of Fisheries and Aquatic Science*, 38, 591–624.

Sabatier, P (1988), 'An advocacy coalition framework of policy change and the role of policy-oriented learning therein', *Policy Sciences*, 21, 129–68.

Sadler, B (1996), 'Environmental assessment in a changing world: evaluating practice to improve performance'. Final Report of the International Study of the Effectiveness of Environmental Assessment, Canadian Environmental Assessment Agency and International Association for Impact Assessment, Ottawa.

Sadler, B and Jacobs, P (1989), 'A key to tomorrow: on the relationship of environmental assessment and sustainable development', in P Jacobs and B Sadler (eds) *Environmental Assessment and Sustainable Development: Perspectives on Planning for a Common Future*, Canadian Environmental Assessment Research Council, Ottawa, Canada, pp. 3–31.

Schout, A and Jordan, A (2005), 'Coordinated European governance: self-organizing or centrally steered?', *Public Administration*, 83, 201–20.

Stinchcombe, K and Gibson, R (2001), 'Strategic environmental assessment as a means of pursuing sustainability: ten advantages and ten challenges', *Journal of Environmental Assessment Policy and Management*, 3, 343–72.

Taylor, S (1984), *Making Bureaucracies Think: The Environmental Impact Statement Strategy of Administrative Reform*, Stanford University Press, Stanford.

Thérivel, R and Partidário, M R (1996), 'Introduction', in R Thérivel and M R Partidário (eds) *The Practice of Strategic Environmental Assessment*, Earthscan, London, pp. 3–14.

Tonn, B, English, M and Travis, C (2000), 'A framework for understanding and improving environmental decision making', *Journal of Environmental Planning and Management*, 43, 163–83.

Turner, R K (1993), 'Sustainability: principles and practice', in R K Turner (ed) *Sustainable Environmental Economics and Management: Principles and Practice*, John Wiley & Sons, Chichester, pp. 3–36.

Wandesforde-Smith, G and Kerbavaz, J (1988), 'The co-evolution of politics and policy: elections, entrepreneurship and EIA in the United States', in P Wathern (ed) *Environmental Impact Assessment: Theory and Practice*, Routledge, London, pp. 161–91.

Wathern, P (1988), 'An introductory guide to EIA', in P Wathern (ed) *Environmental Impact Assessment: Theory and Practice*, Routledge, London, pp. 3–30.

Webler, T, Kastenholz, H and Renn, O (1995), 'Public participation in impact assessment: a social learning perspective', *Environmental Impact Assessment Review*, 15, 443–63.

Wood, C (2003), *Environmental Impact Assessment: A Comparative Review*, Pearson Education, Harlow.

Wood, C and Djeddour, M (1992), 'Strategic environmental assessment: EA of policies, plans and programmes', *Impact Assessment Bulletin*, 10, 3–22.

Wood, C and Jones, C E (1997), 'The effect of environmental assessment on UK local planning authority decisions', *Urban Studies*, 34, 1237–57.

World Bank (1999), *Environmental Management Plans*, World Bank, Washington, DC.

APPENDIX

Table 7.1 Stakeholder involvement methods employed in the case studies and approximate number of consultees

	Mines stabilization	Offshore windfarm	Land remediation
Information provision Stakeholder involvement methods employed[1,2]	Newsletters (13) Fact sheets (1) Exhibitions (7) Press releases Media interviews Website 'Drop in' centre Briefings with councillors and local MP Public talks (5, various issues) Outreach events to publicize exhibitions and road closures		Press releases Media interviews
Consultation	Public meetings (4) Consultation on methods (1) Exhibition (18) and accompanying comment form Questionnaire survey (1) One-to-one surgeries (56)	Scoping report (1) Consultation on alternatives Exhibitions (3) and accompanying questionnaire	Scoping report (1) Media interviews Exhibitions Ad-hoc consultation
Participation	Workshops (6) Community association meetings		Working Group meetings (5) Workshops (3)
Delegated decision-making			Single Issues Working Group meetings
Number of consultees	51[3]	124	50

Notes:
1. Categories of stakeholder involvement are based on Arnstein (1969). Stakeholder involvement methods were divided into Arnstein's four categories in advance of the case study analyses.
2. The number of times a particular method was employed is cited in brackets where known.
3. Excludes the public, but all 3,500 residents of the local ward were sent a questionnaire.

*Table 7.2   Discernible institutional consequences of environmental
              assessment in the UK*

Institution/Sector	Discernable changes
Environment Agency	• Approximately 150 planning liaison staff working on environmental assessments external to the agency. • Approximately 25 staff working on environmental assessments conducted by the agency.
Local planning authorities	• 472 authorities, each needing to deal with environmental assessments and having staff to do so.
Environmental consultancies	• 280 consultancies with specific expertise in environmental assessments in the UK.
Planning consultants	• 431 organizations out of 450 on the Royal Town Planning Institute database claiming expertise in environmental assessment.
Education	• 63 separate courses. • 10 schemes taught at 9 different institutions have environmental assessments as a focus and teach upwards of 200 students per year in the UK. • Remaining programmes have some component of environmental assessments (possibly optional) and teach upwards of 500 students per year at another 29 institutions.

Source: Adapted from Bond (2003).

Table 7.3 Practical experience of, and training in, environmental assessment within the government bureaucracy

Stakeholder	Practical experience of environmental assessment	Training in environmental assessment
Planning officer	More than 20	Continual professional development training courses; self-taught.
Planning officer	6–10	None.
Planning officer	11–20	Attendance of seminars; guidance from colleagues.
Planning officer	2–5	None.
Planning officer	11–20	Self-taught.
Local councillor	1	Council training.
Local councillor	1	None.
Local councillor	1	Informal training from a planning officer and the Environment Agency.
Archaeological officer	More than 20	None.
Ecologist	Not specified	Training course run by English Nature in 1993.
Ecologist	0	None.
Public health specialist	2–5	Health impact assessment course introduced environmental assessment.
Hydrologist	More than 20	1-day training seminar in 1998.
Centre for Environment, Fisheries and Aquaculture Science	More than 20	Training as part of undergraduate education; attendance of conferences and workshops.

*Table 7.4   The contribution of environmental assessment to design
outcomes*

	Mines stabilization	Offshore wind-farm	Land remediation
Type of alternative (number of options evaluated)	1. Strategic solutions (e.g. controlled collapse versus infill) (7) 2. Infill options (4) 3. Location of work-site (13) 4. Transport of infill material (2) 5. Do-nothing	1. Site choice (2) 2. Site layout (1) 3. Turbine choice (n/a[1]) 4. Foundation design (5) 5. Electricity connection point (7) 6. Landfall and onshore cable route (6) 7. Do-nothing	1. General waste disposal method (7) 2. Treatment method for specific waste streams (17) 3. Landfill location[2]
Number of mitigation measures proposed	217	145	91
Average number of mitigation measures per impact prediction[3]	4.8	1.6	2.4

Notes:
1. It was concluded in the environmental assessment documentation that the developer would opt for the turbines with the largest generation capacity available at that time.
2. The do-nothing option was not considered in this case as the owner of the site was legally required to remediate the land.
3. These calculations take into account that single mitigation measures are sometimes applied to multiple impacts.

8. How useful are computable general equilibrium models for sustainability impact assessment?

Serban Scrieciu

I. INTRODUCTION

The concept and practical implementation of sustainable development has become a key issue for policy agendas, research topics and even business plans. The Brundtland Report (or 'Our Common Future') officially initiated the on-going concern for sustainable development by defining it as a process that 'seeks to meet the needs and aspirations of the present without compromising the ability to meet those of the future' (Bruntland 1987). The need to provide a comprehensive and reliable analysis of the effects of major policy changes on sustainability outcomes has been increasingly recognized, and has led to the on-going development of integrated methodological or conceptual frameworks for assessing the impact of policy on sustainable development.

The sustainability impact assessment (SIA) methodology constitutes a response to this need.[1] It represents a relatively new conceptual approach for the ex ante appraisal of the potential impacts of policy reform on sustainable development that has been particularly applied to trade negotiations and trade liberalisation measures.[2] The SIA methodology includes major improvements from previous traditional policy assessments in the sense that it adopts an integrated approach covering the economic, environmental and social impacts of policy reforms, it incorporates a consultation process with the active involvement of stakeholders in the assessment process, and, in addition to the identification of potential effects, it puts forward accompanying measures that would allow for both the enhancement of positive effects and the mitigation of negative impacts (George and Kirkpatrick 2004a).[3]

SIA does not however, recommend a particular tool or set of tools for quantitatively or qualitatively assessing potential economic, environmental and social effects, or trade-offs. It draws on a wide range of methodological

approaches, tools and applications, largely depending on the policy category
to be assessed, the level of analysis and the typology of effects under investigation. However, recent studies have argued that potential trade-offs
between the economic, social and environmental pillars of sustainability may
be more adequately addressed through the greater use of numerical modelling techniques, particularly computable general equilibrium (CGE) models[4]
(Böhringer and Löschel 2006; Böhringer 2004; Ferguson et al 2005). These
papers generally argue for the incorporation of sustainability indicators into
numerical equilibrium modelling frameworks, and implicitly for the intensive
use of these techniques to undertake sustainability impact assessments:

> The quantification of tradeoffs requires the use of numerical model techniques.
> There is simply *no other way* to think systematically and rigorously about the
> interaction of the many forces that interact in the economy affecting potential
> indicators of Sustainable Development. (Böhringer 2004: 10) (italics added)

This chapter critically evaluates the proposition put forward in the literature, which advocates the use of computable general equilibrium models as
the main analytical tool for effectively assessing sustainability outcomes of
policy interventions. While acknowledging the usefulness of CGE modelling for some dimensions of policy analysis, the chapter seeks to question
the legitimacy of extensively, or even exclusively, relying on this particular
modelling tool for the analysis of the multi-dimensional, interdisciplinary,
dynamic and complex concept of sustainability. It focuses particularly on
the weaknesses and shortcomings emerging from the theoretical assumptions and model specification features underpinning CGE models.[5]

The chapter is structured into four sections. The following section briefly
discusses the concept of computable general equilibrium modelling. Section
III evaluates to what extent the literature on CGE modelling has addressed
sustainable development issues. Section IV offers a critical appraisal of the
appropriateness of using CGE models as a main tool or fundamental analytical framework for an effective SIA. Section V concludes.

II.   CGE MODELLING: SOME CONCEPTUAL ISSUES

CGE models usually cover economy-wide impacts on relative prices,
resource allocation and incomes (Kousnetzoff and Chauvin 2004), and in
addition, account for inter- and intra-industry foreign trade links. They
represent a relatively recent category of modelling methods that convert
Walrasian general equilibrium models from an abstract representation of
an economy to a realistic representation of actual economies (Shoven and

Whalley 1984).[6] The theoretical underpinning of CGE models heavily draws on the neoclassical (micro-) economic theory of the optimisation behaviour of rational economic agents against the background of general equilibrium theoretical structures. Although the computer representation of the economy is complex enough to reflect its essential features, it may still retain the tractability characteristics of their analytical counterparts (Kehoe and Kehoe 1994). In other words, the CGE methodology allows models of large dimensions to be quantitatively solved whilst retaining the basic general equilibrium structure of their theoretical counterparts (Glebe 2003). This is because CGE models have emerged as the result of combined efforts of theorists that laid the foundations of general equilibrium theory, applied economists who looked at the real economy using the theoretical foundations, and mathematicians who have developed tools to bring about the feasibility of numerical computations (Grassini 2004).

A more compact definition may thus present a CGE model as an analytical deterministic integrated system of non-linear equations derived from the economic theory of optimizing behaviour of rational economic agents that describes the simultaneous linkages between markets, institutions and factor resources that renders an all-markets clearing equilibrium numerical solution. It could be compared to a scientific laboratory experiment where the modelled economy constitutes the subject of the experiment, the assumptions made are the necessary conditions for the experiment to work, and the exogenous policy changes are the shocks that are administered to the subject in order to investigate their potential effect. In other words, the aim of CGE modelling is '. . . to evaluate policy options by specifying production and demand parameters and incorporating data reflective of real economies' (Shoven and Whalley 1984: 1007).

Numerical CGE models are based on classical analytical equilibrium models (formalized by Arrow and Debreu in the 1950s), according to which a unique (optimal) general equilibrium solution in competitive markets may arise if three equilibrium conditions are simultaneously satisfied (Mathiesen 1985; Paltsev 2004): (i) the 'zero profit condition' requiring that any activity that is functioning and operating must earn zero profit (ii) the 'market clearance condition' requiring that supply and demand for any good and factor of production must balance, and (iii) the 'income balance condition' requiring that for each economic agent the value of income must equal the value of factor endowments. However, CGE models represent an extension to classical equilibrium analytical models in the sense that they are mostly policy driven and aim to provide numerical solutions to large multi-sectoral models.[7] Their main task is to simultaneously find equilibrium prices, quantities and incomes of an economy where all economic flows are accounted for. In other words, they ensure that there is a 'sink' for every 'source' (Paltsev 2004). Furthermore, they are capable of illustrating the respective economic flows in much more detail and complexity than analytical models, which can only afford to work in small dimensions.[8]

CGE modelling hence represents a flexible analytical and simulation device for distinguishing between the multiple effects that might be brought about by the implementation of a set of combined policy issues (FAO 2003). It also has the main advantage of addressing the workings of an economy in an integrated manner and considering the complex inter-link-ages, feedback and spill-over effects between all the sectors and economic agents operating in the modelled economy, whether at a national, regional or global level. Nevertheless, CGE models are, in a nutshell, quantitative expressions of neoclassical economic theory, which tends to impose a number of strict assumptions on the modelling (Barker 2004). In other words, specific functional forms or restrictions need to be employed in order to ensure a unique and stable equilibrium, though the economic realism of these restrictions has often been overlooked (Ackerman 2002). This typically renders the CGE simulation approach often too stylized and rigid for sustainability impact analysis.

III. CGE MODELLING AND SUSTAINABILITY IMPACT ASSESSMENT

The modelling literature dealing simultaneously with interactions between all three – economic, social and environmental – components of sustainable development is extremely sparse. This is because both the SIA concept and CGE economic modelling techniques to incorporate sustainability issues have only recently emerged. However, there are several studies that model the impact of policy changes on individual relationships/aspects of the sustainability process, for example issues pertaining to economic and environmental development or between economic and social aspects.

On the one hand, an increasing number of studies address the relationship between economic policy reforms and environmental performance or environmental policies. For instance, a large number of this type of studies, investigate the interactions between trade policy reforms or greater trade liberalisation and the environment. These are performed at various aggregation levels, from a global perspective (Perroni and Wiggle 1994; Cole and Rayner 2000; Copeland and Taylor 2004; Nijkamp, Wang and Kremers 2005), on a regional scale (Brown, Deardoff and Stern 1992; Anderson 2001, for NAFTA, Löschel and Mraz 2001; Zhu and van Ierland 2006, for an extended EU) or at a country level (Anderson and Strutt 1998, for Indonesia; Townsend and Ratnayake 2000, for New Zealand; Dean 2000, for China). The modelling approach generally attaches an environmental module to production or consumption functions often under the form of technical coefficients of emissions (for example Nijkamp, Wang and Kremers 2005, add an explicit capital-energy composite input into the production structure).

On the other hand, a growing body of CGE modelling literature investigates the impact of policy proposals or policy changes not only on economic growth but also on social welfare, poverty and equity. For example, Mbabazi (2002) analyses short-run welfare impacts of trade liberalisation in Uganda, Humphreys (2000) evaluates within a CGE modelling framework, poverty and distributional impacts of trade liberalisation in South Africa, and Coady and Harris (2004) adopt an augmented CGE approach[9] that addresses the welfare impact of cash transfers targeted at rural areas in Mexico.

This chapter does not go into more detail pertaining to the literature just mentioned because the present analysis deals with issues of measuring the impacts of policy initiatives on all three pillars of sustainable development from an integrative and not separated standpoint. The chapter hence focuses on studies that have attempted to use CGE modelling as a tool for providing an integrative assessment of the sustainability dimension. The particular suitability of computable general equilibrium models for measuring all three pillars of sustainable development has been particularly advocated, for example, in Böhringer and Löschel (2006) and Böhringer (2004), for which a critical discussion is presented in the remainder of this chapter.[10]

Böhringer and Löschel (2006) present the case for the use of computable general equilibrium modelling as a flexible backbone tool for quantifying the impacts of policy changes or proposals on the three pillars (economic, environment and social) of sustainable development. The authors assert that CGE modelling may represent a good fit of the requirements for a comprehensive sustainability impact assessment (SIA):[11]

> We argue that CGE models can incorporate several key sustainability (meta-) indicators in a single micro-consistent framework, thereby allowing for a systematic quantitative trade-off analysis between environmental quality, economic performance and income distribution. (Böhringer and Löschel 2006)

The authors start their arguments by displaying two lists of policy-relevant systems of sustainable indicators that may be partially addressed within a CGE modelling framework. These refer to the list of *Indicators of Sustainable Development* developed by the United Nations Commission on Sustainable Development (CSD) and a list compiled by the European

Commission with the aim of evaluating the progress of the EU towards sustainable development. Both sets of indicators of sustainable development are constructed for use at a national level.[12] A large number of these sustainability indicators can be included within a CGE modelling framework according to Böhringer and Löschel (2006). This would provide a quantitative approach to SIA and lead to better-informed policy decision-making (Böhringer 2004).

The authors develop a generic ('core') CGE model to which they propose several extensions that would increase the policy relevance and would cover a wider range of indicators for SIA. The generic model represents a standard comparative-static multi-sector and multi-region model of trade and environmental or energy policies that employs three primary factors of production (labour, capital and resource of fossil fuels) and non-energy intermediate inputs. The assumptions of no change in the employment of resources, constant returns to scale and perfect competition are generally associated with standard/generic CGE models.[13] However, the Böhringer and Löschel (2006) core model has limited application for SIA purposes in the sense that besides the fact that it addresses only a limited number of economic and environmental indicators for sustainable development,[14] when it comes to the latter it provides only a quantitative assessment in terms of emissions from fossil fuel combustion (namely CO_2) and may simulate only a very narrow spectrum of environmental policy responses, such as the application of a carbon tax.

A state of the art in the use of energy–economy–environment (E3) CGE models for SIA is further assessed in Böhringer and Löschel (2006). The authors acknowledge that although this type of CGE model displays a good coverage of key economic indicators, environmental indicators are only partly covered (with an emphasis on energy-related emissions and hardly any assessment of more complex ecological processes such as biodiversity loss or water stress), whereas social indicators stand out for their very weak coverage, due to difficulties in defining and measuring the social dimensions of development. However, despite these deficiencies of CGE models to cover key sustainability indicators, the authors advocate a so called 'hard link' approach that makes use of a single integrated modelling framework, implying that the 'data and functional relationships from other models must be condensed and synthesized in a way compatible to the structure of the core [CGE] model' (Böhringer and Löschel 2006). In other words, the authors argue for the supremacy of the CGE modelling tool over other methods in assessing sustainability impacts. This may pose a serious danger to sound policy-making, particularly if this simulation device fundamentally mis-represents (as argued in this chapter) the complexity of the development process and sustainability systems.

Furthermore, several extensions are discussed in Böhringer and Löschel (2006) that may develop the core model towards a better assessment of potential interactions and trade-offs between various sustainability indicators. These refer to the inclusion of non-CO_2 greenhouse gases, accounting for market distortions such as taxes or subsidies, involuntary unemployment and imperfect competition, adding dynamic specifications and endogenous technological change. The disaggregation of the representative agent into heterogeneous households would allow for the analysis of equity issues, as well as linking models to ensure a more comprehensive coverage of SIA requirements. However, the authors merely present how each of the proposed extensions may be capable of widening the policy relevance for SIA, but do not provide greater detail on their practical implementation and the appropriateness of their incorporation into a CGE modelling framework.

A more detailed explanation of possible CGE methodological extensions and their relevance for SIA is put forward in Böhringer (2004). The author acknowledges that one of the main weaknesses of CGE numerical modelling is that it is very difficult to distinguish between the numerous general equilibrium effects that are at work and that drive the simulation results, i.e. the black box critique.[15] The study then presents in more depth two alternative decomposition techniques that would identify the economic channels through which international trade may transmit policy impacts. Further extensions to the core CGE model are represented in terms of specifying and solving optimal policy problems, or undertaking systematic sensitivity analysis for key elasticities. Nonetheless, although the proposed extensions to the core model are important for a more reliable CGE analysis, they once again do not particularly address sustainability issues. This is because, despite the fact that such proposals to model development are welcome in the modelling literature, they tend to address CGE modelling limitations in general, and do not necessarily provide satisfactory answers to a range of questions particularly pertaining to the dynamics of sustainable development. In other words, the major assumptions that underpin CGE models and their associated limitations raise the question of how useful are these models in providing an effective and reliable assessment of the sustainability impacts of policy changes.

IV. THE INHERENT LIMITATIONS AND DRAWBACKS OF CGE MODELLING FOR AN EFFECTIVE SIA

At first glance, CGE modelling, as suggested in the Böhringer and Löschel (2006) and Böhringer (2004) studies, appears to provide the much needed single consistent framework necessary to quantitatively perform sustainability impact assessments. Nonetheless, when one looks into the detail of the workings, underpinnings and assumptions of computable general equilibrium modelling, one starts to question their ability to deliver plausible assessments of crucial aspects linked to the complex process of sustainability, particularly when referring to environmental and social dimensions. The following sections discuss the inherent limitations and drawbacks of CGE modelling for an effective SIA.

The Problem of Quantifying Sustainability

The first argument pertains to the capacity of quantitative methods in general (and CGE models as a sub-category of these) relative to qualitative approaches in providing a meaningful assessment of sustainability impacts. Although the need to deliver robust and rigorous quantitative SIAs is widely acknowledged, at the same time it is also increasingly acknowledged that many environmental, social and even economic aspects of sustainable development are very difficult to estimate quantitatively (and in some cases, it may not even be desirable).[16] For example, in a multitude of cases the natural capital may have an intrinsic value (not quantifiable in monetary terms), and integrating it within a pricing system based on individual preferences may actually be in conflict with ecological concerns.[17] The difficulty of mathematically formulating and quantifying interactions between economic activities and the environment becomes more pronounced, for example, in the case of agriculture, which plays a multi-functional role and provides, in addition to corresponding private commodities, a series of rural amenities and public goods. Besides the fact that major aspects of the agriculture–environment nexus are not suited for modelling (for example biodiversity and landscape), those elements of the relationship that may be adequate for modelling continue to be the focus of intense discussions amongst modellers.[18]

Limitations of the Economic Theory Underpinning CGE Models

The CGE theoretical framework draws on a combination of general equilibrium theory, neoclassical micro-economic optimization behaviour of rational economic agents, and some macro-economic elements that attempt to explain economic, and recently, also social and environmental phenomena. In other words, to many economists, the conventional neoclassical approach that extends well known established liberal concepts, such as supply and demand forces, market equilibrium, profit maximisation, utility maximisation, prices, and monetary valuation to address ecological challenges represents a viable solution in tackling environmental problems. Nevertheless, as Söderbaum (2000) also argues, this encompasses a mechanistic, monetary reductionist approach that places a strong emphasis on the market as the solution to all kind of problems (including environmental and social issues) and fails to appropriately account for the institutional arrangements, ethical issues and the developmental needs of a society within an interdisciplinary, pluralistic, holistic and dynamic approach. When economic and environmental linkages are assessed within a CGE modelling framework, their complexity tends to be narrowed down, for example to the attachment of an environmental module to production or consumption functions often under the form of technical coefficients of emissions. Moreover, the elegance of the theory underlining CGE models and its apparent ability to explain the world relies on a truism, as these models, which are typically based on one year's data, are inherently not falsifiable and fit the data perfectly (Barker 2004).

Conventional neoclassical theory also assumes that individual behaviour reflects the rational pursuit of self-interest, and consequently, the optimal policy is one that best allows individuals to maximize their personal utility and meet their preferences. However, individual preferences or personal welfare concerns play only a limited role in human behaviour, as persons generally base their choices on a much more complex set of values. For instance, they may display altruistic or sympathetic preferences or may have goals that transcend maximizing utility objectives, such as moral values or socially valuable choices.[19]

Hence, the theory of optimisation behaviour represents a very specific view of human beings, society and nature. Other theoretical perspectives in both economics and other social and physical sciences, hence, tend to be marginalized or even excluded. Furthermore, neoclassical economists tend to over-emphasize people's autonomy and self-interest, and downplay the influence of others on individual preferences and decision-making, thus ignoring the social networks, interactions and context within which people are generally embedded (Surowiecki 2005). This raises important questions related to the effectiveness of CGE models based on neoclassical theoretical underpinnings to investigate those social impacts that are significantly determined by social interactions and processes (e.g. education, empowerment, health, intra-household income distribution). In other words, following the path of objectivity (namely a mechanistic observation of regularities) and value neutrality, neoclassical economists claim to provide 'optimal solutions' from a societal point of view to environmental and development problems. But, in relation to these latter problems there is no value-free science, as environmental and development issues go much further beyond the limited monistic view of a single discipline (Söderbaum 2000).

The general equilibrium assumption that is inherent to CGE models is also fragile and over-simplistic. A steady-state equilibrium may never be reached, as society tends to always find itself in a never-ending process of change and disequilibrium. The general equilibrium assumption on which CGE models lay their foundations hence suddenly seems very unstable, as there is no theory to explain what may happen out of equilibrium and there is no reason to believe that equilibrium is achieved in the real world (Grassini 2004).

Classical GE assumptions typically include perfect competition, full employment of resources and perfectly mobile factors of production. In addition, the general equilibrium theory behind CGE models assumes that there is complete information about all prices now and in the future, and that economic agents implicitly have unlimited computational abilities. Although some of these assumptions have been relaxed in recent and more advanced CGE models, further research needs to be undertaken in order to bring model specifications closer to realistic behavioural relationships, for example those characterizing transitional or developing economies. Moreover, market clearing conditions and the GE rule that every source needs to find a sink (a factor cannot be employed in two different places, households cannot spend more than they earn, society is a waste-free economy) represent a relatively strong reductionist view on the workings of the real economy. The CGE model builder tends to be satisfied with the choice of some specific functional forms and closure rules, and modifies the available representation of the real world instead of rejecting the model (Grassini 2004).[20] In other words, specific functional forms or restrictions need to be employed in order to ensure a unique and stable equilibrium, though the economic realism of these restrictions has often been over-looked (Ackerman 2002). In addition, on the environmental side there is considerable research showing that ecological systems rarely exhibit equilibrium behaviour, which questions the general equilibrium idea and the hegemony of the neoclassical model of ecological price determination (Patterson et al 2006).[21] This typically renders the CGE simulation approach often too stylized and rigid for sustainability impact analysis.

The Problem of Dynamic Representation

General equilibrium modelling often produces a static equilibrium, whereas an open society is grounded in instability and subject to dynamic disequilibrium forces (Soros 1990). The assumption of a steady-state equilibrium becomes even more uncertain in the case of developing or transition economies that continue to undergo rapid and substantial changes (the so called 'transition' handicap outlined in Piazolo 2001). CGE models focus on equilibrium positions, and are, consequently, unsuited to adequately investigate transitional adjustment paths (Barker 2004).

Furthermore, though more recent developments in CGE modelling allow for the insertion of 'dynamic' elements, these are limited in scope and provide an unsatisfactory description of dynamism within an economy. For instance, CGE models may account for capital accumulation effects but remain silent with respect to regulatory and institutional changes that an economy may need to undergo in order to be on the modelled or 'desired' adjustment path. The dynamic representation in some CGE models that do incorporate pseudo-dynamic features is over-simplistic and merely extends the usual CGE snapshots of comparative statics to a series of annual snapshots based on artificially perfect macro-economic stability (Ackerman 2005). In other words, CGE models fail to adequately explain adjustment paths and what may happen during disequilibrium.

Other Shortcomings

Other disadvantages that are particularly associated with the workings of CGE modelling in general include the use of very complicated models and the simultaneous running of several policy scenarios that makes it difficult to identify the triggering factors and mechanisms leading to final outcomes; the borrowing of parameter estimates from other sources and hence difficulty in validating or falsifying in the traditional sense (econometric critique);[22] and a limited macro side that is based upon the money neutrality assumption and that typically fails to address monetary policies and the role of nominal variables (inflation, interest rates) in influencing economic outcomes.[23] Furthermore, several crucial limitations related to the appropriateness of CGE models to simulate policy reform and sustainable development issues, particularly pertaining to climate change, and the interactions between energy and output have been highlighted in Barker, Köhler and Villena (2002). These refer to limited disaggregation of productive sectors and factors of production, high uncertainty of the assumed values of substitution elasticities between factors of production, and especially the very limited representation of technical progress.

The nature of CGE modelling and the underlying assumptions that it employs pose the risk of generalizing and homogenizing completely different economies and societies, thus failing to account for key country- and context-specific differences. For instance, with regard to the economic background of a nation, CGE modelling is weak in dealing with structural details and often starts from the assumption that economic agents are fully capable of responding to the incentives provided under the new policy change and hence act accordingly. Nonetheless, there may be a multitude of structural barriers and institutional impediments that constrain supply responsiveness, particularly in countries that continue to face important market dysfunctions.

Finally, with regard to the assessment of the social dimension of sustainable development, CGE models perform poorly, as also acknowledged in the Böhringer and Löschel (2006) study. Those that do evaluate social implications tend to focus on poverty impacts, usually employing simplistic poverty measurements (headcount index or the number of poor lifted out of poverty), and, to a lesser extent, on distributional concerns, without consideration for other major social issues such as education, health or justice. Moreover, CGE modelling typically works at high levels of aggregation and focus on representative agents, without special consideration to household heterogeneity and inter- or intra-household distributional concerns. Complementing general equilibrium work with detailed household modules, though still in its emerging phase, may provide valuable insights into spelling out micro–macro links and assessing distributional impacts. However, at the very least, the use of other techniques should be considered in conjunction or in parallel with CGE modelling tools, and the latter should not be seen as holding supremacy over other assessment methods, particularly when informing policy decision makers on the potential sustainability impacts.

V. CONCLUSIONS

The chapter critically assessed the appropriateness of computable general equilibrium models to effectively provide consistent insights into the sustainability impacts of policy proposals. Though CGE models may render useful information on some individual, particularly economic aspects of policy appraisal and SIA studies, by design they are unlikely to perform well when it comes to integrated sustainability impact assessment, and particularly when assessing the environmental and social dimensions of sustainable development. The use of this approach as a main or 'backbone' tool for assessing sustainability outcomes may result in inappropriate or even misleading results and policy suggestions. This is largely because of the often over-simplistic and unrealistic assumptions underlining general equilibrium theory, and the inherent nature of CGE models that allows only for a limited, often static (or at the most pseudo-dynamic) and mostly mis-represented view of the complex process of sustainable development.

Using CGE modelling as a 'backbone' tool for integrated SIA may lead to the domination of an exclusively quantitative technique that draws heavily on a rather narrow view of economic realities, human behaviour and the interactions between economic, social and environmental dimensions of development. This may seriously infringe upon the basic values promoted by the SIA methodology, namely heterogeneity and the reliance of assessment work on both quantitative and qualitative approaches. It is important hence to understand the weaknesses of evaluating indicators of sustainability using CGE models. In other words, whilst acknowledging the strengths, advantages and potential of employing general equilibrium modelling techniques in evaluating certain aspects of sustainability, a certain degree of variety and 'competing' assessment tools would be essential in rendering useful and integrated SIAs. CGE models may be useful particularly in the context for which they have been initially developed (e.g. the potential impact of fiscal or trade policy on factor allocation and sectoral outputs). However, the range of questions that they can answer pertaining to sustainable development and potential mitigating and enhancing policy measures is greatly limited.

NOTES

1. The sustainability impact assessment (SIA) methodology was originally developed at the Institute for Development Policy and Management, University of Manchester at the initiative of the European Commission (Kirkpatrick, Lee and Morrissey 1999). Ex ante assessment of policies has developed since the late 1990s, when the European Commission began to incorporate economic, environmental and social concerns into its policy formulation process (EC 2004).
2. SIA studies include assessments undertaken at multi-national and national level, such as those conducted by the European Commission for the appraisal of EU major policy proposals (also known as extended impact assessments, ExIA) (EC 2005); the evaluation of the impact of greater trade and investment on sustainable development as part of the UK White Paper 2004 on trade and investment (Kirkpatrick, George and Scrieciu 2004); the assessment of national sustainable development strategies in transition economies (Cherp, George and Kirkpatrick 2004); and the sustainability impact assessment of WTO's Doha Development Agenda (Lee and Kirkpatrick 2001; George and Kirkpatrick 2004; Kirkpatrick, George and Scrieciu 2006).
3. Hence, the SIA methodology broadly addresses two complementary issues that feed into each other at various stages, namely an economic, environmental and social assessment undertaken in a clear, scientific and objective manner, and a consultation and dissemination process among stakeholders (EC 2004).
4. Computable general equilibrium models (CGEs) are also referred to in the literature as applied general equilibrium models (AGEs). Although the latter would represent a more appropriate name for these models (as their aim is to turn general equilibrium structures 'from an abstract representation of an economy into realistic models of actual economies', Shoven and Whalley 1984: 1007), the former label is employed in this chapter in order to conform to the common practice found in the modelling literature.
5. However, other limitations of the methods may be further identified if one evaluates in detail the appropriateness of functional forms, closure rules, 'dynamic' modelling elements and other aspects related to modelling performance (see, for example, Grassini 2004; McKitrick 1998, for a more in-depth critical evaluation of CGE models).

6. The Walrasian general equilibrium theory states that in an economy where consumers are endowed with factors and demand produced goods, and firms demand factors and produce goods with a fixed coefficients production technology (or more generally, a constant returns to scale production function), both output and factor markets clear, whilst perfect competition assures that producer prices equal the costs of production for every operating activity.

7. General equilibrium problems have been approached in the last three decades more from a computational and practical perspective due to the pioneering work undertaken in the 1950s, 1960s and 1970s notably by James Meade, Harry G Johnson, Arnold Harberger, H Scarf, John Shoven and John Whalley.

8. Because CGE models usually work at a level of detail halfway between micro and macro variables, some authors have labelled their level of detail as being 'meso', namely the level at which policy makers are interested (Grassini 2004).

9. These represent latest developments in CGE modelling techniques that attempt to link a computable general equilibrium model with a micro-simulation model based on household survey data, allowing the researcher to evaluate welfare and poverty impacts consistent with the macro-economic policies captured in the general equilibrium model (World Bank 2003).

10. Although Ferguson et al (2005) mention in their title 'incorporating sustainability indicators into a computable general equilibrium model', their study addresses only the economic–environment relationship, and within this relationship only environmental aspects pertaining to output emissions and global warming.

11. In this regard, Böhringer and Löschel (2006) and Böhringer (2004) acknowledge that their exclusive focus on quantitative CGE-based analysis should not downplay the role that other numerical modelling approaches may play in sustainability impact assessment studies. However, note that the authors do argue for the exclusive use of numerical modelling techniques, which in turn is largely dominated by CGE modelling techniques.

12. The list compiled by the United Nations CSD contains a set of 58 'core indicators' that are grouped within 15 themes and 38 sub-themes, covering the three main pillars of sustainable development (economic, social and environmental) plus an institutional component reflecting the framework and capacity of each country to implement corresponding sustainability measures. The list forwarded by the European Commission encompasses only fourteen structural indicators that facilitate the process of evaluating the progress made by EU member states towards sustainable development.

13. In a standard model output is derived from a Leontief combination (namely zero elasticity of substitution) of intermediate inputs and aggregate value added, the latter consisting of nested constant elasticity of substitution cost functions. The Armington assumption is also employed to differentiate domestically produced goods from imported commodities.

14. The core model includes in its framework only six (GDP per capita, balance of trade in goods and services, intensity of material use, annual energy consumption per capita, intensity of energy use and emission of greenhouse gases) out of fifty-eight indicators on the United Nations CSD list and four (GDP per capita, labour productivity, greenhouse gas emissions and energy intensity of the economy) out of the fourteen structural indicators on the European Commission's list.

15. The sheer size of CGE models and the difficulty in pinpointing the precise source of a particular result often render these as 'black boxes'.

16. However, a more in-depth discussion of the pros and cons of quantitative versus qualitative analysis for sustainability impact assessment is not pursued here.

17. This view corresponds in fact to the 'strong sustainability' approach to sustainable development that argues that the full contribution of component species and processes to life-support capacity is not fully measurable in (economic) value terms at all (Turner 2002).

18. However, in the last few years there tends to be a convergence in the CGE modelling approach, for example in response to the EU's future shift towards a multi-functional agriculture, namely as a joint production of a pure public good (induced by the government through decoupled direct payments) and an agricultural private good (Cretegny

2002). The author argues for the importance in considering the multi-functionality of agriculture when analysing the policy impacts on consumer welfare, as it might even lead to opposite conclusions if it is ignored.

19. These are labelled by Amartya Sen as meta-preferences or second-order preferences, as opposed to first-order preferences derived from the standard 'rational' economic behaviour.

20. CGE modelling studies have been criticized for their recourse to models characterized by internally inconsistent assumptions, and their choice of model structure, parameter values and functional forms that best serve their purpose (Panagariya and Duttagupta 2001).

21. Patterson et al (2006) argue against the general equilibrium assumptions of neoclassical ecological pricing methods and outline a new method for determining ecological prices in complex ecology–economy systems where non-equilibrium prices are more likely to prevail.

22. CGE models derive the values for various crucial model parameters from mathematical manipulation (calibration), and typically on the basis of one year's data, or are questionably borrowed from the literature, and, hence, are not estimated from statistical fittings of empirical data. They generally ignore the availability of rich sources of time series data and 'do not model observations on the long-term processes of income growth, adjustment to price changes (such as responses to oil price shocks) or technological change' (Barker 2004: 3).

23. The zero homogeneity of demand functions coupled with the linear homogeneity of profits in prices implies that only relative prices affect consumer and producer behaviour, and that the absolute level of prices has no effect on equilibrium outcome (Shoven and Whalley 1984).

REFERENCES

Ackerman, F (2002), 'Still dead after all these years: interpreting the failure of general equilibrium theory', *Journal of Economic Methodology*, 9 (2), 119–39.

Ackerman, F (2005), 'The shrinking gains from trade: a critical assessment of Doha round projections', GDEI Working Paper No. 05-01, Global Development and Environment Institute, Tufts University, Medford MA.

Anderson, K and Strutt, A (1998), 'Will trade liberalisation harm the environment? The case of Indonesia 2020', CEPR discussion paper no. 1933, Centre for Economic Policy Research (CEPR), London.

Anderson, S (2001), *Seven Years Under NAFTA*, Institute for Policy Studies, Washington DC.

Barker, T (2004), 'The transition to sustainability: a comparison of general-equilibrium and space–time–economics approaches', Tyndall Centre Working Paper No. 62, Tyndall Centre for Climate Change Research, University of East Anglia, Norwich.

Barker, T, Köhler, J and Villena, M (2002), 'Costs of greenhouse gas abatement: meta-analysis of post-SRES mitigation scenarios', *Environmental Economics and Policy Studies*, 5, 135–66.

Böhringer, C (2004), 'Sustainability impact assessment: the use of computable general equilibrium models', *Économie Internationale* no. 99, 3ᵉ trimester, 9–26.

Böhringer, C and Löschel, A (2006), 'Computable general equilibrium models for sustainability impact assessment: status quo and prospects', *Ecological Economics*, forthcoming (made available via email by A Löschel).

Brown, D, Deardoff, A and Stern, R (1992), 'A North-American Free Trade Agreement: analytical issues and a computational assessment, *World Economy*, 15 (1), 11–29.

Bruntland, G (1987), *Our Common Future: The World Commission on Environment and Development*, Oxford University Press.

Cherp, A, George, C and Kirkpatrick, C (2004), 'A methodology for assessing national sustainable development strategies', *Environment and Planning C: Government and Policy*, 22, 913–26.

Coady, D and Harris, R (2004), 'Evaluating targeted cash transfer programs: a general equilibrium framework with an application to Mexico', IFPRI research report 137, International Food Policy Research Institute, Washington DC.

Cole, M and Rayner, A (2000), 'The Uruguay Round and air pollution: estimating the composition, scale and technique effects of trade liberalisation', *Journal of International Trade and Economic Development*, 9 (3), 339–54.

Copeland, B and Taylor, S (2004), 'Trade, growth and the environment', *Journal of Economic Literature*, XLII (March), 7–71.

Cretegny, L (2002), 'Modelling the multifunctionality of agriculture in a CGE framework'. Paper presented at the International Conference on Policy Modelling, Brussels, July 4–6.

Dean, J (2000), 'Does trade liberalization harm the environment? A new test', CIES Policy Discussion Paper 0015, Centre for International Economic Studies, University of Adelaide.

EC (2004), 'Impact assessment: next steps – in support of competitiveness and sustainable development', Commission staff working paper, SEC (2004) 1377, European Commission, Brussels.

EC (2005), 'The 2005 Review of the EU Sustainable Development Strategy: initial stocktaking and future orientations', Communication from the Commission to the Council and the European Parliament, COM (2005) 37 final, European Commission, Brussels.

FAO (2003), 'WTO agreement on agriculture: the implementation experience – developing country case studies', Food and Agriculture Organisation (FAO), Rome.

Ferguson, L, McGregor, P, Swales, JK, Turner, K and Ping Yin, Y (2005), 'Incorporating sustainability indicators into a computable general equilibrium model of the Scottish economy', *Economic Systems Research*, 17 (2), 103–40.

George, C and Kirkpatrick, C (2004), 'Putting the Doha principles into practice: the role of sustainability impact assessment', chapter 14 in Katrak, H and Strange, R (eds) *The WTO and Developing Countries*, London, Palgrave Macmillan, pp. 315–38.

George, C and Kirkpatrick, C (2004a), 'Trade and development: assessing the impact of trade liberalisation on sustainable Development', *Journal of World Trade*, 38 (3), 441–69.

Glebe, T (2003), 'Assessing the agricultural trade and environment interaction: taking stock and looking ahead', TUM Discussion Paper 02-2003, Technische Universität München.

Grassini, M (2004), 'Rowing along the computable general equilibrium modelling mainstream'. Paper presented at EcoMod conference on 'Input-output and general equilibrium: data, modeling, and policy analysis', Brussels, September 2–4.

Humphreys, N M (2000), 'A poverty focused CGE model for South Africa, working paper, Oxford University, http://www.columbia.edu/~mh2245/papers 1/.

Kehoe, P and Kehoe, T (1994), 'A primer on static applied general equilibrium models', *Federal Reserve Bank of Minneapolis Quarterly Review*, 18 (1), 2–16.

Kirkpatrick, C, George, C and Scrieciu, S (2004), 'The implications of trade and investment liberalisation for sustainable development: review of literature'. Report for the UK Department of Environment, Food and Rural Affairs (Defra), Institute for Development Policy and Management, University of Manchester, July.

Kirkpatrick, C, George, C and Scrieciu, S (2006), 'Sustainability impact assessment of proposed WTO negotiations: final global overview trade SIA of the Doha development agenda – mid-term report', Consultation Draft, Impact Assessment Research Centre, Institute for Development Policy and Management, University of Manchester, April.

Kirkpatrick, C, Lee, N and Morrissey, O (1999), *WTO New Round: Sustainability Impact Assessment Study*, Phase One Report, Institute for Development Policy and Management, University of Manchester.

Kousnetzoff, N and Chauvin, S (2004), 'Workshop summary: methodological tools for assessing the sustainability impact of the EU's economic policies, with application to trade liberalisation policies', *Économie Internationale*, 99, 3e trimester, 81–9.

Lee, N and Kirkpatrick, C (2001), 'Methodologies for sustainability impact assessments of proposals for new trade agreements', *Journal of Environmental Assessment Policy and Management*, 3 (3), 1–19.

Löschel, A and Mraz, M (2001), 'EU enlargement and environmental policy', ZEW Discussion Paper no. 01-52, Centre for European Economic Research (ZEW), Mannheim.

Mathiesen, L (1985), 'Computation of economic equilibrium by a sequence of linear complementarity problems', *Mathematical Programming Study*, 23, 144–62.

Mbabazi, J (2002), 'A CGE analysis of the short-run welfare effects of tariff liberalisation in Uganda', WIDER Discussion Paper 2002/114, United Nations University.

McKitrick, R R (1998), 'The econometric critique of computable general equilibrium modelling: the role of functional forms', *Economic Modelling*, 15 (4), 543–73.

Nijkamp, P, Wang, S and Kremers, H (2005), 'Modeling the impacts of international climate change policies in a CGE context: the use of the GTAP-E model', *Economic Modelling*, 22 (5), 955–74.

Paltsev, S (2004), 'Moving from static to dynamic general equilibrium economic models (notes for a beginner in MPSGE)', Technical Note No. 4, Joint Program on the Science and Policy of Global Change, Massachusetts Institute of Technology, Cambridge.

Panagariya, A and Duttagupta, R (2001), 'The "gains" from preferential trade liberalization in the CGE models: where do they come from?', chapter 3 in S Lahiri (ed) *Regionalism and Globalization: Theory and Practice*, London and New York, Routledge, pp. 39–60.

Patterson, M G, Wake, G C, McKibbin, R and Cole, A O (2006), 'Ecological pricing and transformity: a solution method for systems rarely at general equilibrium', *Ecological Economics*, 56 (3), 412–23.

Perroni, C and Wiggle, R (1994), 'International trade and environmental quality: how important are linkages?', *Canadian Journal of Economics*, 27 (3), 551–67.

Piazolo, D (2001), 'Investment behaviour in transition countries and computable general equilibrium models', *Applied Economics*, 33, 829–37.

Shoven, J and Whalley, J (1984), 'Applied general equilibrium models of taxation and international trade: an introduction and survey', *Journal of Economic Literature*, 22 (3), 1007–51.

Söderbaum, P (2000), 'Ecological economics: a political economy approach to environment and development', London, Earthscan Publications.

Soros, G (1990), *Opening the Soviet System*, Weidenfeld & Nicholson.

Surowiecki, J (2005), *The Wisdom of Crowds: Why the Many are Smarter than the Few*, London, Abacus.

Townsend, B and Ratnayake, R (2000), *Trade Liberalisation and the Environment: A Computable General Equilibrium Analysis*, Singapore, World Scientific.

Turner, K (2002), 'Speculations on weak and strong sustainability', CSERGE working paper GEC 92–96, Centre for Social and Economic Research on the Global Environment, University of East Anglia and University College of London.

World Bank (2003), *A User's Guide to Poverty and Social Impact Analysis*, Washington, World Bank.

Zhu, X and van Ierland, E (2006), 'The enlargement of the European Union: effects on trade and emissions of greenhouse gases', *Ecological Economics*, 57, 1–14.

9. Methods and tools for integrated sustainability assessment (MATISSE): a new European project

Paul Weaver, Jan Rotmans, John Turnpenny, Alex Haxeltine and Andrew Jordan

I. INTRODUCTION

Sustainable development has become an over-arching policy target for the EU. It represents an essentially contested notion, because it is complex, normative, subjective and ambiguous. There are, nonetheless, a number of commonalities even in diverging interpretations, upon which the notion of sustainable development can be implemented in practice. These commonalities include:

- it is an inter-generational phenomenon
- it operates at multiple scale levels
- it covers social–cultural, economic and environmental dimensions.

The overall challenge is to make the tensions between these scale levels and dimensions explicit and to develop strategies to alleviate them.

The need for integrated sustainability assessments (ISAs) to support the development of integrated sustainability policies is a challenge not only for policy makers but also for science. The multi-dimensionality of sustainable development requires an integrated and interdisciplinary approach. In principle, integrated assessment (IA) is a suitable approach to address the phenomenon of sustainable development. IA is the science that deals with an integrated systems approach to complex societal problems embedded in a process-based context. IA aims to analyse the multiple causes and impacts of a complex problem in order to develop policy options for a strategic solution of the problem in question. IA itself involves a process whereby IA tools form the equipment to perform the assessment. The IA toolkit is rich, including both analytical tools/methods (such as models, scenarios, uncertainty and risk analyses), and participatory methods (such as focus groups, policy exercises and dialogue methods).

The EU policy-making process and that of its member states remains largely sectoral in nature: a wide spectrum of EU policies pursues narrow sectoral concerns and does not contribute fully enough to the achievement of broader sustainability targets. New policy tools, such as extended impact assessment (ExIA) have, therefore, been adopted by the EU to ensure that sectoral policies can be evaluated in relation to their wider, sustainability impacts. In 2004 more than 40 policies were subject to extended impact assessments before their adoption (EC 2003). However, the new regime of ExIA is, arguably, still too narrowly conceptualized to support the development of effective, cross-sectoral, sustainability-oriented policies, albeit that such policies will be needed to tackle the set of persistent development problems that currently besets the EU.

These persistent problems concern unsustainable trends that threaten our environmental, economic and social security and are contextualized by the powerful on-going forces of globalization, resource depletion, environmental change, and shifts in the basis of geo-political power and influence. They have a systemic pathology and are immune to the usual sectoral problem-solving approaches that frame different policy objectives as mutually inconsistent, and therefore constrain the solutions that can be proposed for tackling problems to ones that trade-off gains on one policy front against losses on others. In principle, sustainability assessment could play a central role in a new approach to policy-making that is specifically oriented to supporting more sustainable development and achieving synergies among policy objectives. This depends on a new conceptualization of sustainability assessment, not used for screening already-proposed sectoral policies for unacceptable impacts these might have on the sustainability of development, as is the role today of extended impact assessment or sustainability impact assessment,[1] but in a more strategic, long-term and constructive role as the central element of a co-evolutionary and, essentially, participative approach to policy development.

Such an approach would focus on developing and exploring visions of alternative socio-ecological futures and development pathways for reaching these as part of a continuous, social-learning process that has the potential to achieve transformational outcomes, including changes of socio-political institutions and contexts. Policy proposals would be developed endogenously as part of the assessment process and not, as now, provided to the assessment process exogenously. It is therefore likely that the necessary regime of ExIA, which has an immediate and pragmatic role in sectoral policy appraisal, will be complemented by a form of strategic sustainability assessment purposed specifically to support the long-term development of cross-sectoral sustainability-oriented policies.[2] An appropriate term for such a strategic sustainability assessment process is integrated sustainability assessment, since to be effective such an assessment process must be integrated and embedded in its socio-political context, i.e. policy makers, stakeholders and scientific experts must work together, probably under new institutional arrangements (perhaps as characterized by the term 'sustainability governance') in order for it to deliver on its potential to support sustainable development.

The term 'integrated sustainability assessment' (ISA) has a very specific meaning in this context, which has been developed in detail by Weaver and Rotmans (Weaver and Rotmans 2005) as the conceptual basis for the MATISSE project. This conceptual basis is outlined briefly in the following paragraphs and is encapsulated by Weaver and Rotmans' definition of integrated sustainability assessment as 'a cyclical, participatory process of scoping, envisioning, experimenting, and learning through which a shared interpretation of sustainability for a specific context is developed and applied in an integrated manner in order to explore solutions to persistent problems of unsustainable development'.

Others, also, have used this term, notably Varey (2004) and Brinsmead (2005), but in neither instance do these authors associate integrated sustainability assessment with a purpose so essentially different from proposal appraisal against a set of static (albeit context-specific) sustainability values as is implied by Weaver and Rotmans in their conceptualization of ISA.

Weaver and Rotmans (2005) stress the co-evolutionary nature of integrated sustainability assessment as a social learning process through which stakeholders' understanding and interpretation of what sustainable development means in a particular applications context evolves through the process. This requires cyclical process architecture. Lessons learned during earlier cycles of an assessment process are used in subsequent cycles to reformulate understandings of both problems and potential solutions. This includes the possibility that stakeholders' interpretations of sustainability will change through the process. Indeed, a successful outcome from such an iterative process would depend in significant part upon this, and, as such, transformational outcomes are specifically targeted as process objectives. By contrast Varey, in particular, places emphasis on the consistency of an assessment process with sustainability values that, although context-specific, are time invariant throughout a specific assessment process.

Weaver and Rotmans (2005) propose that what can be accomplished through sustainability assessment depends on achieving progressively higher levels and strengths of integration within the assessment process. There are multiple possible dimensions of process integration including, for example, the integration of multiple objectives within the assessment process;[3] the formulation, integration and reformulation of sustainability values and principles and their use throughout the process as criteria for proposal design, evaluation and decision-making; the integration of the different dimensions or pillars of sustainable development within the process; the integration of multiple time scales, spatial scales and levels within the process, the integration of multiple perspectives and knowledges of different stakeholders, experts and policy makers; the integration of quantitative and qualitative tools, methods and information; and the integration of multiple process phases (scoping, envisioning, experimenting and learning) within an iterative, cyclical process. A strongly and comprehensively integrated sustainability assessment process is likely to provide for more integrated outcomes to emerge from the process: problem descriptions, sustainability interpretations, visions, descriptions of the system of interest, strategies and policies. In turn, these outcomes should be more robust. Integration holds the potential for developing cross-sectoral strategies and the capacities needed for their effective implementation.

Integrated assessment is now exploring new challenges in fields such as sustainable development. However, the current toolkit of IA is not sophisticated enough to address the multi-dimensional complexity. In order to perform ISA at the EU level, many more new tools and methods are needed which are rooted in a new paradigm.

Although significant progress has been made over the past decades, obvious deficiencies and limitations of current IA tools have become clear: the imbalance between the socio-economic–technological dimension versus the environmental dimension, the purely rational representation of actors, the poor treatment of uncertainties and the single-scale process representation. Sustainable development, however, puts new requirements on IA tools, in terms of trade-offs between multiple scales and multiple generations, and between socio-economic-technological and environmental processes. The new paradigm has not yet taken shape in a mature form, but can be portrayed in terms of the following characteristics: (i) better integration of science (ii) co-evolution of sub-systems and underlying processes (iii) synthesis between participatory methods and IA models (iv) more stochastic than deterministic (v) more explorative than predictive, and (vi) more demand (stakeholder)-oriented than supply-oriented. The time is ripe to start developing new ISA tools without discarding the current IA tools. This is a time-consuming activity, so we therefore propose a two-track strategy: find new ways to use the current portfolio of ISA tools as efficiently and effectively as possible, while at the same time developing building blocks to support the next generation of ISA tools.

Hence, the objective of the MATISSE (Methods and Tools for Integrated Sustainability Assessment) project is to advance the science and application of integrated sustainability assessment (ISA) of EU policies by improving the tool kit available for conducting policy appraisals.[4] MATISSE is designed to support the objectives of the European Commission's Sixth Framework Programme (FP6), by developing tools and methods that can handle the complex challenges expressed in the EU Strategy on Sustainable Development. Within FP6, the EU demands, in support of the EU Strategy, a broad sustainability assessment approach, capable of addressing a wide spectrum of sustainability integration tasks for EU policy. The total spectrum of tasks to be addressed ranges from analysing the driving forces behind unsustainable trends (in terms of the intricate interplay between autonomous trends, market forces, policies and surprises) to developing better policy alternatives and facilitating the comparison of different policies in terms of sustainability objectives.

Within the context of the MATISSE project the choice has been made to focus on IA models in relation to participatory methods. In concrete terms this means that ISA involves the whole palette of: (i) analysing human activities as driving forces (ii) estimating the impacts on ecosystems' functioning and human health (iii) indicating critical thresholds and potential damage (iv) setting policy targets (v) developing mitigation and adaptation strategies, and (vi) monitoring the process. As a consequence, we need a portfolio of IA models and participatory methods to support ISA at the various stages in specific contexts and domains. No single tool or instrument can capture all stages and dimensions of ISA. Furthermore, given the range of applications, contexts and domains, a flexible, hierarchical approach to linking elements together is needed. In practice, ISA encompasses the following tasks and tools:

(i)   analysing the dynamics of sustainable development, using IA models;
(ii) forecasting (un)sustainable trends and developments, using IA models and scenarios of the future;
(iii) assessing the sustainability impact of policy options, using model-based cost-benefit and cost-effectiveness analyses;
(iv) monitoring the long-term process of sustainable development, using model-based indicators;
(v)   designing the process underlying integrated sustainability assessment, using participatory methods.

In other words, the over-arching objective of the MATISSE project is to achieve a step-wise advance in the science and application of ISA by:

- producing a systemic inventory of current tools and methods for integrated sustainability assessment, including the development of procedures for benchmarking;
- anchoring sustainability assessment within a rigorous scientific and theoretical context through the development of a conceptual framework for ISA;
- improving and adjusting existing tools and methods for integrated sustainability assessment according to the specific needs of ISA users;
- developing new tools and methods for integrated sustainability assessment that capture the multi-domain, multi-level and multi-actor complexity of ISA;
- applying existing and new tools and methods for ISA in case studies selected in order to test the strengths and weaknesses of the ISA tools and methods and to deliver case-specific sustainability assessments useful to policy makers and other stakeholders;
- engaging users and stakeholders throughout the development and application of ISA tools and methods in order to ensure a co-production of knowledge, build competences/capacities, and secure take-up in the EU policy process.

The overall challenge is to assess sustainability at the EU level, using the best available current ISA tools in a more coherent and interlinked manner, but also developing new ISA tools in a process of co-production with stakeholders at the science-policy interface. Both existing and new ISA tools need to be based on 'best practice' operational procedures that encapsulate the learning experiences gained with the use of diverse tools and methods over the past decades.

II.   THE WIDER CONTEXT

The leaders of the EU have stated their objective of making the EU 'the most competitive and dynamic knowledge-based economy in the world, capable of sustainable economic growth with more and better jobs and greater social cohesion'[5] by 2010. If this bold target is to be achieved, there is an urgent need for instruments by which policies in all three domains (environmental, economic and social) can be assessed in an integrated fashion. There is currently a proliferation of potentially incompatible tools and methods jeopardizing consistent integrated sustainability assessments. The urge to continuously undertake ISA of major policy instruments stems in particular from the Gothenburg decision, which established the EU Strategy on Sustainable Development and identified sustainability assessment as one of the main 'grips' by which the strategy can be implemented for specific policies/directives. The need for sustainability assessment is reinforced by decisions at the Barcelona Summit to integrate external dimensions into policy-making and by commitments reached at the Johannesburg Summit.

Despite the ambitious environmental considerations informing all EU policy domains, many environmental problems in Europe are (at least partly) aggravated by policies and other regulatory instruments (such as taxes and incentives). There is a clear ambition within the EU to integrate sustainability issues into all policy domains, through the Cardiff Process (begun in 1998 – see, for example, the 2004 review (EC 2004), and continued through the EU Sustainable Development Strategy (EC 2001, 2005), and the Sixth Environment Action Programme (EC 2002).

The MATISSE initiative builds upon several informal and formal networks of scientists and research groups across Europe. The need for, and also added-value of, a European level project can be described by many different aspects, such as the need for a comprehensive approach and the formulation of bold objectives; the need to encompass a wide range of European landscapes with different social and cultural settings; the need to encompass countries and regions in different stages of political, economic and scientific development; the need to encompass countries and regions in different stages of a sustainability transition; and the need to use the final results of the project primarily at the EU level.

III. OUTLINE OF THE IMPLEMENTATION PLAN

A 'full' integrated assessment of SD is so complex and time-consuming that it is beyond the scope of any single research project. This implies that specific choices have to be made with regard to context, themes and tools/methods of ISA aimed at creating a balance between being realistic and pragmatic on the one hand, and ambitious and innovative on the other, whilst focusing on meeting the objectives of the European Commission research programme. The following choices form the context of the MATISSE approach:

- ISA and impact assessment are considered as complementary, and both will be used in a harmonious manner.

- No single ISA tool can capture the complexity of SD, so a diversity of ISA tools and methods will be used. However, diversity without coherence will lead to fragmentation, therefore, a common set of principles is needed for using and developing ISA tools.
- The ISA tools that can be used are: integrated assessment models, scenarios, indicators and participatory methods. The main focus in MATISSE will be on quantitative ISA tools, in particular on integrated assessment models.
- A limited number of case studies will be carried out in order to use ISA tools and perform a partial ISA. The selection of case studies is based on the priorities of the EU SD-strategy.
- Different aspects of ISA, such as forecasting, monitoring or impact assessment, will be treated in different case studies.

The aims of the project are structured around four main activities. The four activities are presented in more detail as follows:

Activity 1: Developing the Toolkit for Integrated Sustainability Assessment

The challenge of improving the ISA toolkit is divided into two broad tracks. Firstly, there is the challenge of improving existing tools and linking of existing tools and methods together to provide the means to address interactions between developments and policies that span different domains and, also, the means to make more comprehensive assessments. In essence, this is aimed at serving joined-up governance, at avoiding perverse policy outcomes or problem shifting, and at clarifying potential conflicts between policy objectives. This track will use a portfolio of existing ISA tools and methods in a more creative and coherent manner, while also adjusting and improving them, in order to better enable current policies and programmes to be assessed. To overcome the deficiencies and limitations of current tools for sustainability assessment, it is necessary to inter-link them. This enables estimation of how policies contribute to specified sustainability targets, and it allows assessment of the distance between a future projection and specified sustainability targets, and exploration of the reasons for any gap between them. There is also much room for improvement of current ISA tools and instruments, in particular the limited level of integration between the various sub-systems and the high level of abstraction of the processes represented. The focus will be on quantitative tools and methods, in particular on integrated assessment models (IAMs). The challenge is to use IAMs in conjunction with sustainability indicators and scenarios, and to provide them with an appropriate and adequate participatory setting. For instance, a hierarchical set of indicators might be dynamically linked to IAMs: in this way, indicators can serve as vehicles to communicate IAM results and as a basis for mapping response strategies. IAMs might also provide scenarios with quantitative rigour and accuracy, whereas scenarios could provide communication vehicles for models (as tested in the EU-VISIONS project, Rotmans et al 2000). Existing IAMs could be used in a participatory context (as tested in the EU-ULYSSES projects, Kasemir et al 2003). Systematic uncertainty and risk analyses performed with IAMs can help in conveying the nature of the uncertainty and provide a link to different risk strategies.

Secondly, to address the complexity of SD we need to develop the next generation of ISA tools, in particular the next generation of IAMs. These should handle multiple scale levels, in particular micro-scale dynamics that can deal with the dynamic behaviour of actors, and are rooted in a new paradigm, that is rooted in complex systems theory, evolutionary economics, multi-level governance and multi-agent modelling. New concepts are needed which are based on the aforementioned characteristics of the new paradigm. Since developing new ISA tools is a time-consuming activity, our strategy is to proceed step-wise: first conceptual models and modules will be developed, then these modules/conceptual models will be implemented and tested in case studies, and if done successfully these modules can be incorporated in existing ISA models, gradually evolving into the next generation of ISA models. In developing new ISA tools, learning from past experiences, both in terms of failures and successes, plays an important role. Therefore, the guidance from Activity 2, by providing a set of principles, priorities and needs for the next generation of ISA tools, is of crucial importance.

Activity 2: ISA Methods and the Contextual Framing for ISA

The main objective of Activity 2 is to support the development of quantitative models for ISA. This may be achieved first by providing a conceptual framework for ISA, and second, by providing an analysis of the demand and supply sides for ISA.

ISA development and implementation are processes that hold the potential for recursive and reflexive learning and capacity building. The goal of the MATISSE project is to advance the state of the art of ISA by broadening the scope of assessment, extending the domains in which assessment is practised, enhancing the ISA toolkit, and developing ISA methods, principles and examples of best practice. There needs to be an iterative and adaptive learning process that will lead to a consortium-wide consensus on key definitions, concepts, priorities, principles and approaches to the challenges of ISA development and testing. This is necessary in order to emerge from the MATISSE process with tools, lessons, principles and examples that will help secure an improved, broadened, extended and harmonized approach to ISA, appropriate for a wide set of application domains.

A second, and related, aspect is that the consortium needs to start from a common understanding of both the current status of ISA and its pattern of use in relation to different domains and contexts of application, including, especially, the important institutional factors that play a key role at the science-policy interface, and an ambitious future vision of the potential role of ISA as a key instrument in support of decision-making and sustainable development. This contextualization of ISA is critical for coordinating the work of the MATISSE consortium and for identifying priorities, criteria and principles that will need to be integrated into the development and testing work in order for ISA to fulfil its potential. This requires an understanding of the complex mechanisms that shape policy-making, including fundamental questions of how policy preferences are formed, and what the decision-making context is in terms of actors, interests, information needs and what the role of the assessment should be. The supply side requires insights into the scientific potential of ISA, and the toolkit currently available. A systematic inventory of ISA tools is therefore needed, including tools and methods that are available but not widely used in the policy arena, and including critical gaps, deficiencies and overlap between tools and methods. The systematic inventory has been fully designed to utilize and build upon the Sustainability A-Test[6] and the IQTools[7] projects, parts of which have gathered inventories of tools (see, for example, de Ridder et al 2005), and examined the use of tools and methods in policy-making.

Activity 3: Scenarios and Case Studies to Implement, Evaluate and Improve the ISA Toolkit

In order to test the improved tools portfolio developed through Activity 1, and advance the state of the art concerning the process by which ISA tools may be applied, the project requires a set of case study applications. Activity 3 thus consists of a set of four case study applications of the new and improved tools developed through Activity 1. These will address the following areas: agriculture, forestry and land-use; resource use, waste and dematerialization; water; and sustainable environmental technology development.

The case studies have been selected to exemplify priority substantive policy issues and urgent analytical challenges that face ISA development. They have also been chosen because of the linkages between the cases, giving the possibility for further integration by considering interactions between them.

As a common starting point for all case studies, a limited set of global and more detailed European scenarios will be created. The value of the scenarios does not lie in their capacity to predict the future, but in their ability to provide insights into the present. By helping to identify weak signals of change that could become major future developments, the implications of those changes could be unfolded. Within this context, the MATISSE project involves taking a limited set of currently used global scenarios, as developed within the framework of the IPCC, Millennium Ecosystem Assessment, and the Global Scenario Group, defining key denominators, time frames and spatial scales, and translating this integrated set of scenario assumptions into a specific European context. In practice this means a limited (three to four) set of European scenarios that are integrated and coherent.[8] The proposed time horizon will be one or two generations (i.e. 25–50 years), with a policy outlook of 10–15 years as 'zooming in' focus. Finally, as a type of sensitivity analysis, surprises and discontinuities will be introduced in the common set of global and European scenarios, to analyse to what extent IA models can cope with these non-linear trends and developments, and how sensitive they are to abrupt external changes. The scenarios will then be used by each case study to explore the implications of different future pathways.

Activity 4: Dissemination and Capacity Building within a Co-development Paradigm

Learning, interaction and feedback are crucial elements in the cyclical and iterative MATISSE approach. Results from the case studies form the input for the further development of existing and new ISA tools. These are then used in the case studies, which in their turn feed back into the development of ISA tools and methods and so on. Obviously, dissemination of these learning experiences and feedback is of crucial importance in MATISSE.

This is a cross-cutting capacity building, communications and outreach activity. In parallel with the philosophy that underpins Activity 2, according to which the concept of ISA represents a process of adaptive management and learning with the object of building capacities and shared understanding, Activity 4 will secure the involvement and engagement of stakeholders throughout all the activities of the project. MATISSE thus aims to secure a wider and harmonized use of an improved set of ISA tools and methods as a means of contributing to better informed and more transparent decision-making processes.

This goal can only be achieved if stakeholders, such as ISA commissioners, practitioners and information users, are involved in the process of ISA tools development, implementation and use in each and every activity within MATISSE. This is needed if ISA tools development is actually to address users needs and also if perceptions of needs and of the possibilities of meeting these are to be re-conceptualized. Equally, there is a need to ensure outreach to ISA stakeholders beyond those directly engaged in the development work. In the spirit of this learning-by-doing and doing-by-learning approach, in which knowledge development is a co-production process, Activity 4 will engage a wide range of stakeholders within the project, provide a contact and advisory service to prospective users and interested parties, and train young ISA scientists to build a community of experienced practitioners capable of implementing ISA in accordance with the ambitious vision for ISA set out in Activity 2.

IV. PROGRESS OF WORK AND CONCLUDING REMARKS

The project intends to deliver an improved toolkit for ISA, focused on improvements to existing quantitative tools and a small set of innovative new tools (from Activity 1); a range of research deliverables to advance the scientific state of the art for ISA, including the conceptual framework for ISA and the inventory and use-analysis of ISA (from Activity 2); a completed set of case study ISA applications that will provide reference application cases for conducting ISAs (from Activity 3); a focused dissemination and capacity building programme that will have made a major contribution to the advancement of an ISA-user community with Europe and especially the new EU member countries (Activity 4); an evaluation of the effectiveness of MATISSE and of the usefulness of its products (facilitated through Activity 4); and a set of integrated policy scenarios that combine the results of all four case studies.

The project aims to facilitate the development of improved approaches or methods for conducting ISA at both the EU and member state level. The dissemination programme will allow these groups to benefit from the scientific results of MATISSE in the practical implementation of ISA in policy-making. The project will facilitate the harmonization of ISA tools and methods within the EU, whilst allowing flexibility to custom build an ISA appropriate for any context. The project addresses two main issues. On the one hand, it seeks to benchmark existing elements and approaches for ISA, assessing their strengths and weaknesses, overlaps, fitness for purpose, context-specificity, transferability, and any critical gaps and linkage problems. MATISSE works closely with other EU and national research initiatives to incorporate the latest work in the field. By making best use of what is already available, duplication of effort will be avoided, enabling resources to be focused where they are most needed, i.e. on filling gaps, securing compatibility and developing the 'best-practice' operational methods for ISA. On the other hand, it addresses the need to improve, develop and apply tools and methods for ISA including sustainability progress monitoring; sustainability impact assessment and evaluation; integrated policy assessment and development; back-casting and forecasting of sustainable development; and managing the transition towards sustainable development. Within the Integrated Project, the overall task will be made manageable by developing different facets of ISA in different parts of the project. Some of the tools (e.g. integrated modelling tools) will be used to assess the sustainability impact of EU policies, some (e.g. scenario tools) to explore the sustainability of future trends and policies, while other tools (i.e. indicators) will deal with monitoring sustainability progress, and participatory methods will focus on the active participation of stakeholders in the development of sustainability tools; most important, however, will be the development of improved ways of using these tools and methods in conjunction with each other.

Therefore, the MATISSE project intends to address the overall need for developing tools and methods that integrate the social, economic, environmental and institutional dimensions of sustainability. This is required for integrating sustainability into EU decision processes and for securing greater cohesion and coordination in sectoral and cross-sectoral policy-making by highlighting conflicts and trade-offs between EU policy objectives and by identifying opportunities for enhancing the compatibility of policy objectives. The project will characterize the disparate sustainability dimensions of EU policies by developing tools and methods that blend quantitative, qualitative, analytical, participatory and deliberative elements and approaches. Because the multitude of temporal and spatial scale levels cannot be covered by a single tool or method, multiple tools and methods are required, which are then tested through multiple case studies, including place-based and chain-based analyses.

MATISSE adopts a multi-disciplinary, trans-disciplinary and participatory research model in order to engage users and civil society, secure a co-production of knowledge, build capacities and competence and secure take-up. This will support capacity building in undertaking integrated sustainability assessments across the European Research Area, and will eventually bring together a critical mass of resources from across the EU-25 member countries to ensure harmonization of methods at the European level.[9]

NOTES

1. These two regimes are referred to hereafter by the abbreviation (S)IA.
2. Today's assessment regimes are used predominantly to screen sectoral policy proposals for unintended impacts that spill over into other policy domains. These may include sustainability-related spill-overs. The assessment is therefore a 'negative test' of the degree of incompatibility of a proposal with sustainable development. (S)IA can increase transparency and support more 'joined-up' government, but cannot deliver sustainability-oriented policies. Nor does it have the potential to change the socio-political context in which it is used.
3. Process goals include, among others, sustainability interpretation, proposal development, capacity building, strategy building, attitude changing, network building and a wide range of transformational and context-changing outcomes associated with creating support for sustainability-oriented policies and strategies.
4. The MATISSE consortium consists of 21 European partners led by the Dutch Research Institute for Transitions (Drift) at the Faculty of Social Sciences (FSW), Erasmus University of Rotterdam (EUR). The project is funded under the European Commission's Sixth Framework Programme and runs for three years. The project began on 1 April 2005.
5. Strategic goal for 2010 set at the Lisbon European Council, March 2000.
6. EU 6th Framework Programme (FP6) for Research, Technological Development and Demonstration (European Commission, DG Research, contract GOCE-CT-2003-505328).
7. FP6 Project 'IQ Tools' (Call No. FP6-2002-SSP-1, Proposal No. 502078).
8. Coherence refers to the inclusion of all relevant dimensions and all relevant inter-linkages between the various processes considered.
9. Further details and progress on the project can be found on the website for the MATISSE project, www.matisse-project.net.

REFERENCES

Brinsmead, T S (2005), 'Integrated sustainability assessment: identifying methodological options', available at, www.naf-forum.org.au/papers/Methodology-Brinsmead.pdf.

EC (2001), 'A sustainable Europe for a better world: a European Union Strategy for Sustainable Development', COM (2001) 264 final, European Commission, Brussels, 15 May.

EC (2002), 'The Sixth Environment Action Programme' [Decision No. 1600/2002/EC of the European Parliament], European Commission, Brussels.

EC (2003), 'The Commission's Legislative and Work Programme for 2004', COM (2003) 645, European Commission, Brussels.

EC (2004), 'Integrating environmental considerations into other policy areas: a stocktaking of the Cardiff Process', COM (2004) 394 final, 1 June 2004, European Commission, Brussels.

EC (2005), 'The 2005 review of the EU Sustainable Development Strategy: initial stocktaking and future orientations', COM (2005) 37 final, 9 February, European Commission, Brussels.

Kasemir, B, Jäger, J, Jaeger, C C and Gardner, M T (eds) (2003), *Public Participation in Sustainability Science: A Handbook*, Cambridge University Press.

Ridder, de W et al (2005), *Sustainability A-Test Inception Report*, Report 555000001/2005, Netherlands Environmental Assessment Agency [www.SustainabilityA-Test.net], accessed 29 Sep 2005.

Rotmans, J, van Asselt, M B A, Anastasi, C, Greeuw, S C H, Mellors, J, Peters, S, Rothman, D S and Rijkens, N (2000), 'Visions for a sustainable Europe', *Futures*, 32 (9/10), 809–31.

Varey, W (2004), 'Integrated approaches to sustainability assessment: an alignment of ends and needs'. Paper presented at the International Association for Impact Assessment Conference, Vancouver, Canada, 27 April.

Weaver, P M and Rotmans, J (2005), 'Integrated sustainability assessment: what, why and how?'. Paper presented at the Matisse Conference, Barcelona, Spain, 4–6 November.

10. The selection of suitable tools for sustainability impact assessment[1]

Marjan van Herwijnen and Wouter de Ridder

I. INTRODUCTION

Assessment tools play an important role in decision-making processes. The variety of tools that can be used to carry out assessments is huge. Each tool has its own specific qualities and contributes in a particular way to decision-making processes. Each tool can be used to address different issues, like costs and benefits, short- and long-term effects, global competitiveness and many more key aspects in relation to sustainable development. The Sustainability A-Test project evaluates tools that can be used for sustainability assessments.

The overall goal of the Sustainability A-Test is to support the definition and implementation of the EU Sustainable Development Strategy. The project will do this by describing, assessing and comparing tools that can be used to measure or assess sustainable development. At the same time the project strives to improve the scientific underpinning of sustainable development impact assessment. This will be done by building further on on-going work by the UNFCCC secretariat (2005) and UNEP (1998), literature review of the applications of the tools, and a case study. Within the project an evaluation framework will be developed in which the various tools and a number of assessment methods are compared with the requirements of sustainable development assessments. The final output of the project will be an electronic handbook[2] to support the selection of suitable tools for SIA.

This chapter gives an overview of the primary results of the project and at the same time some insight into the electronic handbook on the worldwide web. To do this, Section II briefly describes the project and explains some terminology, after which it shows one of the results of the project: an overview of the tools and incorporated methods. The third section then presents the evaluation framework followed by the preliminary results of the evaluation of the tools according to this framework. To give insight in how the handbook will offer maximum usability and, at the same time, link the reality of assessment practice with the information presented in the handbook, Section IV first describes the users of the web-book and subsequently the expected functionality of it. The final part of this section shows how the web-book will be designed (using a database) and presented (using a tool search) to the user. The chapter finishes with some concluding remarks in Section V.

II. OVERVIEW OF TOOLS

Terminology

Within the Sustainability A-Test project the word 'tools' is interpreted in the broadest sense, ranging from small aids to complex methodologies for carrying out an assessment. 'Assessments' in turn refers to all kinds of evaluations to determine if and to what degree an observed development, or certain policy proposal, contributes to sustainable development. Both ex ante and ex post assessments are taken into consideration within the Sustainability A-Test, thus addressing various stages of the policy cycle.

So, in the project the word 'tool' is a collective term used only as such to prevent us from having to write 'tools, methods, methodologies and procedures' each time we want to refer to all kinds of tools. Obviously, different types of tools exist. Some have a more procedural character, whereas others have a more instrumental character. Different types of tools have different functions in assessments, and in order to be able to distinguish between them, we use the following tool types within the Sustainability A-Test: methods, tools, procedures (along the lines of UNFCCC (2005)) and recipes:

- A *method* is a tool type at the most detailed level within the Sustainability A-Test. It is a specific analytical procedure within a tool; a specific 'way of doing something'. Most tools contain multiple methods. Methods themselves can have many levels, and methods can be embedded in other methods. An example of this is the method of non-market valuation (that is a methodology to estimate the benefits of a policy intervention) within which contingent valuation is another method (a specific non-market valuation methodology to estimate the benefits of a policy intervention).
- A *tool* is an instrument that makes up a recognizable methodological approach (for example cost-benefit analysis, scenario analysis and so on). Tools can use various methods. An example of a tool is the cost-benefit analysis. Different methods exist to estimate the costs and the benefits.

- A *procedure* is a tool type, which describes how tools can be used to accomplish a type of assessment. Procedures can use various tools and/or methods, but they do not consist of certain tools and/or methods *per se*. Examples of procedures are the Commission's impact assessment procedures (CEC 2002) and the strategic environmental assessment procedure, describing which elements should be included in the assessment (whilst the choice of which tools or methods to use is left open).
- A *recipe*, to conclude, is a combination of procedures, tools and methods to undertake (parts of) sustainability assessments. A recipe could be one procedure with pre-described tools and methods, but it could also be a combination of different procedures, tools and methods.

Combinations: the Heart of the Sustainability A-Test

Tools are seldom used alone, and for the most part they are used in combination with other tools, with or without procedures describing which tools to use and how to use them. The heart of the Sustainability A-Test is to analyse common assessment practices and to identify leads for making combinations of tools that could strengthen assessments. Combinations that will be evaluated within the Sustainability A-Test shall be referred to as 'recipes'. This word has been chosen to capture the fact that recipes refer to more than just the creation of combinations of tools. Instead, it is a combination of tools and an instruction outlining how to create and use it.

In principle the project will consider all tools commonly used in Europe for carrying out assessments. However, not all of these will be evaluated: only those that are most common and/or promising. Eight groups of tools have been distinguished, although it is difficult to apply a strict classification to them. This is because some tools overlap, and the applied classification is also partly shaped by the concentration of expertise with certain tool types within the project's consortium, solely for the purpose of efficiency. The classification presented here forms a useful starting point, but should remain open for discussion until the end of the project.

The following tool groups are distinguished within the project:

1. Physical assessment tools: tools that assess some physical parameter
2. Monetary assessment tools: tools that assess some financial/economical parameters
3. Models: tools that use (computer) models
4. Scenario analysis: tools with a prospective character

5. Multi-criteria analysis: tools that help with the consideration of various criteria
6. Sustainability appraisal tools: tools prescribing how sustainability appraisals could/should be done
7. Participatory tools: tools that aim to involve stakeholders
8. Transition management: tools that can support transition management.

So far, the tool papers that were reviewed have resulted in the identification, description and (preliminary) evaluation of 44 tools. Figure 10.1 gives an overview of the groups and their tools. Note that the (vertical) 'hierarchy' suggested by this figure is roughly based on those tools that could be considered a building block for other tools. Obviously, such a single true hierarchy does not exist. Figure 10.1 therefore provides mainly an overview, and the hierarchy should not be afforded too much value. By means of an additional review of all tool papers (both within the project team and outside) it should be further analysed if all tools commonly used in assessments have indeed been included.

III. EVALUATION FRAMEWORK

The evaluation framework for the project was designed in cooperation with all partners involved. Tool experts have used this evaluation framework for a preliminary evaluation of all tools covered by the project (the results of which are incorporated in a report (Ridder et al 2005) and in the web-book). The criteria that compose the evaluation framework are grouped in three categories: policy processes, sustainable development and operational aspects. Each of these is now discussed.

Policy Processes

Each tool will be evaluated for its ability to support assessments made in the various stages of decision-making (from, e.g., policy initiation to termination). Based on a theoretical framework for policy analysis (Brewer and deLeon 1983) and in combination with frameworks for integrated assessment (e.g. Sadler 1996; Rotmans 1998; Ravetz 2000; Norse and Tschirley 2000; George 2001) an indicative list of policy processes has been created (see Table 10.1). Using such theoretical frameworks ensures a structured approach for the identification of different stages in decision-making and different roles of tools in integrated assessments. Note that the project goes beyond analysing how well tools support ex ante impact assessments.

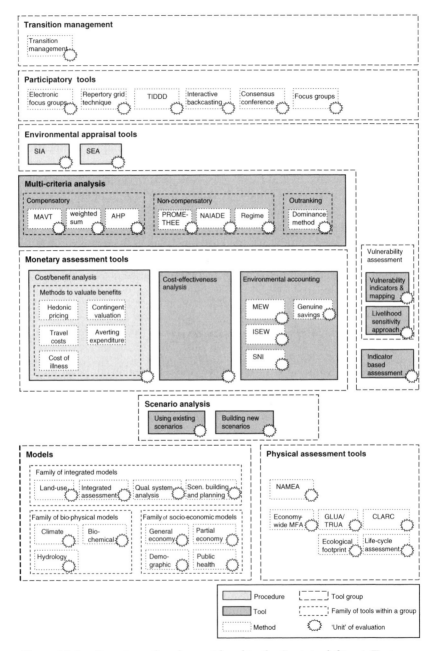

Figure 10.1   Overview of tools considered in the Sustainability A-Test

Table 10.1   List of policy processes

Policy processes	Explanation
Recognition of a problem	The process of analysing if (or discovering that) an observed development/trend leads to a problem (including drawing conclusions from monitoring and strategic outlooks, and the process of getting the problem on the political agenda)
Investigating the nature of a problem and identifying conflicting assumptions with respect to the problem situation	The process of analysing the problem in further detail, in order to understand the nature of the problem (that is conceptualizing and outlining the problem, identifying the driving forces underlying the problem, causal relations between the driving forces and the observed problems, and the identification of conflicting assumption) by means of strategic outlooks, models and so on
Identification of possible solutions to alleviate, mitigate or resolve the problem	The process of generating ideas to address the problem, including the collection of information and data needed to lay out a range of possible responses and the further specification of potential policy choices within that range, including the process of tentative burden sharing analysis
Analysis of policy proposals (ex ante)	The process of analysing the likelihood that any of the policy proposals will prove to be a success or failure by means of predetermining the risks, costs and benefits associated with each proposal, using empirical, scientific and/or projective knowledge (including the process of screening for possible impacts)
Selection of a policy option	The process of the authoritative policy maker or body debating and exploring and comparing in detail all policy proposals in order to reduce the level of uncertainty and to reach the best decision, incorporating into the decision-making process all the work that has been done prior to this stage
Implementation of the selected policy option	The process of developing directives, regulations, guidelines and so on to execute the selected policy option, including the definition of policy goals (targets) and the burden sharing analysis supporting that

Table 10.1   (continued)

Policy processes	Explanation
Evaluation of the selected and implemented policy option (ex post)	The process of assessing the efficiency and results (and possibly other aspects) of the selected and implemented policy option, including the process of determining what aspects/impacts should be accounted for during this evaluation and the process of actually carrying out the evaluation
Discontinuation of poorly performing or unnecessary policy options	The process of the authoritative policy maker or body debating and exploring in detail if policy options are poorly performing or unnecessary, in order to reach a decision on the termination of the policy and to specify new problems stemming from termination, if any

Aspects of Sustainable Development

The aspects of sustainable development are divided into topics that can be found in the often-mentioned 'three pillars of sustainable development' (Pope et al 2004). These three pillars refer to the environmental, social and economic domains. There are also so called 'cross-cutting aspects of sustainable development'. These cross-cutting aspects are topics that cannot be attributed unambiguously to any one of the three pillars, but that are important for sustainable development. The number of aspects that could belong to each of the three pillars and the category of cross-cutting aspects is in principle inexhaustible. A number of lists exist which suggest aspects that could be taken into consideration during an impact assessment. The lists that have been analysed are:

1. The European Commission's handbook, *How To Do an Impact Assessment* (CEC 2003)
2. Sustainable development indicators, developed by the SDI-taskforce[3]
3. Structural indicators, developed by Eurostat[4]
4. Factors for sustainability appraisals, developed by the European Commission's Joint Research Centre[5]
5. The list of the European Environment Agency (EEA) of the cross-cutting sustainability aspects (unpublished).

These five lists have been integrated into an indicative list of aspects that can be placed in each pillar of sustainable development, and a list of aspects that

*Table 10.2   List of main categories of environmental, social and economic
aspects*

Environmental	Social	Economic
• Air, water, soil or climate • Renewable or non-renewable resources • Biodiversity, flora, fauna • Land-use • Natural and cultural heritage • Waste production/ generation or recycling • Human safety or health • The likelihood or scale of environmental risks • Mobility (transport modes), or the use of energy	• Social cohesion • Employment quality • Public health • Health systems and security • Social protection and social services • Consumer interests • Education • Social capital • Liveable communities • Equality of opportunity and entitlement • Culture • International cooperation • Governance and participation • Fundamental human rights • Security, crime or terrorism • Ageing of society and pensions	• Economic growth • Price levels and stability • Effects on public authority budgets • Human capital formation and employment • Economic cohesion • Innovation • International performance • Market structure • Micro-economic effects on enterprises, non-profit organizations and so on • Effects on households • Global partnership

belong to the cross-cutting aspects. Table 10.2 shows the main categories of
the impacts within each pillar of sustainable development. Further details
of what can be found within each category can be found in Annex 3 of the
project's inception report (see Ridder et al 2005). The result of the list of
cross-cutting aspects is given in Table 10.3. Both lists function as a starting
point for the evaluation. However, it is likely that these lists will be adjusted
for improvements during the course of the project.

Operational Aspects

Each tool has its own costs, data needs and so on. These so called operational aspects are important when determining which tool is best to use for
a specific assessment. Table 10.4 lists the operational aspects that shall be

Table 10.3   List of cross-cutting aspects of sustainable development

Short name	Explanation
Inter-generational effects	Long-term (at least one generation, 25-odd years) effects in the social, economic and environmental potential – 'potential' can be conceptualized by looking at stocks, or capacity, found in the economic, social and environmental domains
(De-)coupling	Effects on the economy's resource use compared to the economic development, or effects on welfare growth compared to consumption of natural resources
Adaptability	Changes in the capability of the economic, environmental and social system (or the system as a whole) to adapt to external influences
(Ir-)reversibility	The arising of (ir-)reversible and long-term effects to economies, societies/humans and/or ecosystems
Distributional effects	The distribution of (dis-)advantages over different regions, societal/income groups, sectors, etc.
Global dimension	Worldwide effects, or effects outside Europe
Spatial scale	Magnitude of impacts in terms of spatial scale (local, regional, national, European and/or global)

used for the evaluation of tools. Note that some of the following operational aspects might be too specific or detailed, and therefore be unnecessary. Thus, this list can also be adjusted for improvements during the project.

Preliminary Tool Evaluation

During the first phase of the project some experience has been gained by considering the applicability of the evaluation framework. The evaluation with respect to the policy processes supported by the tools worked well. For most tools it appeared feasible to assess which policy processes can be supported with them and which cannot. With respect to the sustainable development aspects, the preliminary evaluation has shown that a tool's coverage of the three pillars of sustainable development has mostly been done at the highest level, that is, coverage of the 'environment', 'social' and 'economic' pillar, without further specifying what topics within each pillar can actually be covered with the tool. The tool's ability to address the cross-cutting

Table 10.4 Operational aspects

Category	Criteria
Input/output	Costs of applying the tool
	Manpower needs for applying the tool
	Time needed for making the assessment
	Data needs
	Data availability
	Data type input
	Data type output
	Technical equipment required
Complexity/transparency	Complexity (of the tool itself)
	Transparency
	User friendliness
	Reliability
	Uncertainty
Tool characteristics	Marginality
	Intensity
	Experience (of applying the tool)
	Mandatory usage
	Time before results become outdated
	Time scale/time horizon
	Geographical coverage
	Geographical resolution
	Specificity of results

aspects of sustainable development is mostly specified, though for some of these aspects, the exact meaning appeared to be ambiguous and needs to be further explained. The operational aspects are mostly specified, although not all operation aspects are relevant for each tool. For most tools it appeared difficult to assess criteria like the costs and time needed to apply the tool. This problem could be partly solved by asking for a range for these criteria (so, a minimum and maximum value) rather than a specific value.

The preliminary tool evaluation has further shown that for the physical assessment tools and the multi-criteria analysis tools, the evaluation framework manages to capture the most relevant characteristics of each tool. However, for the other tool groups this does not seem to be the case. For those tools, the evaluation does not provide the basic information needed for showing which tools can be part of assessments, in combinations with other tools and approaches, to measure and assess the three pillars of sustainable development. There are two main reasons for this. First, the evaluation framework does not contain the most relevant evaluation criteria for each tool (for example the tool sustainability impact assessment requires specific criteria focusing on its role in the decision-making process). Second, the evaluation framework is not being used at the most relevant level of tools (for example being applied at the level of cost-benefit analysis rather than at the level of methods that can be used to monetize benefits).

The evaluation framework and tool evaluation will be developed further in the next phases of the project, in an iterative process, analysing in particular the most suitable level at which the tools within each tool group will be evaluated, and the need for additional criteria for some tools to address the most relevant tool characteristics.

IV.   THE WEB-BOOK

The main output from the project is a handbook. This should enable anyone who is interested to be able to find out all the information generated during SustainabilityA-Test. More specifically, it will help those preparing to carry out an assessment to find the most suitable tools to use. The handbook will be based on the tool overview papers, the tool information sheet and the evaluation framework, all developed during the course of the project. The tool overview papers contain all relevant information of the tools evaluated in the project and are drafted under the responsibility of the tool experts in the project team. The papers form the core of the handbook and can be used as a book of reference in which all details regarding the tools can be found. The tool information sheet summarizes the main characteristics of each tool and therefore provides a useful introduction to each tool, whereas the evaluation framework and the criteria used therein will form the criteria for looking up the tools in the handbook.

The bundle of tool overview papers already contains over 400 pages of text (excluding the tool information sheets and output of the case study). In order for this information to become manageable and useful, we decided to produce an electronic handbook available via the web. This allows both easier distribution of and better access to the information acquired during the project. In addition, updating the information becomes simpler, thereby extending the lifetime of the Sustainability A-Test's output. The electronic handbook on the web is referred to as the web-book.

Users of the Web-book

The web-book will be designed to support various user groups including policy makers and consultants, policy analysts and others (such as researchers). We expect the people in the first group (policy makers and consultants) to use the web-book to identify tools to carry out or complement a specific sustainability assessment. In this case the web-book should identify tools to execute a certain assessment task within the context of sustainability impact assessment. The second group, the policy analysts, are expected to analyse whether a completed assessment has been carried out with the most suitable tools available. The web-book serves this group of users in much the same way as it does the policy makers and consultants. The remaining group, researchers (but also including the other groups of policy makers, consultants and policy analysts), are expected to use the web-book as a book of reference (or a tool catalogue) in order to look up specific information related to the tools, and any additional information needed to apply the tools in real cases.

Functionality of the Web-book

Based on these three groups of users, the functionality of the web-book will be to assist users in the search for a suitable tool and in finding specific information relating to a specific tool. The second function will be achieved by giving the users access to the information through the tool-scheme and by a book of reference. The window to the left in Figure 10.2 shows the scheme that provides the user with a graphical overview of the tool groups and the tools. This scheme serves as a menu. By selecting a tool in the scheme menu, information about the tool will be given in the right window. A legend is implemented that will provide the user with the ability to show precisely the information desired by the user. The book of reference provides the users of the website with a more traditional way of accessing the information. Here, the tool groups are listed in the form of a table of contents (or a folder list), through which users can navigate by folding and unfolding tool groups, thereby revealing or hiding detailed tool information taken from the tool overview papers.

Database

All the important information about a tool is captured on a tool information sheet (TIS), covering a maximum of two A4 pages. This serves two purposes. First, these TISs provide the user with a summary of the information available for each tool. Second, fitting such information on a maximum of two pages forces the tool team members to draw sharp and succinct conclusions about each tool.

The first page of the TIS describes the methodology of the tool, the experiences, possible links with other tools and strengths and weaknesses.

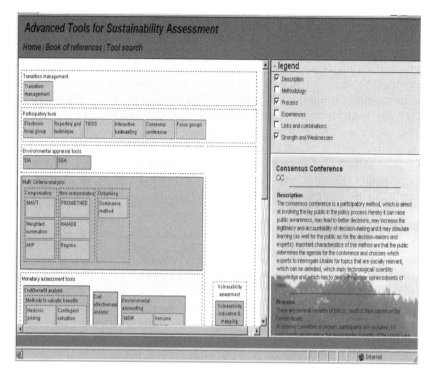

Figure 10.2   Home page of the web-book

The information on this page is presented in the right window of the home page of the web-book (see right panel of Figure 10.2). The second page contains the scores of the criteria in the evaluation framework together with an argumentation. These scores are used in the tool search program of the web-book.

The information on the TISs of all tools is incorporated in a database. The advantages of such a database are multiple. First, information stored in a database is easily accessible for participants in the project. They can access the database through the web and adapt the tool information for which they are responsible (see Figure 10.3). Second, the information is also easily accessible for the web-book builder, through which tool search capacity can be provided. This capacity is further described under the next heading. Third, a database with standardized tool information enables us to extract tool information in any way imaginable, either on-screen or in printed reports. An example of this can be seen in the right panel of Figure 10.3. The legend provides the user with the possibility to select the required information. A user only interested in the methodology, process and

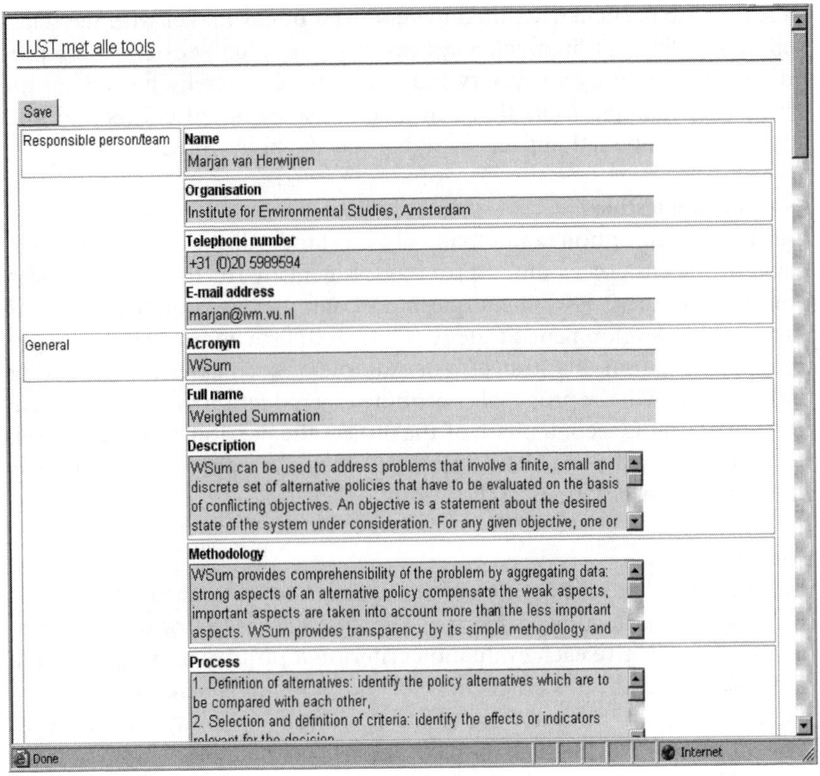

Figure 10.3   Database entry for the participants

strengths and weaknesses of a tool can limit the information provided to these topics should they so wish.

Tool Search

The tool search program will be designed in such a way that it can help users to find tools and promising tool combinations, and so that it can propose realistic solutions for carrying out assessments. To obtain this functionality three types of tool search options are envisaged: matrices, assessment questions and prioritizing.

Matrices
Matrices will provide the user with the opportunity to list all tools that comply with one of the criteria of the evaluation framework. Examples of this could be all tools that can be used to assess distributional effects, or all

tools that are particularly suited to support a policy maker with the selection of a policy option. Such a system can be gradually extended by providing the possibility to specify multiple criteria, thereby narrowing the search (for example tools that can assess distributional effects and also certain environmental impacts, within a specific policy process).

Assessment questions

Another search option could make use of standardized assessment questions. In the case of ex ante impact assessment by (or for) the European Commission, these assessment questions could be based on the European Sustainable Development Strategy (CEC 2001), or more specifically, the priorities set out in this strategy. An example of such assessment could be the question, 'will the proposal contribute to a reduction of greenhouse gas emissions?' In the second phase of the project the possibility to include this search option will be further explored to formulate appropriate and relevant assessment questions in the web-book.

Prioritizing

Prioritizing will be an extension of the matrices tool search and is the most complex search function to develop. The difference is that within prioritizing the user can give each evaluation criterion a priority or weight to indicate how important this criterion is for the tool that is being searched for. These weights will be used to calculate an overall suitability score for each tool. The tools will then be ranked in order of suitability based on the scores. Direct links from the ranked tools to more specific information on the tools will give the user an insight into the recommended tools. The matrices tool search described earlier assigns weights equal to 0 and 1 to all criteria. The criterion that is examined receives a 1 and all other criteria receive a 0.

The challenge in this approach lies in the fact that not all aspects incorporated in the evaluation framework are suitable for assigning weights. In principle, two types of aspects can be distinguished: criteria and thresholds. Criteria are those aspects that are scored with an index on a scale from 1 (best) to 3 (unsuitable). The user has to indicate the importance of each aspect. Thresholds are those aspects that indicate a specific process, geographic resolution or a quantitative aspect like the costs or time needed. The aspect 'costs of applying the tool' is an example of an aspect that is treated as a threshold. The user then has to indicate the maximum costs that are allowed (according to the available funds).

After the user has established thresholds and weights for the criteria, the prioritizing tool search mechanism will start and will perform its selection and ranking of tools according to the following steps:

1. All tools will be put in the set of possible tools.
2. Those that do not fulfil the thresholds will be deleted from the set of possible tools.
3. The remaining tools will be ranked according to their scores and weights given to the criteria.
4. The ranking of possible tools will be presented to the user.

V. CONCLUSIONS

The Sustainability A-Test project aims to assist policy makers on the verge of carrying out a sustainability impact assessment. A lot of tools and techniques are available to measure to what extent the policy proposed is sustainable, and these tools offer various possibilities and suitability for answering specific questions relating to the assessment at stake. This project aims to support the policy maker in making a carefully considered decision on the tool(s) that are most suitable for use in the assessment. An evaluation framework has been developed to achieve this, and tools have been selected and evaluated using the framework. From the primary evaluation it appeared that the evaluation framework, with respect to the policy processes supported by the tools and most of the operational aspects, works well. The evaluation of the tool's coverage of the three pillars of sustainable development has mostly been done at the highest level (that is coverage of the 'environment', 'social' and 'economic' pillar, without further specifying what topics within each pillar can actually be covered with the tool). The tool's ability to address the cross-cutting aspects of sustainable development has mostly been specified.

The preliminary tool evaluation has further shown that for the physical assessment tools and the multi-criteria analysis tools the evaluation framework manages to capture the most relevant characteristics of each tool. For other tool groups, however, this seems not to be the case. Therefore, in the next phases of the project, the evaluation framework and tool evaluation will be developed further. This will be done in an iterative process, during which the most suitable level at which the tools within each tool group will be evaluated, together with the need for additional criteria for some tools to address the most relevant tool characteristics.

In the next phase, a case study on bio-fuel is being used to further deepen the evaluation. Furthermore, based on concrete policy decisions, this case study will be used to investigate commonly seen, but also promising, combinations of tools. A lot of information has been gathered about the tools and evaluation of the tools. The risk arising from this is that policy makers may get lost in the large amount of information available. Therefore, an electronic handbook (web-book) is under development to present the information in a structured way and to provide the policy maker with a tool search program to find the most suitable tool(s) for the assessment. Part of this web-book is available already; part of it is still under development. A review by real policy makers will be used to improve and enhance the functionality of the web-book and, at the same time, to familiarize policy makers with the possibilities the web-book can offer.

NOTES

1. This publication was funded under the EU 6th Framework Programme for Research, Technological Development and Demonstration, Priority 1.1.6.3. Global Change and Ecosystems (European Commission, DG Research, contract 505328). Its content does not represent the official position of the European Commission and is entirely under the responsibility of the authors.
2. Address of the electronic handbook is, www.SustainabilityA-Test.net.
3. See, http://forum.europa.eu.int/Public/irc/dsis/susdevind/library.
4. See, http://europa.eu.int/comm/eurostat/newcronos/reference/display.do?screen= welcomeref&open=/&product=EU_strind&depth=2&language=en.
5. See, http://www.jrc.es/projects/iastar/.

REFERENCES

Brewer, G and DeLeon, P (1983), *Foundations of Policy Analysis*, Homewood, Dorsey.
CEC (2001), 'A sustainable Europe for a better world: a European Union Strategy for Sustainable Development (Commission's proposal to the Gothenburg European Council)', Communication from the Commission of the European Communities (COM(2001)264 final), Brussels.
CEC (2002), 'Communication from the Commission on impact assessment', Communication from the Commission of the European Communities, COM (2002) 276 final.
CEC (2003), *A Handbook for Impact Assessment in the Commission – How To Do an Impact Assessment*, Commission of the European Communities, Brussels.
Eurostat (2004), 'The EU Sustainable Development Strategy: a framework for indicators', SDI Workshop 9–11 February 2004, Stockholm (see 'SDI-TF-030 Rev. 5 SDI Framework' at, http://forum.europa.eu.int/Public/irc/dsis/susdevind/ library?l=/policysdocuments&vm=detailed&sb=Title).
George, C (2001), 'Sustainability appraisal for sustainable development: integrating everything from jobs to climate change', *Impact Assessment and Project Appraisal*, 19 (2).
Norse, D and Tschirley, J B (2000), 'Links between science and policy making', *Agriculture, Ecosystems and Environment*, 82, 15–26.
Pope, J, Annandale, D and Morrison-Saunders, A (2004), 'Conceptualising sustainability assessment', *Environmental Impact Assessment Review*, 24, 595–616.
Ravetz, J R (2000), 'Integrated assessment for sustainability appraisal in cities and regions', *Environmental Impact Assessment Review*, 20, 31–64.

Ridder, W de (ed) (2005), 'SustainabilityA-Test inception report: progress to date and future tasks. Deliverable D5 of *SustainabilityA-Test*', RIVM report 555000001, Bilthoven, RIVM.

Rotmans, J (1998), 'Methods for IA: the challenges and opportunities ahead', *Environmental Modelling and Assessment*, 3, 155–79.

Sadler, B (1996), 'Environmental assessment in a changing world: evaluating practice to improve performance'. Final report, International Study of the Effectiveness of Environmental Assessment, Canadian Environmental Assessment Agency and International Association for Impact Assessment.

UNEP (1998), *Handbook on Methods for Climate Change Impact Assessment and Adaptation Strategies*, United Nations Environment Programme (UNEP).

UNFCCC (2005), *Compendium on Methods and Tools to Evaluate Impacts of, and Vulnerability and Adaptation to, Climate Change*, Secretariat of the United Nations Framework Convention on Climate Change (UNFCCC).

PART II

Impact assessment and sustainable development: European perspectives

11. Assessing the cost-effectiveness of environmental policies in Europe

Benjamin Görlach, Eduard Interwies, Jodi Newcombe and Helen Johns

I. INTRODUCTION[1]

Economic analysis for policy appraisal is generally interested in answering two questions, 'is a given policy objective worth achieving?' and 'if so, has the policy objective been achieved in the most cost-effective way?'. While the first question is addressed in a cost-benefit analysis (CBA), the second question can be answered with the help of a cost-effectiveness analysis (CEA).

Cost-benefit analysis (CBA) is carried out in order to compare the economic efficiency implications of alternative actions. The benefits from an action are contrasted with the associated costs (including the opportunity costs) within a common analytical framework. To allow comparison of these costs and benefits related to a wide range of scarce productive resources, measured in widely differing units, a common *numeraire* is employed: money. This is where most problems usually start for economic policy or project appraisal since some resources, especially environmental resources are difficult to evaluate in money terms. Many of the goods and services provided by ecosystems, such as amenity, clean air, and biodiversity sustenance, are not traded on a market, hence, no market price is available which reflects their economic value. Such prices need to be estimated instead through the use of valuation studies, for example eliciting people's willingness to pay for a particular environmental good. By comparing costs and benefits in monetary terms, a CBA provides an assessment of whether a policy option is worth implementing (that is whether the benefits outweigh the costs).

A cost-effectiveness analysis (CEA) seeks to find the best alternative activity, process or intervention that minimizes resource use to achieve a desired result. An ex ante CEA is performed when the objectives of the public policy have been identified and an analyst or an agency has to find the least-cost option of achieving these objectives. An ex post CEA addresses the question of how far objectives have been achieved, and at what cost. In either case, the cost effectiveness of a policy option is calculated by dividing the annualized costs of the option by a quantified measure of the physical effect, such as animal or plant species recovered, tons of emissions of a given pollutant reduced, kilometres of river length restored and so on. In this context, the effects of a policy can be both reduced pressures (for example the least-cost option to reduce CO_2 emissions) or avoided impacts (for example the cheapest way to keep global warming below 2°), where the latter is usually more difficult to assess. Different options that achieve/have achieved the same effect are then compared based on their cost. CEA, therefore, does not ask, nor attempts to answer, the question of whether the policy is justified, in the sense that its benefits to society will exceed its costs to society. CEA is sometimes used as a second-best option when a full-blown CBA would be desirable, but many effects cannot be captured in monetary form.

Cost-effectiveness analysis can be applied both as an ex ante appraisal and as an ex post evaluation tool. If applied ex ante, a CEA will help to determine the most cost-effective way of achieving a given target, assisting policy makers to allocate resources and efficiently realize policy objectives.

The focus of this paper is on ex post CEAs. Where it is applied ex post, a CEA may help to assess whether a policy measure has been effective in addressing the problem it was designed for, and at what cost. It can take the form of an ex ante/ex post comparison, assessing whether expected effects were realized in the projected cost; it can consist of a cross-country comparison (benchmarking), or, if ex post CEAs are carried out repeatedly, it can determine whether efficiency has increased over time.

Although some European countries have moved ahead in this respect in the last years, ex post evaluation of environmental policy performance remains a relatively recent phenomenon and is not widely applied. At the European level, there is little experience with carrying out such assessments, and even less with using their results to feed back into policy implementation. Whether at the European level or at the level of member states, the problems encountered in ex post assessments are similar. First, the main challenge is to establish the causality between observed effects and influencing factors, thereby disentangling the different effects of policies and relating them to individual policy measures, and separating out the influence of other factors. Second, a related problem is that of data gathering: unless specifically tailored monitoring requirements have been specified up front, it is often difficult to find the data that measure the impact a policy has had. For this reason, data gathering ex post can easily become very costly and time-consuming. And third, another main issue relates to the scale of the analysis: traditionally, CEAs were mainly applied at the local level, in order to evaluate individual, well defined measures. Upscaling the analysis to assess the cost effectiveness of strategies or policies at national or European level necessarily increases the uncertainty of relating observed impacts to a particular action.

Next to these practical problems, there are also some theoretical issues that merit further discussion, but which are only touched upon in the available literature. There is some discussion on which types of costs should be considered in a CEA, ranging from the purely financial private costs (investment and operational costs) of specific measures to general-equilibrium estimates of costs to the wider economy, including efficiency losses (foregone welfare). Regarding the treatment of effectiveness, there is an interesting issue of whether measures of effectiveness should be discounted even though they are in non-monetary terms. Other issues include the distinction between intermediate goals and final goals of a policy intervention, which are often confused. Thus, the effectiveness term in a cost-effectiveness analysis can either capture a pressure (tons of emissions reduced) or an impact (avoided damage or improvements in environmental quality). Which of the two is applicable depends on the original goal of the policy measure. In practice, most assessments tend to focus on pressures, since they are less challenging to measure, and since the causality between measures and effects is easier to establish.

The chapter is structured into six sections. The next section provides an overview of legal requirements for ex post CEA in European environmental policy, whereas Section III summarizes the guidance documents and manuals for carrying out ex post CEAs. Section IV presents selected case studies of applied ex post CEA for environmental policy measures, and Section V provides an interpretation of the results. Section VI concludes and suggests a number of recommendations.

The gathering of information and literature involved the following sources: consultation with members of the network of economists in the framework contract; consultation with the EEA project steering group; consultation with EEA national focal points; a detailed web-search, including on-line resources of major research institutes, international bodies, relevant national government departments and European Commission DGs; consultation with in-country contacts in ministries; and searches in relevant academic journals.

II. LEGAL REQUIREMENTS FOR EX POST CEAs

In 2001, the European Environment Agency (EEA) noted that 'very few items of EU environmental legislation request information on policy

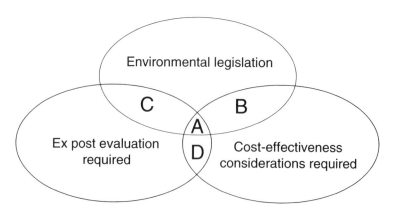

Source: Authors' diagram.

Figure 11.1 Grouping of environmental legislative items

effectiveness . . . even though some EU measures are very costly to implement and should be subject to some kind of cost-effectiveness scrutiny' (EEA 2001, p. 14). This observation still seems to be valid, although a (small) number of recent directives do include a requirement to perform an ex post cost-effectiveness analysis.

This project identified eighteen legislative items that require some type of evaluation, and can be related to environmental policy. In Figure 11.1, these items are visualized by grouping them in four categories. As the analysis shows, only a small subset (A) indeed meets all three requirements: (i) environmental legislation that (ii) mandates a cost-effectiveness analysis (iii) to be carried out ex post. If any of these three criteria are relaxed, the scope of relevant items can be expanded.

This means that the eighteen general items covered in this project may be subdivided as follows:

A – Environmental legislation that requires an ex post evaluation of cost effectiveness, at least as one of several factors to be considered in a wider evaluation framework. The current study has identified four items in this category: directives on cogeneration, bio-fuels, renewable energy and emission ceilings (see next list).

B – Environmental legislation that requires an ex ante evaluation/analysis of cost effectiveness, or at least consideration of cost effectiveness as one of several factors. In this category, six items have been identified. The cost-effectiveness requirements in this category may take different forms, for example in the case of the Water

Framework Directive (WFD), it is not so much the cost effectiveness of the directive as such that is considered, but rather the cost effectiveness of combinations of measures mandated by the directive. Several directives (for example large combustion plants, and ozone and benzene in ambient air) require that experiences with the implementation of the directive be taken into account when deciding on the cost effectiveness of stricter standards, thus connecting ex post evaluation and ex ante CEA.

C – Environmental legislation that requires an ex post evaluation, but not (necessarily) the analysis of cost effectiveness. Four items have been identified that fall into this category, including directives on marine and air pollution. While none requires explicitly the consideration of cost effectiveness, some items refer to the overall efficiency or the effectiveness of the regulations, implying at least a contributing function for cost effectiveness.

D – Legislation and regulations requiring ex post CEA that is not strictly environmental, but has a significant impact on the environment. This category comprises four items related to funding instruments of the Community regional policy (Cohesion Fund, Structural Funds, the Instrument for Structural Policies for Pre-accession (ISPA) and the Financial Instrument for the Environment (LIFE)). It should be noted that this list is not exhaustive. Depending on which policies are regarded as having a significant impact on the environment more could be included in this category.

This also means that while there are several more directives that involve effectiveness assessments in one way or another, the set of environmental directives calling for an ex post evaluation of cost effectiveness is limited to four directives:

- **Directive 2001/77 (electricity from renewable energy sources).** Article 4.2 of the directive demands that '[the] Commission shall, not later than 27 October 2005, present a well documented report on experience gained with the application and coexistence of the different mechanisms [. . .]. The report shall assess the success, including cost effectiveness, of the support systems [. . .] in promoting the consumption of electricity produced from renewable energy sources'. The reporting may include a proposal for a framework for Community activities with regard to support schemes for Community activities. This framework should 'promote the use of renewable energy sources in an effective way, and be simple and, at the same time, as efficient as possible, particularly in terms of cost'.

- **Directive 2001/81 (national emission ceilings).** Article 9.1 of the directive demands that 'in 2004 and 2008, the Commission shall report to the European Parliament and the Council on progress on the implementation of the national emission ceilings', and on the extent to which the objectives of the directive are likely to be met. The reports shall include 'an economic assessment, including cost effectiveness, benefits, an assessment of marginal costs and benefits and the socio-economic impact of the implementation of the national emission ceilings on particular member states and sectors'.
- **Directive 2003/30 (promotion of bio-fuels and other renewable fuels).** Article 4.2 of the directive states that 'by 31 December 2006 at the latest, and every two years thereafter, the Commission shall draw up an evaluation report [. . .] on the progress made in the use of bio-fuels and other renewable fuels in the member states'. The report shall assess 'the cost effectiveness of the measures taken by member states in order to promote the use of bio-fuels and other renewable fuels', as well as 'the economic aspects and the environmental impact of further increasing the share of bio-fuels and other renewable fuels'.
- **Directive 2004/8 (cogeneration).** Article 7.3 of the directive demands that the Commission should provide 'a well documented analysis on experience gained with the application and coexistence of the different support mechanisms' in order to 'assess the success, including cost effectiveness, of the support systems in promoting the use of high-efficiency cogeneration'.

All of these directives have entered into force in 2001 or later. Consequently, they are still in their first reporting cycle. The first assessments of the directives' performance was expected for the end of 2004 (for the National Emission Ceilings Directive), but has not been published at the time of writing. Most of the assessments will be repeated at intervals of two or four years.

A further question is how the evaluation of cost effectiveness should be conducted. For the four directives that require an ex post CEA, neither guidelines nor standards are provided regarding the content or the methodology to be applied. For some of the other directives and regulations, more guidance exists. The guidance is most developed in the case of the Water Framework Directive, Article 11/Annex III of which requires an ex ante appraisal of the most cost-effective combination of measures to achieve good ecological status. To support the selection of measures, the European working group WATECO (established under the WFD Common Implementation Strategy) has produced an extensive guidance document. In addition, some member states have come up with

While the focus of this study was on requirements for ex post effectiveness in European environmental legislation, it also became evident that the legal requirements for ex post evaluation on the level of the member states differ markedly. Considerable experience with such assessments exists in the Netherlands and the United Kingdom, where requirements are in place to evaluate policies and their impacts, including their (cost) effectiveness.

- In the Netherlands, Article 20 of the Government Accounts Act (Comptabiliteitswet) states that ministers shall be responsible for the effectiveness and efficiency of the policy underlying their budgets. This includes conducting regular audits of the effectiveness and efficiency of the policy, and reporting back to the Ministry of Finance. Guidance for this requirement is presented inter alia in the draft 'guidance for ex post evaluation research' (Concept wegwijzer evaluatieonderzoek ex-post, VROM (2003)).

- For the UK, the *Green Book* on appraisal and evaluation in central government (HM Treasury 2003) states that 'all new policies, programmes and projects, whether revenue, capital or regulatory, should be subject to comprehensive but proportionate assessment, wherever it is practicable, so as best to promote the public interest'. In this context, the *Green Book* mentions cost-effectiveness analysis as one possible assessment method.

Source: Authors' analysis.

Figure 11.2   National-level requirements in the member states

handbooks and guidance documents for the national implementation (see Figure 11.2).

III.   GUIDANCE DOCUMENTS

There are a large number of textbooks on the use of economic appraisal, most of which focus on cost-benefit analysis but also sometimes cover cost-effectiveness analysis. Textbooks on cost-benefit analysis in the environmental sector typically only mention cost effectiveness in passing.

For the selection of the guidance documents covered in this study, emphasis was placed on providing a range of the best examples, in order to make an overall assessment of the state of play. For selecting guidance documents, four selection criteria were employed:

- The guidance was up to date (thus only the latest government guidance from one issuing body is presented).
- The guidance is focused on the analysis of environmental policies (or explicitly mentions them as one of a number of policies to be assessed).

- The guidance is issued by or directed at EU member states (except where other country-level guidance offers additional insights, as is the case with the US).
- Public sector guidance is preferred.

Forty-four potential guidance documents, mostly guidelines from various national and international public sector bodies, but also academic papers and books, were identified during the course of this project, of which twenty-four were deemed to be relevant for the purposes of this study. The relevant guidance documents are summarized in Table 11.1 (a bracketed '(X)' in the ex post or ex ante column indicates that the document is relevant, but does not explicitly address ex post/ex ante evaluation; a question mark indicates that we were informed of the document's existence, but were unable to obtain a copy).
Of the fifteen guidelines summarized, there are:

- three documents dealing with cost-effectiveness analysis for implementing the Water Framework Directive (RPA 2004; Ecologic 2004; Wateco 2003);
- six government or international body-issued guidance documents for the public sector in general (HM Treasury 2003; OMB 1992; PEEM and WHO 1993; UNESCO 1997; DG Budget 2001; VROM 2003);
- two government-issued guidance documents for evaluation of environmental policies (EPA 2000; eftec 1999);
- two guidelines on using cost effectiveness for project appraisal (ADB 1997; Government of Canada 2004);
- one document primarily concerned with data collection and management as a prerequisite for cost-effectiveness analysis (EEA 1999);
- one academic background paper on cost-effectiveness analysis of agri-environment schemes (Pearce 2004).

The guidance documents and manuals identified in the study vary substantially in the level of detail they provide about how to undertake cost-effectiveness analysis, especially with regards to technical issues such as discounting, distributional impacts, effects on competitiveness and so on. However, the basic descriptions of the core stages of the cost-effectiveness analysis differ only a little.

As discussed in greater detail in the next section, the overall picture that emerges is that many useful elements are present in the different documents, which together provide good insights on how to conduct an ex post cost-effectiveness analysis. However, there is not one single document that would combine all of these elements into one volume.

Table 11.1 A summary of relevant guidance documents

No.	Title	Policy area	Country	Author/client	Type of analysis	Ex post	Ex ante	Summary
G2	CEA and Developing a Methodology for Assessing Disproportionate Costs (2004)	WFD	UK	Risk and Policy Analysts Ltd/ DEFRA and UK Environment Agency	CEA & CBA		X	X
G3	Guidelines for Defining and Documenting Data on Costs of Possible Environmental Protection Measures (1999)	Environment general	EU	European Environment Agency/no client	Neither			X
G8	The Green Book: Appraisal and Evaluation in Central Government (2003)	General	UK	UK Treasury/no client	CBA & CEA	X	X	X
G9	Guidelines for Preparing Economic Analyses (2000)	Environment general	USA	US Environment Protection Agency/no client	CBA & CEA	(X)	X	X
G12	Basic Principles for Selecting the most Cost-Effective Combinations of Measures as Described in Article 11 of the Water Framework Directive Handbook (2004)	WFD	Germany	Ecologic/German Federal Environment Agency	CEA		X	X
G14	Economics and the Environment: the	WFD	EU	WATECO/no client	CEA		X	X

Table 11.1 (continued)

No.	Title	Policy area	Country	Author/client	Type of analysis	Ex post	Ex ante	Summary
	Implementation Challenge of the Water Framework Directive, Guidance Document (2003)							
G18	*What Constitutes a Good Agri-Environmental Policy Evaluation? (2004)*	Agriculture	OECD	Pearce, David/no client	CEA & CBA	(X)	(X)	X
G20	*Guidelines and Discount Rates for Benefit-Cost Analysis of Federal Programs (1992)*	General	USA	US Office of Management and Budget/no client	CBA & CEA		X	X
G21	*Guidelines for the Economic Analysis of Projects (1997)*	Development projects	Asian countries	Asian Development Bank/no client	CBA & CEA		X	X
G22	*Opportunities Envelope Guidelines for Proposals (2004)*	Climate change	Canada	Government of Canada/no client	CEA		X	X
G24	*PEEM Guidelines 3 – Guidelines for Cost-Effectiveness Analysis of Vector Control. (1993)*	Vector-borne diseases	International	Panel of Experts on Environmental Management for Vector Control (PEEM), WHO/ no client	CEA	X	X	X

Code	Title	Topic	Country	Author/client	Methods			
G25	*Review of Technical Guidance on Environmental Appraisal (1999)*	Environment general	UK	eftec/former UK DETR	CBA & CEA	X	X	X
G27	*Guide to Cost-Benefit Analysis of Investment Projects*	General	EU	Evaluation Unit, DG Regional Policy, EC/no client	CBA & CEA		X	
G29	*Cost-Effectiveness Analysis a Tool for UNESCO*	General	International	SPM consultants/ UNESCO	CEA	X	X	X
G30	*DTLR Multi-Criteria Analysis Manual*	General	UK	former UK DETR/no client	CBA, CEA & MCA		X	
G32	*Making Choices in Health: WHO Guide to Cost Effectiveness Analysis*	Health	International	World Health Organisation/no client	CEA		X	
G33	*A Handbook for Impact Assessment in the Commission: How to do an Impact Assessment*	General	EU	Strategic Planning and Programming unit, Secretariat-General, EC/no client	CBA, CEA & MCA	(X)	X	
G34	*Samfundsøkonomisk vurdering af miljøprojekter.*	Environment general	Denmark	Danish National Environmental Research Institute/ no client	?	?	?	
G35	*Kosten en baten in het milieubeleid, definities en berekeningsmethoden*	Environment general	NL	Dutch Ministry for Spatial Planning, Housing and the	?	?	?	

Table 11.1 (continued)

No.	Title	Policy area	Country	Author/client	Type of analysis	Ex post	Ex ante	Summary
				Environment (VROM)/no client				
G36	*Evaluating EU Activities*	General	EU	European Commission DG Budget/no client	CBA & CEA	X	X	
G37	*A Framework for Evaluating Environmental Policy Instruments*	Environment general	Finland	Mickwitz, Per/no client	CBA & CEA	X	X	
G38	*Kosteneffectiviteit natuurbeleid: Methodiekontwikkeling*	Environment general	NL	Rijksinstitut voor Volksgezondheid en Milieu (RIVM)/no client	CEA	X		
G39	*Evaluating EU Expenditure Programmes: A Guide: Ex post and Intermediate Evaluation*	General	EU	European Commission DG Budget/no client	CBA & CEA	X		
G40	*Ex-ante Evaluation: a Practical Guide for Preparing Proposals for Expenditure Programmes*	General	EU	European Commission DG Budget/no client	CBA & CEA		X	X
G43	*Ympäristöpolitiikan Taloudellisten Vaikutusten*	Environment general	Finland	Porvari, M and Hildén, M	?	?	?	

Arviointi (Economic Assessment of Environmental Policy)			(Finnish Environment Institute)/no client	Neither	X
G44 *Wegwijzer Evaluatieonderzoek ex post (2003)*	General	NL	Dutch Ministry for Spatial Planning, Housing and the Environment (VROM)/no client	X	

Source: Authors' analysis.

This section ends with a few observations regarding the distribution and the focus of the respective documents:

- In many cases, guidance documents will generally be written with ex ante analysis in mind, treating ex post analysis as a special case, and in far less detail (see, for example, the HM Treasury *Green Book* (HM Treasury 2003) or the *Handbook for Impact Assessment in the European Commission* (undated) as well as the DETR Review of Technical Guidance on Environmental Appraisal (Eftec 1999)). Where organizations are not legally required to perform ex post analysis, the need for guidance will be less pressing, and the focus of the guidance less clear-cut. Good examples can be found in three countries in particular: the UK (RPA 2004; HM Treasury 2003; eftec 1999), the US (EPA 2000; OMB 1992) and the Netherlands (VROM 1998; RIVM undated; VROM 2003).
- The general guidance documents issued by governments or their agencies or international bodies are for the most part not specifically related to the analysis of environmental policy, but have a much broader scope. In this way, for example the HM Treasury *Green Book* (HM Treasury 2003), the guide to cost-benefit analysis of investment projects issued by the European Commission, the DG Regional Policy (undated) or the Dutch guidance on ex post policy evaluation (VROM 2003) do provide general guidelines for assessing the cost effectiveness of policies, but pay less attention to the specific needs of evaluating environmental policies, such as the valuation of environmental goods and services, or the incorporation of long-term effects and irreversible damages. The HM Treasury *Green Book* provides examples of data sources for a range of impacts, including environmental impacts, with an entire annex devoted to the valuation of non-market goods. However, this type of data is more commonly used in a CBA than a CEA.
- Several guidance documents focus specifically on the evaluation of environmental policy, including, for example, the OECD guide on evaluating economic instruments for environmental policy (OECD 1997), the US EPA guidelines for preparing economic analyses (EPA 2000, ex ante only), the eftec/DETR study on review of technical guidance on environmental appraisal (eftec 1999), the Danish economic assessment of environmental projects (Samfundsøkonomisk vurdering af miljøprojekter, NERI 2000) or the Dutch guidance on costs and benefits in environmental policy (Kosten en baten in het milieubeleid, VROM 1998).

- An explicit distinction between financial and economic costs is made in most of the guidance documents. The documents use different terms to make this distinction, and sometimes the same terms are used to mean different things. In some cases, the terms 'direct' and 'indirect' costs are used instead of 'financial' and 'economic', in other cases 'social welfare losses' are used to mean economic costs. The US EPA guidelines (EPA 2000) are the most detailed in this respect, differentiating between compliance costs, government regulatory costs, social welfare losses, transitional costs and indirect costs. However, environmental costs are not always explicitly mentioned. The focus of some of the guidelines is on the social costs of the options assessed, while others are more interested in the costs to industry of proposed environmental regulation.

- At least one of the documents (the HM Treasury *Green Book* (HM Treasury 2003)) recommends cost-benefit analysis over cost-effectiveness analysis. A similar tendency to regard CEA as a simpler but inferior alternative to a CBA can also be discerned in the UK Water Framework Directive Guidance (RPA 2004). Other documents note that cost-effectiveness analysis should be performed when there are substantial doubts about the theoretical basis of the monetization of benefits, or if environmental targets are set politically without a cost-benefit analysis.

- Finally, some of the guidelines (RPA 2004; HM Treasury 2003; VROM 2003) point out that performing the cost-effectiveness analysis or the evaluation itself can be a significant drain on resources, and the effort put into the analysis should be commensurate with the proposed programme or policy.

IV. CASE STUDIES OF APPLIED EX POST COST-EFFECTIVENESS ANALYSES

This section reviews applications of cost-effectiveness analysis in the evaluation of environmental policies, with a strong focus on European studies and on ex post analyses. To this end, more than seventy potential case studies were identified, out of which eighteen passed the selection criteria and were thus summarized and treated in greater detail. The project did not attempt to give a comprehensive overview of ex post CEA in Europe: due to language limitations an emphasis was placed on studies that are published in English, French, German or Dutch. To identify a broad scope of potential studies, consultations were carried out with some national authorities as well as with the EEA's network of national focal points. Table 11.2 presents a selection of

Table 11.2 A selection of case study applications of CEA in the evaluation of environmental policies

No.	Author	Year	Title	Country	Policy area	Timing	Summary
CS1	NERA	2002	Fleetwide Emissions and Cost-Effectiveness of the Consent Decree Pull-Ahead Requirements for Heavy-Duty Diesel Engines	USA	Air quality	ex ante	
CS2	Wright et al	2001	The Cost-Effectiveness of Reductions in Dioxin Emissions to Air from Selected Sources	New Zealand	Air quality	ex ante	
CS8	Standard & Poor's DRI	1999	The Auto-Oil II Cost-Effectiveness Study	FI, F, D, EL, IRL, I, NL, E, UK	Air quality	ex post	
CS11	IVM	2000	Cost-effectiveness of Dutch water policies	NL	Water	ex ante	X
CS12	RIVM	2000	Cost effectiveness of environmental measures	NL	Acidification	ex ante	X
CS13	RIVM	2004	Environmental costs of energy measures 1990–2010	NL	Energy, climate	ex ante/ ex post	X
CS15	RIVM	2003	Evaluation of the Implementation memorandum for emission ceilings, acidification and large scale-air pollution 2003	NL	Air quality	ex ante	X

CS19	CE Delft	2001	Treatment of plastic packaging waste from households	NL	Waste	ex ante	
CS20	CE Delft	2000	Accelerated introduction of cleaner petrol and diesel engines in the Netherlands	NL	Air quality	ex ante	
CS26	Resources for the Future	1999	The Enhanced I/M Program in Arizona: Costs, Effectiveness, and a Comparison with Pre-regulatory Estimates	USA	Air quality	ex post	X
CS30	Harvard School of Public Health	2000	Are the Costs of Proposed Environmental Regulations Overestimated? Evidence from the CFC phaseout	USA	Ozone	ex post	X
CS31	Swedish University of Agricultural Sciences	2000	Cost efficient reductions of stochastic nutrient loads to the Baltic Sea	Baltic Sea countries	Water	ex ante	
CS47	Macaulay Land Use Research Institute	2002	The cost-effectiveness of biodiversity management: a comparison of farm types in extensively farmed areas of Scotland	UK	Biodiversity	ex post	X
CS49	Beamount, N and Tinch, R	2003	Cost Effective Reduction of Copper Pollution in the Humber Estuary	UK	Water	ex post	X

Table 11.2 (continued)

No.	Author	Year	Title	Country	Policy area	Timing	Summary
CS51	IIASA	1999	Economic Evaluation of a Directive on National Emission Ceilings for Certain Atmospheric Pollutants. Part A Cost-Effectiveness Analysis	EU	Air quality	ex ante	X
CS52	VTT	1999	Integrated cost-effectiveness analysis of greenhouse gas emission abatement: the case of Finland	FI	Climate change	ex ante	X
CS53	AEA Technology	1998	Options to Reduce Nitrous Oxide Emissions	EU	Climate change	ex post	X
CS54	AEA Technology	1998	Options to Reduce Methane Emissions	EU	Climate change	ex ante	
CS56	WRc	Un-known	Examination of Existing Policy Options . . . to Implement Directive 76/464/EEC	EU	Water	ex post	
CS57	eftec	2001	The Potential Cost and Effectiveness of Voluntary Measures in Reducing the Environmental Impact of Pesticides	UK	Agriculture	ex ante	
CS63	Entec	2004	Review of the Large Combustion Plant Directive	EU	Air quality	ex ante	

CS69	Tyndall Centre	2004	Ex post evaluations of CO2-based taxes: a survey	DK, FI, D, NL, NO, S, UK	Climate change	ex post	X
CS70	DMU	2004	Effectiveness of waste water policies in selected countries – an EEA pilot study	DK, NL, F, E, PL, EE	Water	ex post	X
CS71	European Topic Centre on Waste and Material Flows	2004	Analysis of effectiveness of implementing packaging waste management systems	AT, DK, IRL, I, UK	Waste	ex post	X
CS73	SPRU	2000	The Large Combustion Plant Directive (88/609/EEC): An Effective Instrument For Pollution Abatement? (IMPOL)	F, D, NL, UK	Air quality	ex post	X
CS74	CERNA	2000	The Implementation of the Municipal Waste Incineration Directives (IMPOL)	F, D, NL, UK	Air quality	ex post	X
CS75	SPRU	2000	The Implementation of EMAS in Europe: a case of competition between standards for environmental management systems (IMPOL)	F, D, NL, UK	Population & Economy	ex post	X
CS86	RIVM	2004	Evaluation of the Dutch Manure and Fertiliser Policy, 1998–2002	NL	Agriculture	ex post	X

Source: Authors' analysis.

the total case studies, listing only those that were pre-selected for further analysis.

It emerged that the practical experience with ex post cost-effectiveness evaluations is unevenly distributed in Europe, with much evidence coming from the Netherlands and the UK. The finding that these countries have a long tradition for such assessments is in line with the results of a 1998 study for the European Commission, which surveyed the use of economic evaluation methods for environmental policies in several European countries (Virani 1998).

In general, there is a limited awareness of the precise concept of cost effectiveness, both by consultants conducting the analyses and by the officials administrating them. Reports promising discussions of cost effectiveness sometimes turn out instead to be cost–benefit analyses (for example Entec 2000), discussions on whether static or dynamic efficiency is being achieved (especially with respect to market-based instruments) (for example Agnolucci 2004), or aggregations of cost estimates unrelated to the outcomes achieved (case studies not summarized). Few studies were strict methodical cost-effectiveness analyses of the type outlined in guidance documents (the most complete example of which was the US EPA guidance, EPA (2000)). Where cost-effectiveness ratios are actually calculated, they are sometimes not clearly defined (for example in the IMPOL studies Eames (2000) and CERNA (2000)):

- As stated in EEA (2001) and by Agnolucci (2004), environmental effect and environmental effectiveness should be treated as distinct concepts. The former is the physical outcome of the intervention, while the latter is a measure of this effect in comparison with what was expected or with what other interventions have achieved. This distinction is not made in all case studies. Many of the aspects of cost-effectiveness analysis recommended by guidance documents are not carried out in practice in the studies, presumably because of the difficulties of reconciling theoretical correctness with time, data, resource and skill constraints.[2] For example, none of the studies reviewed included lost consumer or producer surplus in their costs, as recommended by the US EPA guidelines (EPA 2000). Furthermore, discounting, although recommended in almost all guidance documents, was not applied in most studies. This was particularly noticeable in Lehtilä and Tuhkanen (1999), which discussed greenhouse gas abatement costs in Finland far into the future without the use of discounting. As one exception, a study on energy measures in the Netherlands (Boonekamp et al 2004) not only applied discounting, but also investigated the impact of choosing a social or a private interest rate.

- With regard to the choice of a baseline or reference scenario, business-as-usual baselines representing 'the world without the intervention' are found less often than baselines, which use a single year as a reference point. The latter implies that without the intervention, environmental outcomes would have stayed constant at the level of the base year. This can lead to a large underestimation of the actual effect that an intervention has had.

- Some of the studies reviewed discussed the marginal abatement costs of emission reductions. However, it should be remembered that marginal abatement cost is only a proxy for cost effectiveness, and becomes a less accurate proxy the more marginal abatement costs vary for different emission levels. This is because the cost-effectiveness ratio should use the total cost of a measure,[3] whereas the marginal abatement cost is the cost per unit reduction at a particular stage of abatement, and ignores the fact that costs at an earlier stage may very well have been lower.[4] Therefore, the marginal abatement cost is only an exact measure of cost effectiveness if marginal abatement cost is constant across all emission levels, which would be a brave assumption.

- The most widely used sources of information were surveys of regulated business units (Resources for the Future 1999; Wynn 2002; AEA Technology 1998; Eames 2000; Entec 2000), academic studies (RIVM 2000; Hammitt 2000; Wynn 2002; Amann et al 1999; Lehtilä and Tuhkanen 1999; Entec 2000), firms' environmental reports (RIVM 2000; Beamount and Tinch 2003; Entec 2000), official national statistics (Amann et al 1999; Lehtilä and Tuhkanen 1999), data transmitted to the regulatory agency as part of the regulatory obligation (Resources for the Future 1999; Beamount and Tinch 2003; Andersen 2004; ETC/WMF 2004), including data submitted to international bodies such as the IPCC or CORINAIR database (Lehtilä and Tuhkanen 1999; AEA Technology 1998). The latter included three studies where data were supposed to be reported to Eurostat or others (Andersen 2004; ETC/WMF 2004; Eames 2000). Strikingly, some of these studies were conducted in those cases where least data was available. Other sources were realized using market prices from trade journals and newspapers (Hammitt 2000), consultation with technical experts (Hammitt 2000; Entec 2000), and government information on subsidy amounts (Wynn 2002).

- Some case studies addressed lack of data as a restriction for the analysis. One case study (AEA Technology 1998) noted that commercial sensitivity restricted the availability of data; another (Agnolucci 2004) noted that a lack of data on the marginal costs of abating carbon dioxide makes attempts to perform CEA problematic. Other problems with data sourcing were noted in Andersen (2004), namely insufficient data provided by Eurostat, and ETC/WMF (2004), which found that it takes a long time for data to become publicly available. However, none of the studies explicitly discussed the cost of conducting the analysis itself, or of the data gathering in particular.

● Methodological considerations, such as the treatment of confounding factors and sensitivity testing, are variably applied and are sometimes buried in the text rather than explicitly introduced as important parts of the cost-effectiveness analysis. RIVM (2000) is a notable exception in this regard, providing a comprehensive set of sensitivity tests that control for variations in the interest rate, depreciation period applied, indirect costs, effect of interactions between measures, timing of different measures and the impacts of relative price changes. Other case studies reflect uncertainty by using different weightings for different parts of environmental effectiveness (Resources for the Future 1999), different assumptions about baselines (Hammitt 2000), different lifetimes for abatement measures (Beamount and Tinch 2003), to wider influences like reform of the Common Agricultural Policy (Amann et al 1999) and economic growth (Lehtilä and Tuhkanen 1999).

V. INTERPRETATION OF THE RESULTS

Is the current practice of ex post cost-effectiveness analysis making best use of available advice to quantify the effectiveness of policies and relate it to the costs encountered?

For environmental policy at the Community level, systematic ex post assessment of cost effectiveness is a fairly recent phenomenon. Of the total environmental *acquis*, only four directives explicitly mandate that an ex post assessment of cost effectiveness be carried out. As these directives all entered into force after 2000, no assessment has yet been carried out in response to the reporting obligations for these directives.[5] However, several ex post cost-effectiveness assessments have been carried out to assess the performance of other earlier directives and Community programmes, even though the directives and regulations themselves do not mandate such assessments. This includes assessments of the EU Urban Waste Water Treatment Directive (Andersen 2004), the directive on packaging and packaging waste (ETC/WMF 2004), the Large Combustion Plant Directive (CERNA 2000) or the EMAS regulation (Entec 2000). Likewise, there are a few examples where the implementation of European regulations at the member state level has been analysed in a CEA (for example RIVM (2003) for the National Emissions Ceiling Directive in the Netherlands).

From the analysis of ex post CEAs surveyed in this study, it has emerged that the scope, level of detail and methodological focus of ex post CEAs differ substantially. As of yet, it is not possible to identify one 'common approach' to ex post CEA that has been applied in different countries, or to different policy questions. On the contrary, a certain tendency of reinventing the wheel can be discerned, for example in the case of the Water Framework Directive, where different member states have commissioned guidelines and handbooks in addition to the guidance prepared on the European level. This is not necessarily a negative development, as different approaches to implementing one and the same directive may be warranted by different conditions in the member states (for example in terms of available data, complexity of the decision situations, available human resources and so on). Yet it means that much scope remains for policy learning and mutual exchange.

The actual implementation of the CEAs documented in this project differs from the theoretical ideal of a CEA, more so in some cases than in others. The real-life practice combines several different approaches, all of which include assessments of costs and outcomes of some sort, but which do not always closely resemble the textbook ideal of a CEA. Such changes are not always due to a lack of understanding, but are often necessitated by data gaps or by time and capacity constraints. To deal with these, authors will often take methodological shortcuts. For instance, a US study on the cost of CFC phase-out (Hammitt 2000) uses marginal abatement cost as a proxy for cost effectiveness, an EEA study on packaging waste (ETC/WMF 2004) uses budgeted government expenditure as a proxy for costs, and the cross-country study (CERNA 2000) on the implementation of the municipal waste incineration directives uses data from two German *Länder* as representative of the whole of Germany. Three studies (Agnolucci 2004; Andersen 2004 and ETC/WMF 2004) explicitly note that the lack of data makes analysis difficult, but derive their conclusions on the limited database available. Some studies will omit certain parts of the analysis and certain types of impacts, or treat them in a qualitative way. Thus, many studies do not address impacts to the national economy, such as increased expenditure, job creation and so on. (This omission is explicitly noted in a study on copper pollution in the Humber estuary (Beamount and Tinch 2003), but also applies to other studies.) Other studies do not address secondary environmental impacts of abatement technologies used, or describe them only in qualitative terms (for example Entec (2000) for the case of the EMAS scheme). In some cases, cost estimates are sometimes taken over from previous studies, even though these may not be recent ones (for example Beck et al 2004; Amann et al 1999).

Confounding factors and parameters, such as economic growth, technological change, policy developments, the interactions and inter-dependencies between measures, the presence of side-effects, or the difficulty of relating measures to outcomes, are discussed in many studies. Most studies would either mention them, but not incorporate them into the subsequent analysis (Beck et al 2004; Hammitt 2000; Andersen 2004; ETC/WMF 2004), or they are treated in the sensitivity analysis only (RIVM 2000; Amann et al 1999). For presenting results, a particular shortcut was applied in the IMPOL study on the Large Combustion Plant Directive (Eames 2000), which described the cost effectiveness of the compared options only in qualitative terms as low, medium or high.

The variety of methodological shortcuts employed means that only a minority of case studies has actually applied the different parts of a CEA that are described in guidance documents. Thus, for example, a third of the summarized case studies do not consider sensitivity testing of any sort. While some others employ sensitivity testing or at least some type of plausibility check (for instance by comparing results with other studies), only two provide an elaborated sensitivity analysis (RIVM 2000; Amann et al 1999). In two studies, a reduced form of sensitivity analysis is applied by using different baselines (Hammitt 2000; Lehtilä and Tuhkanen 1999). Only four studies (RIVM 2000; Beamount and Tinch 2003; Amann et al 1999; AEA Technology 1998) apply discounting and discuss the effect that the choice of discount rate has on the results, while other studies skip this part altogether. Also, only four studies (RIVM 2000; Amann et al 1999; Lehtilä and Tuhkanen 1999; AEA Technology 1998) made use of models to estimate the cost effectiveness of policies. While many studies simply applied the status quo (or the situation in a given year) as the baseline for the analysis, one study (Andersen 2004) did not specify a baseline for the analysis, making interpretation of the findings rather difficult. And in addition, none of the studies provided a monetary valuation of environmentally beneficial side-effects, as suggested, for example, by the WFD-related guidance document (RPA 2004).

The majority of these simplifications, shortcuts and omissions can be related to a lack of data, or respectively to a lack of resources for gathering the necessary data. While the reviewed case studies are not very transparent about the cost of conducting the analysis and of gathering the data, some of the guidance documents contain insights on this point. The particular difficulties of gathering ex post data on costs and effectiveness are discussed, for instance, in VROM (2003) and UNESCO (1997), both of which note that data gathering ex post can be more tedious than for ex ante analysis. For example, the UNESCO guidance on CEA (1997) notes that 'systematic C-E analysis presumes the existence of clear objectives, cost data and results indicators. Many times, however, organizations request ex post evaluations of the effectiveness of interventions that were never designed with any of these aspects in mind'. Consequently, all these steps that should have been taken up front have to be repeated ex post.

When comparing different ex post CEAs, it has to be considered that not all policy initiatives are equally suited for an ex post evaluation by means of a CEA. Two main conditions would appear most relevant for a successful ex post CEA (see also VROM 2003). First, the objectives of the policy intervention have to be clearly identified and defined, ideally connected with a quantified target and a clear baseline. And second, the policy should be connected to a fixed time period, identifying when policy targets should be achieved.

This diversity in terms of depth and detail can also be related to the guidelines used. None of the guidance reviewed for this study is an 'uncluttered', easily digestible general guidance document for performing CEA with respect to environmental policies. It is either a little too comprehensive, for example the US EPA's 'Guidelines for preparing economic analyses', or too general, for non-economists, for example the UK Treasury *Green Book*, or too specifically focused on one policy area, for example the Water Framework Directive documents. Also, while most guidelines for ex post cost-effectiveness analyses strive to be theoretically comprehensive, which, by itself, is positive, they also need to take into account the likelihood of data gaps and other practical difficulties in conducting analysis, and make practical recommendations for dealing with these limitations.

On this point, the available guidance documents are mostly confined to a reasonably concise technical description of cost-effectiveness analysis and its strengths and weaknesses. However, they give much less guidance on how to deal with real-life difficulties, for example by specifying which methodological shortcuts can be advisable or at least justifiable. The exceptions to this are the guidelines aimed at the WFD (RPA 2004; Ecologic 2004 and Wateco 2003), which are already embedded in a specific regulatory context, the section on communicating assumptions and methods in EPA (2000), the Dutch guidance on ex post evaluation VROM (2003), and the outlining of issues surrounding the practicalities of data reporting in EEA (1999). For instance, the WFD-related guidance RPA (2004) argues for a tiered approach in determining the level of detail of the analysis. Thus, it is suggested that the analysis can be limited if there is widespread agreement among stakeholders on the measures to be implemented, if different alternatives differ strongly in the results that they deliver, or if either of the alternatives delivers significant additional benefits. Likewise, the US EPA

Guidelines for Preparing Economic Analyses (EPA 2000) recognize that some impacts may escape quantification, and provide brief guidance on which of the markets affected by a measure can be left out of the analysis. The Dutch guidance on ex post evaluation (VROM 2003), by contrast, pays ample attention to the everyday problems encountered by policy makers, including scarce resources, lack of time, political pressures and so on. However, the document only describes evaluation in general and provides no information on how these findings relate to conducting a CEA.

Practical limitations of CEAs, and ways of overcoming them are also sometimes touched upon in discussions on dealing with risk and uncertainty, but it is not explained how this can be related back to carrying out the assessment (see, for instance, the US EPA Guidelines for Preparing Economic Analyses (EPA 2000) or the European Commission handbook for impact assessments (undated)).

The emerging picture is thus that there is a considerable amount of guidance on cost-effectiveness analysis, which sheds little light on ex post CEA, and that there is sufficient guidance on the practical aspects of ex post policy evaluation, which however, says little about cost effectiveness and the way it can be assessed. That is to say, the knowledge of how to conduct an ex post evaluation of cost effectiveness is available, but it needs to be combined from different sources. There is as yet not one single document that provides all the relevant guidance in a consistent way.

As just noted, ex ante CEAs are relatively more abundant than assessments carried out ex post, a fact that is also reflected in the focus of most guidance documents. There are few cases where the results of an ex post CEA were directly compared to an ex ante analysis previously conducted for the same policy measure. The assessment by Resources for the Future of the enhanced inspection and maintenance programme in Arizona (Resources for the Future 1999) is one of the rare examples of such comparisons, concluding that the ex ante estimates of the costs of achieving the forecasted emission reductions were underestimated. Another assessment by James Hammitt (Hammitt 2000) of the cost of CFC phase-out found mixed evidence: while some ex ante assessments substantially overestimated the marginal costs of limiting CFC consumption, others modestly under-estimated this cost.[6] The small amount of studies comparing directly the results of ex ante and ex post analysis prevents us from inferring specific conclusions regarding the relationship between ex ante and ex post CEAs. What can be said, however, is that an ex post CEA will be much easier to perform in cases where an ex ante assessment has been carried out. Certain points that are crucial for a successful ex post CEA will have been clarified in cases where an ex ante assessment has been carried out. This includes clearly defined and quantified targets for a policy intervention, a baseline scenario, and a timetable for achieving the targets. Carrying out an ex ante assessment presents an opportunity to formulate at an early stage the questions that should later be addressed in the ex post CEA. This means that monitoring and reporting requirements can be designed accordingly, meeting the data needs of an ex post CEA.

VI. CONCLUSIONS AND RECOMMENDATIONS

When summarizing the results of this project, it should be emphasized again that the findings are preliminary and should be considered as work in progress. Nevertheless, the results shed some light on the trend in European environmental policy towards more and better assessment of the impacts of policies, both ex post and ex ante. At the same time, policy evaluation is clearly not a goal in and of itself, but has to serve a specific purpose. Considering the time and resources that flow into evaluation exercises like an ex post cost-effectiveness analysis, it is clear that the expenses will be justified only if the results of the analysis have a practical impact on policy-making. Thus, the evaluation of policies becomes a useful tool once the results feed back into the policy process, be it for the further implementation of the same policy, or for future policy initiatives in a related field.

The main findings of this project – a diversity of approaches followed in real-life CEAs, and a lack of guidance targeted specifically at ex post CEA – are clearly relevant for the implementation and evaluation of those directives that require an ex post evaluation, including cost-effectiveness aspects. For the four directives identified in Section I, the first round of evaluation is either underway or imminent, highlighting the need for specific guidance and good-practice examples of ex post CEAs. At the same time, the findings of this project are also relevant for the implementation of other directives identified in this study, which either provide for an ex ante cost-effectiveness analysis or which require ex post reporting of effectiveness in a broader sense. In both these cases, findings related to the methodology and practice of ex post CEAs, including specific guidance, can provide important inputs. Two possible applications are outlined as follows:

1. In policy areas where an ex ante CEA is required, to support the learning from policy implementation, it seems advisable to re-consider the results of such an ex ante analysis during, and after the implementation, in order to see if the ex ante analysis succeeded in assessing expected impacts, and if the judgment made regarding the most cost-effective solution was indeed correct. Such knowledge can be a valuable input for the further implementation process, or for other subsequent

policy initiatives in the same field. The Water Framework Directive provides an example of this. The WFD requires programmes of measures to be drawn up in order to reach good ecological status in all water bodies by 2015. The selection and combination of measures shall be guided *inter alia* by cost-effectiveness considerations. It is foreseen that the programme of measures will be adapted and revised at six-year intervals, repeating the cost-effectiveness analysis for the selection of potential measures. Although there is no formal requirement to do so, it seems highly advisable to base the selection of measures after 2015 on an assessment of how far the judgments made in the first planning cycle regarding the cost effectiveness of measures were indeed correct. To this end, an ex post analysis would be necessary to assess the extent to which the planned objectives have actually been reached, and if not, then why not. Similar arguments can be made for other directives that are implemented over a longer time period and with more than one implementation and reporting cycle.

2. The second possible application concerns those directives that mandate an ex post evaluation of the policies' performance or effectiveness, but do not explicitly require a cost-effectiveness analysis. However, even a loose evaluation that does not qualify as a CEA in the proper sense will often involve a qualitative description of cost effectiveness, or an unrelated juxtaposition of information on costs and on effects. With some guidance and better data, such assessments could be developed further towards a CEA. Here, it needs to be assessed whether the evaluation would benefit from giving a greater weight to cost-effectiveness considerations, in order to make it more stringent and more coherent.

As previously mentioned, there are notable differences between individual member states when it comes to evaluating the (cost) effectiveness of environmental and other policies. Judging by the number of case studies and guidance documents surveyed in this study, systematic and institutionalized procedures for evaluation and appraisal would appear to be most fully developed in the UK and in the Netherlands, supported by cross-cutting requirements to evaluate the performance and cost effectiveness of major policy initiatives. This observation is also supported by Virani (1998), who surveyed the use of economic evaluation methods for environmental policies in several European countries. For those European directives that require member states to report on cost effectiveness, it can be expected that the capacity and experience built up will also be reflected in the quality of the assessments (for example Directive 2000/60 (WFD); Directive 2002/30 (noise-related operating restrictions at Community airports) and Directive 2004/8 (cogeneration)).

As many of the directives requiring an ex post evaluation of (cost) effectiveness are still in their first reporting period, the number of ex post evaluations carried out both at the EU and the member state level will increase in the near future. This raises the question of how the assessments themselves will be assessed: what constitutes a successful assessment, and how can the value of an assessment for subsequent policy-making be assessed? In this context, it also needs to be established which institutions will be responsible for reviewing assessments, and how the results of assessments will flow back into the policy-making process.

NOTES

1. This chapter is based on research that was carried out by Ecologic, eftec and IVM on behalf of the European Environment Agency in 2004 and 2005. The financial support of the EEA is gratefully acknowledged. It should be noted that the analysis presented in this paper should be regarded as work in progress. The positions presented in this paper represent solely the views of the authors, and cannot be attributed to the EEA. The authors would like to thank the members of the EEA national focal point network for their support and input to this paper. The authors would also like to thank Friedrich Hinterberger (SERI), Frans Oosterhuis (IVM), Hans Vos (EEA) and the late David Pearce for reviewing and commenting on this paper.
2. Unfortunately, few of the studies are transparent about which aspects were omitted and why, which difficulties and constraints were encountered, and how they were addressed.
3. Note that total costs here refer only to the additional costs associated with the measure itself, and not the total costs of achieving the environmental outcome.
4. A more formal mathematical explanation would describe this by showing that the total cost of emissions reductions is the integral of the marginal abatement cost between two different emissions levels.
5. For the National Emission Ceilings Directive (2001/81), an extensive ex ante cost effectiveness has been carried out in 1999 in preparation for the Directive (Amann et al 1999). The first assessment of the implementation of the Directive is due at the end of 2004, but was not available at the time of writing. In addition, a national ex ante CEA for the implementation of the NEC Directive has been carried out in the Netherlands (Beck et al 2004).
6. A 1999 study published by the Stockholm Environment Institute, 'Costs and strategies presented by industry during the negotiations of environmental regulations' (SEI 1999), was not considered in detail in this project: while the study did compare ex ante and ex post estimates of costs, it did not relate these to the effectiveness or measures or compare their cost effectiveness.

REFERENCES

ADB (1997), *Guidelines for the Economic Analysis of Projects*, Manila, PH, ADB.
AEA Technology (1998), *Options to Reduce Nitrous Oxide Emissions*, Oxfordshire, AEA Technology.
Agnolucci, P (2004), 'Ex post evaluations of CO2-based taxes: a survey', Tyndall Working Paper 52, June 2004, Norwich, Tyndall Centre for Climate Change Research.

Amann, M et al (1999), 'Economic evaluation of a directive on national emission ceilings for certain atmospheric pollutants. Part A: Cost-effectiveness analysis – Final Report', November, Laxenburg, AT, IIASA.

Andersen, Mikael S (2004), *Effectiveness of Waste Water Policies in Selected Countries*, Roskilde, DK, Danish National Environmental Research Institute.

Beamount, N and Tinch, R (2003), 'Cost effective reduction of copper pollution in the Humber Estuary', Norwich, CSERGE.

Beck, J P, Folkert, R J M and Smeets, W L M (2004), 'Beoordeling van de uitvoeringsnotitie emissieplafonds verzuring en grootschalige luchtverontreiniging 2003', RIVM rapport 500037003/2004, Bilthoven, NL, RIVM.

Boonekamp, P G M, Sijm, J P M and van den Wijngaart, R A (2004), 'Milieukosten Energiemaatregelen 1990–2010 – Overzicht Kosten en Mogelijke Verbeteringen in de Monitoring', Bilthoven, NL, RIVM.

CERNA (2000), *The Implementation of the Municipal Waste Incineration Directives (IMPOL)*, Paris, CERNA.

Directorate-General Budget (2001), 'Ex ante evaluation: a practical guide for preparing proposals for expenditure programmes', Brussels, European Commission.

Directorate-General Regional Policy (undated), 'Guide to cost-benefit analysis of investment projects', Brussels, European Commission.

Eames, M (2000), 'The Large Combustion Plant Directive (88/609/EEC): an effective instrument for pollution abatement?', Brighton, SPRU.

Ecologic (2004), 'Basic principles for selecting the most cost-effective combinations of measures as described in Article 11 of the Water Framework Directive Handbook', Berlin, Umweltbundesamt.

Eftec (1999), 'Review of technical guidance on environmental appraisal', London, Department of the Environment, Transport and the Regions.

Entec (2000), 'Scope for the use of economic instruments in the implementation of the EC Solvent Emissions Directive', Newcastle upon Tyne, Entec.

EPA (2000), 'Guidelines for preparing economic analyses', Washington, D.C., United States Environmental Protection Agency.

ETC/WMF (2004), 'Analysis of effectiveness of implementing packaging waste management systems', Copenhagen, European Environment Agency.

European Commission (undated), *A Handbook for Impact Assessment in the Commission: How To Do an Impact Assessment*, Brussels, European Commission.

European Environment Agency (1999), 'Guidelines for defining and documenting data on costs of possible environmental protection measures,' Copenhagen, European Environment Agency.

European Environment Agency (2001), 'Reporting on environmental measures – towards more "sound and effective" EU environmental policies', Environmental issue report 25, Copenhagen, European Environment Agency.

Government of Canada (2004), *Opportunities Envelope Guidelines for Proposals*, Ottawa, Government of Canada.

Hammitt, James K, Harvard School of Public Health (HSPH) (2000), 'Are the costs of proposed environmental regulations overestimated? Evidence from the CFC phaseout', *Environmental and Resource Economics*, 16 (3), 281–302.

HM Treasury (2003), *The Green Book: Appraisal and Evaluation in Central Government*, London, HM Treasury.

Lehtilä, A and Tuhkanen, S (1999), 'Integrated cost-effectiveness analysis of green-house gas emission abatement: the case of Finland', Espoo, VTT Technical Research Centre of Finland.

NERI (2000), *Samfundsøkonomisk Vurdering af Miljøprojekter*, Roskilde, NERI.

OECD (1997), *Evaluating Economic Instruments for Environmental Policy*, Paris, Organisation for Economic Co-operation and Development.

OMB (1992), 'Guidelines and discount rates for benefit-cost analysis of Federal Programs', Washington, D.C., Office of Management and Budget.

Pearce, David (2004), *What Constitutes a Good Agri-environmental Policy Evaluation?*, Paris, Organisation for Economic Co-operation and Development.

PEEM, WHO (1993), 'PEEM Guidelines 3 – Guidelines for cost-effectiveness analysis of vector control', Geneva, World Health Organization.

Resources for the Future (1999), 'Costs, emissions reductions, and vehicle repair: evidence from Arizona', Discussion Paper 99-23-REV, Washington, D.C., Resources for the Future.

RIVM (undated), 'Kosteneffectiviteit Natuurbeleid: Methodiekontwikkeling', Bilthoven, RIVM.

RIVM (2000), 'Cost effectiveness of environmental measures', Bilthoven, RIVM.

RPA (2004), 'CEA and developing a methodology for assessing disproportionate costs', London, Department for the Environment, Food and Rural Affairs and Environment Agency.

SEI (1999), 'Costs and strategies presented by industry during the negotiations of environmental regulations', Stockholm, Swedish Ministry of the Environment.

UNESCO (1997), 'Cost-effectiveness analysis: a tool for UNESCO', Paris, United Nations Educational, Scientific and Cultural Organization.

Virani, S (1998), 'Economic evaluation of environmental policies and legislation', Report prepared for the European Commission, DG III – Final Report, September 1998, Norfolk, RPA.

VROM (1998), 'Kosten en baten in het milieubeleid, definities en berekeningsmethoden, Publicatiereeks Milieustrategie', 1998/6, The Hague, VROM.

VROM (2003), 'Concept Wegwijzer Evaluatieonderzoek Ex Post: Een Praktisch Handvat voor de Opzet en Uitvoering van Evaluatieonderzoek Ex Post', The Hague, VROM.

WATECO (2003), 'Economics and the environment: the implementation challenge of the Water Framework Directive', Guidance Document.

Wynn, Gerard (2002), 'The cost-effectiveness of biodiversity management: a comparison of farm types in extensively farmed areas of Scotland', *Journal of Environmental Planning and Management*, 45 (6), 827–40.

12. Implementing a monitoring system for the French national strategy for sustainable development

Benoit Simon and Jean-Pierre Sivignon

I. INTRODUCTION

This chapter presents work carried out for the French Ministry of Ecology and Sustainable Development, which aimed to develop a monitoring system for the French national strategy for sustainable development. This focused on the evaluation of sustainability along three axes. First, a reflection on the framework of the national strategy for SD: we asked questions such as how can a hierarchy between strategic objectives be made? How can the multiplication of actions be avoided? Where should the frontiers be between SD policies and other government policies? Second, we discuss the methodology used to elaborate indicators. The partial use of logical diagrams, screening indicators (individually and at the system level) through a quality assessment grid and an Intranet for fulfilling indicators are all considered. Finally, we reflect on the difficulties encountered during the process.

II. THE FRENCH NATIONAL STRATEGY FOR SUSTAINABLE DEVELOPMENT

The development of a national strategy for sustainable development is the response to the commitment made by the French government in the framework of the UN and confirmed during the Johannesburg Summit. This national strategy has to be coherent with the European strategy for SD, adopted in 2001. France first initiated a strategy for SD in 1997. This first strategy was based on the following orientations: taking into account SD in all public policies; carrying out studies to apply SD principles in transport, waste and agriculture sectors; establishing a charter for consultation so as to favour transparency in public decision-making processes; reinforcing education actions in the fields of environment and SD; and producing an annual assessment of international efforts dedicated to SD notably in the framework of aid policies. Unfortunately, this first initiative remained largely unapplied. The development of the present strategy followed several steps. First, in 2002, a secretary of state in charge of SD was nominated within the government. Then, a governmental seminar focusing on SD took place on 28 November 2002. It defined 64 measures to better take into account SD in national policies. Finally, a new national strategy for sustainable development was adopted during spring 2003.

The decision to write a new strategy was made because of several different reasons. On the one hand, the 1997 strategy remained a theoretical exercise without any operational implementation. Because of this previous experience, the 2003 national strategy for sustainable development is based on clear orientations for a fast implementation and action programmes during five years, with concrete objectives and actions to achieve. On the other hand, the national level of this strategy requires a participative elaboration involving all stakeholders. The French strategy text is also articulated around the three pillars of SD: economy, social and environment. However, a fourth pillar, culture, was added to reflect French specific stakes. The French national strategy for sustainable development (NSSD) aims to give ministries, administrative directories, local authorities and citizens a common vision of short- and medium-term stakes and an idea about the changes that are necessary. It also establishes modalities for integrating SD into public policies and for monitoring progress achieved in this field. The development of the strategy was organized through a systematic mobilization of all French ministries, which were asked to review, organize and prioritize actions to be achieved. Because this strategy cross-cuts the interests of all the ministries, it required them to work together to create the strategy. However, some may underline that this strategy is more a governmental than national strategy: objectives and actions were largely defined by governmental bodies, and achievement of the strategy relied on ministries and public agencies. As a matter of fact, civil society has not been much involved in the process: NSSD was validated by the CNDD (Conseil National du Développement Durable) which is the official body for civil society representation, but no action is to be implemented by this organization or any of its members.

A specificity of the French NSSD is its complex architecture and its wideness. The following diagram helps to get a broad picture of this architecture:

The NSSD has a number of specific objectives. These are, to promote a genuine solidarity between generations, people and territories and to fight against exclusion and poverty; to develop strategies for the promotion of health; to apply responsible management of natural resources, by integrating environment and economic and social development by

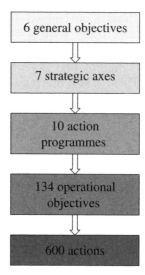

Figure 12.1   Architecture of the NSSD

promoting sustainable production and consumption patterns; to consider
the cultural dimension as an element of identity and value; to promote
the creation of decent jobs, firms and to favour innovation; and to
prepare for the future by reinforcing research, education and training for
ecology and SD.

The French national strategy is designed around seven strategic axes and
ten programmes of action. Each strategic axis is made of orientations and
at least one programme of action:

- *The citizen, actor of SD*: this first strategic axis simultaneously takes
  into account information and awareness-raising, education and participation. Two programmes of action are linked to this axis: social
  and health dimensions and citizens.
- *Territories or domains*: this axis aims to organize the territory or
  domain through the integration of all economic, social and environmental factors, especially through broader decentralization activities.
  A specific programme of action 'Territories' has been set for this axis.
- *Economic activities, enterprises and consumers*: this third axis aims to
  achieve economic growth while being more respectful towards the
  environment. Mechanisms for achieving this include certification,
  labelling, socially responsible investment and a more incentive-based
  fiscal and financial system. An eponym action programme has been
  elaborated.

- *Energy, transport and agriculture sectors*: this axis contains three complementary action programmes aimed at reinforcing SD considerations in the energy, transport and agriculture sectors. Three action programmes are associated with this axis: climate change and energy; transport; agriculture and fisheries.
- *To prevent risks, pollutions and other environmental and health problems*: this includes the implementation of preventive and precautionary strategies, the furthering of research, and the creation of an environmental policing and justice system. The corresponding programme is called 'Natural and technological risks'.
- *Towards an exemplary state*: the government has to be exemplary as regards its management and the development of public policies. One action programme has been established.
- *International action*: this axis seeks to contribute to the fight against poverty, towards the better management of the globalization process and the promotion of SD within the different policies of the EU. One action programme has been established for this axis.

Despite its appearance, the strategy is characterized by a high level of heterogeneity (in terms of the types of actions, objectives, the architecture of actions and programmes and so on). This makes the implementation of a monitoring system very difficult. Consequently, each action programme is organized in different levels and sublevels. At the broadest level are global objectives. There are between 3 to 5 of these per programme. The next level is that of the specific objectives. There are 0–13 of these per global objective. The level below this is that of the operational objectives. There are between 0 to 4 of these per specific objective. Finally, the actions included in a plan of action range in number from 0 to 10 per operational objective. So, as a whole, the NSSD includes seven strategic axes and ten action programmes based on 49 global objectives, 62 specific objectives, 134 operational objectives and approximately 600 actions.

However, the ten action programmes do not share exactly the same architecture, so the similarities between them are very few. Some programmes are built around the entire range of levels of objectives and actions, while others do not include plans of actions, or do not present specific objectives but instead present one plan of action for each operational objective. This degree of homogeneity stops at the first level of the actions programmes: the level of global objectives. In addition, what can be considered as a specific objective in one given programme could be considered as an action in another one.

In addition, we notice that there is no hierarchy between objectives, which means that there is no identifiable priority within the strategy. Even if we may consider from a normative viewpoint that all objectives are equally important, from a pragmatic point of view, this may be a source of concern: the strategy being very ambitious, if it is not possible to achieve all goals, which ones should be prioritized? Also, most objectives of the strategy are not quantified: except for a few objectives for eco-responsibility of administration, it is not clear what should be attained. Even if the quantification of goals is not always easy, this is a major drawback for monitoring and evaluation systems. Finally, there is no budget for the strategy: again, this creates difficulties for identifying who is in charge of what, and what should be done. It is thus not possible to monitor the implementation of the NSSD from a financial point of view.

Consequently, these different limits have important consequences for the design of the monitoring system: the lack of homogeneity between programmes of actions makes it more difficult to build up a full monitoring system based on the most detailed level.

The Monitoring System

The need to elaborate a monitoring system for the NSSD is due to the requirement to send an annual report to Parliament on the progress of the strategy implementation. Indeed, there was no real system of output indicators set for monitoring actions to be achieved. This was considered insufficient by the administration services in order to effectively ensure a continuous monitoring of the implementation of the national strategy. The objectives dedicated to the monitoring system to be realized were threefold: first, to clarify the logic of action and make the NSSD more easy to read by external actors; second, to define outcome indicators for the 10 different programmes; and finally to propose that impact indicators should be linked with the national indicators with regard to the state of SD (context indicators).

III. METHODOLOGY

The methodology developed for this work was based on four different steps. These include the use of impact diagrams, a review of existing indicators, the definition of complementary indicators and finally, the quality assessment of individual indicators. Each of these is now discussed.

Impact Diagrams

From a methodological perspective, it was essential to first clarify the logical framework for the NSSD. Even if the official document displays a breakdown between different levels of objectives within a programme, a schematic presentation allows us to have a synthetic vision of NSSD and at the same time to get an impression of the hierarchy between objectives and actions. This was necessary because of the lack of homogeneity between these different levels (as suggested earlier, some actions could be considered as objective in other programmes and vice versa). For this exercise, we used a common evaluation tool: the impact diagram. This tool gives a good representation of causality links between outputs of a given programme, located on the left of the diagram, and specific and global impacts, located on the right of the diagram. It was thus decided to build up one impact diagram per programme of action and one global impact diagram for the NSSD as a whole in order to obtain a full and clear understanding of how the strategy was designed. In other words, this aimed to show how actions were supposed to produce expected outcomes and impacts in terms of SD.

The second benefit of impact diagrams is the support provided to define indicators. Indeed, each level of objective (operational, intermediary and global) respectively has associated expected outputs, outcomes and impacts. On the basis of this deconstruction, a systematic overview of indicators was achieved by 'zooming' into each box on the diagram successively and by extracting output, outcome and impact indicators. These were then selected according to their quality. This method of indicator definition is illustrated in Figure 12.2.

Review of Existing Indicators

Around 100 indicators were initially developed to monitor some of the concrete actions of the ten different programmes. However, most of these indicators were simply inappropriate (for example they did not provide a real measurement of the state of implementation of corresponding actions). Furthermore, they covered only a small part of the 600 actions. A careful analysis of these indicators during the review process demonstrated that globally, less than a quarter of NSSD actions are defined with indicators, whatever sectors they cover. This shows that the initial system was not useful for the monitoring and evaluation of the NSSD implementation. Indeed out of a total of 75 output indicators (which are directly linked to the actions taken), only half of them can provide effective and satisfactory information about the implementation of actions. This shows that only 5% of NSSD actions could be covered by indicators. A similar situation is apparent for the 30 outcome indicators (corresponding to the 'objectives' level in the NSSD). Thirty of the indicators are from our point of view, simply not exploitable. This is because either they are not referring to the

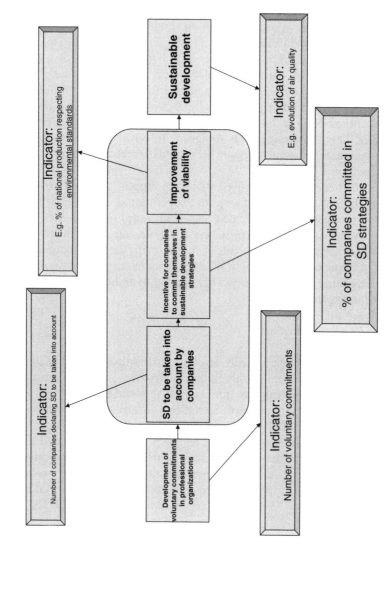

Figure 12.2   Definition of indicators on the basis of a logical diagram

corresponding objective or they are not precise enough or not quantifiable. Finally, four of the ten programmes are not covered by the indicators at all. In summary, there are only 16 outcome indicators that are considered satisfactory, while there are 158 objectives in the ten action programmes of the NSSD.

Definition of New Indicators

The objective was to develop outcome indicators, which should display the expected benefit of the actions undertaken for the different targets. A two-step approach was used for this specific work. First, a 'theoretical' definition was achieved: consultants proposed indicators that they considered as the closest direct counterparts of the different NSSD objectives, without questioning the ability to fulfil them. Second, the indicators were discussed with the different ministries in charge of implementing the strategy in order to refine them and give them a more concrete aspect. On this basis, a full list of indicators has been produced.

Quality Criteria

The list of indicators was screened on the basis of a quality grid at two different levels, according to the quality of the individual indicators and the quality of the system of indicators. The criteria used to select the indicators and verify the quality of the system as a whole are presented as follows. For each indicator, criteria used were:

- Availability: The first quality criterion for an indicator is its actual existence, that is to say, it must be quantified at regular intervals. Sometimes one or more indicators featured in the programming documents have never been quantified, and for all practical purposes do not therefore exist. The actual availability of data is therefore the very first quality criterion.
- Freshness: Once an indicator has been quantified, it may take several months or even years before the information can really be used for monitoring and evaluation. This is particularly true for certain context indicators drawn from annual statistical publications. The freshness of information then becomes an important quality criterion.
- Sensitivity: A programme indicator must vary significantly when the programme is implemented and produces effects.
- Reliability: The programme actors must trust the information produced. Reliability is therefore a quality criterion. Reliability can be

defined as the fact that the same measurement, taken by two different people, will produce the same value for the indicator.

- Comparability: The usefulness of an indicator depends largely on whether it allows for internal comparisons between different measures of the programme or inter-regional external comparisons. The comparability of the indicator is therefore a criterion of its quality. This criterion is important, but difficult to meet.
- Normativity: Indicators must include a reference so that the outcome can be judged to be satisfactory or not. Any value observed by means of the indicator must therefore be compared to a norm, for example according to the objective to be met, norm to be surpassed, European average to be attained and so on.
- Meaning: A good indicator must be understood without ambiguity by everyone who has to use it. In the minds of both decision makers and the public, the meaning of the indicator must be the same as for the programme managers. It must accurately reflect the concept to be measured. This is what is called the validity of construction.

The quality criteria which were applied to the entire system are:

- **Coverage**: The indicators selected must cover a sufficiently large proportion of the programme measures. This coverage must be equal to or greater than three-quarters of the planned expenditure.
- **Balance**: The system must consist of a good balance between indicators in the different categories. In particular, result and impact indicators must be the most numerous.
- **Selectivity**: A system of indicators must be simple. The selectivity criterion requires that the programme managers' capacity to absorb information be respected. The information must therefore be limited to a maximum of a few dozen figures.
- **Relevance**: The relevance of the system implies that the indicators be developed primarily for those measures or themes which have significant implications in terms of decision-making (so, measures with a very high budget, innovative measures, themes considered to be strategic and so on).

IV. RESULTS

Results of this work can be outlined for the three different levels of indicators (output level, outcome level and impact level). The following sections explore these in more detail.

Output Indicators

Output indicators were integrated in an operational board so as to characterize in detail the whole set of NSSD actions, and ease the monitoring of action programmes. For each action, a set of 14 criteria was defined and fulfilled. These were then validated by the Ministry of Ecology and Sustainable Development. These criteria are:

- name of the action
- state of the action: existing or newly created
- description of the action
- objective of NSSD with which it is concerned
- pilot of the action
- partners involved
- level of implementation
- percentage of implementation
- date of start
- financing
- comments
- type of action (two levels)
- target
- reference to SD.

Among the most important information to be collected for this operational board, it is interesting to look in more detail at two of them. The *Level of Implementation* aims to better describe the progress of a given action. This is achieved through consideration of four items:

- Not engaged: the action has not yet been started.
- Engaged: the action has started, but the degree of implementation is lower than 30%.
- Advanced: the action has started, and the degree of implementation is higher than 30%.
- Achieved: the action is achieved, and the objective is reached.

The *type of action* aims to give a description of the different kind of actions which are implemented. A typology of actions has been established, incorporating 12 different types of action. These are broken down into five different categories of instruments, as displayed in Table 12.1.

Table 12.1   Breakdown of categories

Category of instrument	Type of action
Information and social instruments	Communication, information and awareness-raising Vocational training Incentives for 'virtuous' behaviours: chart, labels, quality contracts and so on
Regulation instruments: knowledge	Monitoring tools: information systems, observation systems, indicators and so on Studies, surveys, evaluations, production of technical documents supporting decision-making Scientific and technical research
Regulation instruments: legislation and regulatory action	Legislative and regulatory action
Regulation instruments: organization	Plan or programme of action Governance, organization, structuring of actors
Economic instruments	Financial incentives Fiscal policy Equipment and technological innovations (investments of public authorities)

Outcome Indicators

Based on the methodology just described, outcome indicators have been gathered together in a table. This table (Table 12.2) has been built on the basis of five different columns. These enable us to get a more complete picture of the relevance and usefulness of the indicators, including the improvement of our understanding of the links between objectives and actions, and who is supposed to give the information. Only a brief example is given, as the total number of indicators remains high.

Given the number of objectives to be monitored (158), the total number of outcome indicators remains high: more than 150. This is still very important, even if, for each ministry, the total number of indicators to be informed is rather low. This leads to a second problem which emerged in the process: the relative reluctance of ministries in charge of the implementation of the actions to collect the necessary information.

Table 12.2   Extract from indicators database

Ministry in charge of the action	Global objective	Objectives SNDD	Actions	Outcome indicator
Foreign affairs	To facilitate human development	To support the elaboration and implementation of national health and education politicies as well as supporting most vulnerable populations, in in rural and urban areas	To favour the elaboration of national strategies in ZSP countries To maintain the support to the 'primary education for all' initiative To reinforce cooperation with WHO To support AIDS prevention projects	Evolution of the number of health and education projects in favour notably of most vulnerable populations, in rural and urban areas in ZSP countries

We will review the different arguments against this collection in the next section.

Furthermore, the indicators presented in Table 12.2 are not fully operational at present, since many indicators still question the relevance of the related objective. At this stage, it is not possible to reformulate these objectives, and thus indicators would need to be discussed a second time. A second step which still needs to be carried out is the elaboration of a software interface in order to facilitate the task of information collection for the different ministries.

Impact Indicators

A first set of impact indicators has also been produced, according to the same methodological process as the other indicators. However, it is necessary at this stage to articulate those indicators with the 45 national indicators on

Table 12.3   Themes covered by national SD indicators according to the three pillars of SD

Economic pillar	Environmental pillar	Social pillar
Synthetic indicators	Climate change	Social cohesion
Improvement of potential growth	Environmental resources	Lifestyles and health
Inter-generational equity	Production and consumption pattern	Human resources valorization
Innovation and research	Health and environment	
Insertion pattern in the globalization system		

the state of SD, which have been published by the government (Ministry of Ecology and Sustainable Development). Those indicators are organized according to the three pillars of SD, each of them being split into different themes. These are summarized in Table 12.3.

Indicators have been combined in order to use the majority of those indicators to minimize data collection and ensure a coherence between the two works. Complementary indicators have been defined and, as for outcome indicators, data collection process now needs to be defined.

V.   DIFFICULTIES ENCOUNTERED

During this study, three main difficulties have been faced, which may be useful to share with other European experiences. The first difficulty was the national strategy for sustainable development itself. This was problematic due to the way in which it is organized (in terms of priorities, programmes, objectives with different levels, actions and so on). Also problematic was its size, in terms of the number of objectives and actions it considers. Coupled with this, the number of actors involved (ministries, agencies and so on) is also very large, making it difficult to manage. Finally, because the objectives are rather vague with some having a weak logical chain, it made it more difficult to build a coherent and relevant indicator system. It is almost the case that each individual indicator questions the relevance of the objectives.

The second difficulty was related to the data collection process. The people who are to be involved with data collection are reluctant to spend time on these tasks and do not perceive the immediate advantage of doing it. On the other hand, reporting to another ministry is often perceived as a constraint, and because the Ministry of Ecology and Sustainable Development is less powerful than other ministries, it makes it difficult to convince colleagues to involve themselves in the process.

The third difficulty is linked to the existence of other indicators, which require the search for coherence. The French government is currently implementing a wide reform of the national budget, with the introduction of performance indicators for each governmental programme. This reform, named LOLF (*Loi Organique relative aux Lois de Finances* – organic law on budget law), is supposed to cover all of the actions undertaken by the ministries. Consequently, all actions of the national strategy for sustainable development are theoretically supposed to be linked to a performance indicator. Even where this is not the case, first it has been necessary to verify the interconnection between the two exercises and second, it has been even more difficult to convince people to work on new indicators. The second challenge linked to the NSSD has already been mentioned and concerns the national indicators on the state of SD. Even if these indicators are impact-oriented, unable to give information on the performance of NSSD actions, it was necessary to look for coherence and to minimize the total number of new indicators.

Finally, we believe that when indicators have not been defined at the same time as the strategy, a long and complex process is necessary to organize a performing monitoring system. Our work is only a first step in that direction. Only its implementation can make it better, with learning by doing effects.

13. The quality of impact assessment in Slovakia[1]

Katarína Staroňová

I. INTRODUCTION

This chapter aims to evaluate the type and quality of information on impact assessments contained in the explanatory memoranda of draft legislation adopted by the government of Slovakia. The research is based on the normative content analysis of a sample of 93 government-initiated draft laws and their explanatory memoranda that were submitted for government consideration during the period immediately after EU accession (1 May–31 December 2004). The quality of information on impact assessment is evaluated against a benchmark identified by best practice of OECD countries, and most importantly against the recent draft paper of the European Commission, '*Next Steps*' (2004). In this sense, this chapter discusses whether the decision maker or regulator is enabled to think about legislation more open mindedly as the literature on impact assessment and better regulation suggests. The research reported here is only one part of a larger project on the comparative evaluation of quality of information on impact assessment in explanatory memoranda in Slovakia, Hungary and Estonia.[2]

From 1 May 2004, the eight candidate countries of Central and Eastern Europe became full members of the EU. In the course of the accession process, these countries were preparing for the EU entry, by harmonizing domestic legislation with *acquis communautaire*, meeting the EU entry criteria and undertaking related reforms in the public and private sector. All these countries, including Slovakia, mostly seem to have met the formal criteria for the EU accession and now they are facing regulatory management capacity problems in terms of institutionalization and implementation of impact assessment (IA) and public participation methods in the everyday work of all ministries.

EU member states are not only subject to formal binding legal norms of the EU, but also adhere to some 'soft laws' and standards concerning the professional and efficient making and governance of public policy. In practice, this means that recent and new candidate countries should not only focus on the content of the harmonized legislation, but, above all, on the quality manner of policy-making, which should comply with the principles of democratic and efficient governance. Most past studies assume that the availability and use of information from IA leads to changes in the outcome of policy-making, notably to better law-making and regulatory quality (Hahn and Litan 1997; OECD 1997b, 2005; Mandelkern 2001; European Commission 2002a). It should also improve the accountability and legitimacy of any policy- and law-making system due to the factual efficiency provided by adequate information (Hahn and Litan 2003). According to both OECD and EU intergovernmental agreements, a system of ex ante IA (the projection of the likely effects of a range of proposed programmes or regulations such as draft laws), is an integral part of good government practice.[3] Social, economic and environmental IA in an integrated methodology is now becoming an obligation for policy makers in all EU countries (European Commission 2004).[4] As such, it is an integral part of the policy design process and allows politicians to take their decisions in the light of the best available evidence.

The main aim of the research project discussed in this chapter is to create a framework that will enable researchers to describe and evaluate the quality of information on IAs contained in the explanatory memoranda (EM) of draft laws and legislative amendments. The pilot study in Slovakia is focusing in particular on the existence and quality of IA in the explanatory memoranda of draft laws. These are required by national legislative framework on the proposal of draft laws and other rules. This chapter looks at two levels: first, the legislative background, that is, the formal requirements for IA and public consultations in a national setting; second, the actual practice of IA as manifested in the information contained in the explanatory memoranda attached to the draft legislation. In this way, a preliminary partial evaluation of a country's compliance with the normative requirements and/or recommendations of the EU Commission is also provided.

II. STUDY DESIGN AND METHODOLOGY

Both academics and institutions like the European Commission and OECD are currently debating what the dimensions of IA quality are and how to measure it. Radaelli (2005) distinguishes between two approaches to the measurement of quality: indicators and tests.[5] In both approaches the main aim is to introduce quality assurance mechanisms that would increase the validity, reliability and other properties of quality. Hahn et al (2000) on the other hand, has developed a scorecard where he questions key assumptions and assesses the appropriateness and application of models used in particular analyses. In this chapter, the research will take a different approach and will focus on the quality of information on IA from the perspective of a key stakeholder – the decision maker (politician) who should decide on the appropriateness of a certain policy upon the information contained in the explanatory memoranda attached to draft laws. The IAs are not judged by their validity, truthfulness or appropriateness of assumptions and methods used, but simply by: (a) the existence of certain information contained in the explanatory memoranda, and (b) by indicators of quality of the information.

The research focused on in this chapter considers only the explanatory memoranda of draft laws and legal amendments that became laws. It omits all other material that goes for discussion to the government sessions, such as law intention, concept papers, information, action plans, bilateral agreements and loans. The reason for this focus is twofold. First, most of the policies in CEE countries take the form of a legal document, which is binding to all subjects in the country. Thus, draft laws and amendments usually have a significant impact on the lives of citizens. Second, it is the legislative process that is formally regulated rather than policy process, which again allows the author to evaluate the degree of compliance with national and international standards.[6] The initiators of the draft laws and amendments are mostly ministries (80% of the cases) so the author indirectly assesses the capacity of the administration by evaluating the outputs. Thus, draft laws and amendments initiated by members of the Parliament or other state agencies are not taken into account. Draft laws debated more than once within the government are calculated as one, simultaneously taking the characteristics of all materials into account.

The research is organized in three stages. Stage one focuses on the description and analysis of normative frameworks and requirements in terms of impact assessment (so, the institutional pre-conditions for IA and public participation in public policy- and law-making processes). The second stage introduces the normative content analysis of explanatory memoranda of all ministerial draft laws that were passed by the Cabinet in the given period (1 May–31 December 2004). The main focus of this stage is to determine the type and quality of information on impact assessment present in the explanatory memoranda of draft laws. In the third stage (beyond the consideration of this chapter), in-depth interviews will be conducted with civil servants at the ministries to reveal the factors that led to any drawbacks or successes in the findings during the second stage. The results of the second stage of the study – normative content analysis – are grouped according to certain groups and categories and presented in a table format (see Figure 13.1 for more details). The interpretation of the results follows.

1.1.–1.3. Existence and extent of IA
The first grouping looks at the existence of impact assessment within explanatory memoranda and the extent of its elaboration.

1.1. No IA attached
IA cannot be found in the explanatory memoranda of draft law. This classification indicates that there are no statements and/or other information available in the explanatory memoranda on impacts/changes in given five categories (1.1.–1.5.)

1.2. Formal IA
IA information is found in the explanatory memoranda. However, this takes the form of statements either in verbal or quantitative form without related facts or evidence. The main criterion in this category was the provision of any logic or evidence on how the originating ministry arrived at the statement/quantified figure. If this information or evidence could not be found, then the IA was codified as formal, since this information has a rhetoric value, regardless of whether the statement is true or false.

(a) Verbal
The verbal statements include suggestions such as, 'there is probably no impact', 'there is some/enormous/little impact', 'there is positive/negative impact', or 'there is no direct impact'.

(b) Monetary
Some basic figures, data or quantification expressed in monetary terms are provided, however, without showing how this figure has been achieved.

1.3. Substantial IA
IA is found in the explanatory memoranda, and evidence is provided. The information on the logic and evidence can either be traced, or there may be signs of the utilization of IA scientific methods (even if these are only primary indications and in one segment of IA only). The most important selection criteria for this category are the real existence of evidence on one or more impacts/changes in the fields/relations to be regulated, and also whether the text of explanatory memoranda contain anything beyond the explanation of the juridical text of draft law and predictions based on intuitions.

(a) Partial IA exists
Less than 2 categories from 2.1.–2.5. types of IA are provided (fiscal, social, economic, environmental and administrative)

(b) Complex IA exists
More than 2 categories from 2.1.–2.5. are provided.

2.1.–2.5. Types of IA
The European Commission is currently looking into a systematic application of IA, regardless of the originating DG (or ministry at national level), by integrating social, economic and environmental IA.** As fiscal and administrative burdens of regulations are a standard approach to IA, these categories are included as well.

2.1. Social impact/changes

Identification of target groups and their socio-economic situation, influence on the labour market, health and gender issues or social services provision (ranging from education to health and so on) for certain vulnerable groups in society. It also includes impacts on human capital, fundamental/human rights, compatibility with the Charter of Fundamental Rights of the European Union, changes in employment levels or job quality, changes affecting gender equality, social exclusion and poverty, impact on health, safety, consumer rights, social capital, security (including crime and terrorism), education, training and culture and so on.

2.2. Fiscal, budgetary impact/changes

It looks not only at the impacts on budgets of the state, municipalities or other self-governments or agencies in the country, but at overall financial risks and consequences, taking into account financial sustainability and affordability. Even in cases where the financial implications are minor, a minimum amount of information should be supplied. Ideally, fiscal IA includes estimates of costs for each option on a multi-year basis, implications for the institution's budget, revenue impacts and possible off-setting savings, and an analysis of risks, and impacts on fiscal plan.

2.3. Economic, businesses impact/changes

It looks at the effects on markets, trade and investment flows, direct and indirect costs for businesses, impacts on innovation, effects on the labour market and on the functioning of the internal market, consequences for households, impacts on public authorities and budget expenditure, impacts on specific regions or sectors, effects on third countries and international relations, macro-economic impacts and so on.

2.4. Environmental, sustainability impact/changes

It judges the likely hazards and consequences that may affect the general ecological environment (water, waste, air, soil pollution, land-use change, bio-diversity loss and so on) and climate change. It also considers the effects on specific groups. Indicators of sustainable development, energy saving and so on are also observed.

2.5. Organizational/administrative impact/changes

It considers the various administrative changes and activities that need to be brought about when adopting the policy (for example training). Also, questions on implementation of the draft law and design of public services are considered.

3. References

References for the conduction of IA and used/–ordered studies, analyses, databases, reports and so on.

---

4. Consultations

Consultations with interested and affected parties, internal and external of the government. This category will specifically consider who has been involved in policy planning and draft legislation processes, as well as how they have been involved (in addition to groups to civil servants within the originating ministry). Concrete names of organizations and their representatives are noted, and focus is also on the proceedings of proposals made by external bodies (both private/business and third sector).

(a) Representing public sector (governmental, subordinated agencies, self-governments, etc.)

(b) Representing the private sector

(c) Representing civil society

(d) Representing independent experts (foreign, local, etc.).

Notes:

* This part relies heavily on the Mandelkern Report (2001).

** The terms *Economic IA* and *Administrative IA* are to some extent comparable with OECD (1997) terms *economic regulation* and *administrative regulation*, but in this study the context of target groups and fields is prevailing.

Figure 13.1   The organization of the study*

III.   RESEARCH RESULTS

Formal Framework to Impact Assessment

In Slovakia, the preparation of material for government sessions is guided by two documents, both setting the general requirements for presenting the assessment of possible impacts of draft laws. The first of these is the 'Legislative rules of Slovakia 241/1997'. This was last amended as of November 2001, when the most significant changes occurred in relation to the introduction of the requirement for impact assessment and consultation with the public prior to government sessions.[7] The second document is entitled 'Guidelines for the preparation and submission of material for government sessions of the Slovak Republic (No. 512/2001)'. This was introduced with the amendments to the Legislative Rules with the intention of providing a more detailed explanation of the Legislative Rules.

In reality, the two documents do not provide adequate explanation and standards for conducting impact assessment. Moreover, they contradict each other in certain requirements.[8] Both documents describe the formal procedures and required elements to be attached to a draft law in the form of explanatory memorandum for government sessions (Table 13.1 summarizes elements to be attached to a draft law under both documents). Most of the

Table 13.1   Requirements for government sessions

Legislative rules	Guidelines
(1) Cover	**(2) Draft decision of the government** clear division of feasible tasks within set deadlines
(3) Report of submission (predkladacia správa) • rationale for the preparation of the needs material • short summary of the goals and needs of the proposal • short summary of the material • short summary of IA, mostly on state budget (Legislative Rules also indicate the importance of impact on self-governments) • summary of the opinion of the advisory bodies of the government • rationale for classification if material is to be classified • summary of opinions raised by the public • summary of opinions from the opinion gathering period	• indication of follow-up measures after the material has been adopted
(4) Draft law/amendment edited according to the results of the opinions gathered	**(4) Material** (proposal, report, concept paper, information, etc.) together with appendices – analysis of the current status of the subject area (positive and negative sides) – clear and feasible goals – alternative measures and timescale of achieving goals (short term and long term) – organizational and human resources support in implementation

Table 13.1 (continued)

Legislative rules	Guidelines

(5) Explanatory memorandum (dôvodová správa)
(5a) Impact assessment
Fiscal IA
  – state budget
  – budgets of municipalities
  – budget of public institutions
	(5) Statement of impacts (doložka vplyvov)
	Fiscal IA = impact on public finances
	Proposal to cover expenditures from state budget if any

Economic IA	Economic IA = impact on citizens, business sector and other legal entities
Environmental IA	Environmental IA
Employment = needs for labor and organizational support	Employment
	Business environment
(5b) Opinion of the Ministry of Finance if state budget affected	
(5c) Statement of Conformity with EU legislation	
(5d) Opinion of the Economic and Social Council of the Government (or statement that that opinion is not needed)	
(6) Analysis of the opinions gathered of opinions, accepted/non-accepted (why), public opinion (min. of 500 signatures), etc.	
(7) Proposal for 'communiqué' (short summary)	

information about future effects of the draft law is to be found under the relevant section of the explanatory memorandum entitled 'dopady' or 'doložka vplyvov', depending on the type of document. The practice is that draft laws, amendments to legislation and directives follow the Legislative Rules, whereas all other materials (such as legislative intentions, reports, concept papers, information and so on) follow the Guidelines. Nevertheless, the information about IA is relatively short in both documents and left open for interpretation by individual ministries. Some information that is related to the impact assessment (such as the rationale, purpose and need for the draft laws, results of the consultation process, references to other studies, and organizational support for the implementation and so on) is to be found in different sections of the explanatory memoranda. Some of the same information is requested in different parts of the explanatory memoranda, which contributes to the relative disorganization in presenting the necessary information.

No central body exists (either in the central government office or in the designated ministry) to encourage, monitor, coordinate or check the quality of the IAs conducted by the individual ministries (with the exemption of fiscal impact assessment as discussed later) or at least to provide guidelines and standards for conducting IAs.[9] As a consequence, no additional handbooks or manuals exist for deeper explanation of the terms used or about the process of preparing IAs. This absence of both a coordinating body and additional literature that could assist the civil servants in conducting the assessments might have a decisive influence on the interpretation of the categories where impact assessment is required. It could also influence the quality of the analyses conducted, particularly when we take into consideration that no prior experience with impact assessments existed.

Nevertheless, almost all of the draft laws (and amendments) analysed within this study also encompassed the 'Statement of impact assessment' which is a separate document attached within explanatory notes, and as a concept it is taken from the Guidelines. Both documents require the ministries to include the assessments of impacts in *fiscal, economic, employment and environmental issues*. The Guidelines in addition require information on follow-up measures in administrative and organizational spheres for better implementation. This is not required by the Legislative Rules, and as such it is barely to be found in any draft legislation (see the discussion on the results of the review of draft laws in Slovakia). These categories broadly correspond to the EU's guidelines on impact assessment, to ensure the economic, environmental and social impacts of a proposal (European Commission 2002a).

Fiscal impact assessment in both Legislative Rules and Guidelines is equated with the state budget and/or budget on local municipalities and higher territorial units. Any fiscal assessment that states impacts on the state budget must be referred to the Ministry of Finance, which provides both a qualitative check on the analysis provided and most importantly, formal approval to such an impact. Without such formal approval, the draft legislation will not have the chance to be approved by the government. None of the remaining three categories (economic, employment and environment impact assessment) has a formal body within the Slovak system of impact assessment that checks the quality of the analysis conducted. This may have an influence on IA practice.

Economic impact assessment is not elaborated further in the Legislative Rules and thus is entirely open to the individual interpretation of the ministries. Guidelines specify economic impact assessment as the impacts on citizens, the business sector and legal entities. However, the Guidelines provide a fifth category (business environment), and it is not clear what difference there is between economic and business impact assessment. Impact assessment on employment, on the other hand, is defined by Legislative Rules within the context of the ministry's needs for labour and organization, whereas the Guidelines do not discuss this category. None of the documents elaborate upon environmental impact assessment, mostly due to the existance of a specific law on enviromental impact assessment.

There is no specific requirement for *consultations*, and the only category found in both the Legislative Rules and Guidelines is the so called 'commenting period'. This period asks for opinions on draft legislation from all ministries and relevant subordinated agencies as well as the public. In practice, any draft legislation has to be put on the Internet so the public has the opportunity to provide comments. If more than 500 signatures are gathered, the originating ministry is required to substantiate its potential refusal for incorporating the comments. In this way, consultation is understood primarily as the inter-ministerial process of gathering opinions once a draft law is ready. Consultations with the public (and NGOs) are understood as a passive way of gathering opinions rather than active involvement of specific groups that will be most affected by the draft proposal. The EU approach to impact assessment is more pluralistic than the one just presented because it draws explicitly on notions of participatory governance and on the idea of democratizing expertise (Mandelkern 2001).

Harmonization of two documents guiding the IA process, together with clarifying the IA process and the improvement in the clarity of presentation of assessments (clear guidelines as to the substance, clear indicators and measures) would help individual ministries and civil servants to ensure that they are using consistent approaches towards IAs. Improving the clarity of presentation would also assist stakeholders in understanding the impacts, and in this way improve the quality of policy-making.

Normative Contents Analysis

Information on impact assessment can usually be found in the general explanatory memorandum, in a specialized section on impact assessments (Statement of Impacts according to the Guidelines), or in both. Sometimes a summary can be found in the explanatory memorandum with a referral to a detailed calculation in the Statement of Impacts. Other times it can be the opposite way round. In some of the explanatory memoranda a referral is mentioned for a detailed calculation (analysis, modelling and so on) that can be found in a third document. However, this is often not attached to the explanatory memorandum and thus it is impossible to check the methodology or results of the analysis. Such variable information presentation in the explanatory memoranda makes it difficult for both decision makers or any interested party to check the information contained in the explanatory memoranda. Table 13.2 provides a summary of data evaluation of information in explanatory memoranda on impact assessment.

Existence and Extent of IA Information

Formally, all draft legislation in Slovakia complies with the Slovak requirement of attaching an impact assessment to the material that goes for government sessions (see Table 13.3). However, out of 93 draft laws submitted to the government sessions during the period of 1 May–31 December 2004 (thus the period after the EU accession) as many as 63 draft laws (67%) only formally state expressions such as 'no impact' or 'will bring positive impact'. They offer no quantitative or qualitative substantiation in all four required categories (fiscal, economic, environmental and employment). An additional 11% (10 draft laws) also provide only formal information, although expressed in monetary terms. However, again any evidence or information as to how the figures have been calculated is lacking, and thus there is no possibility of checking the validity of the estimates. Only twenty draft laws (22%) have undergone substantial impact assessments which not only quantify the estimates of impacts but also show exactly how the quantification has been calculated (and even provide alternatives). However, none of the draft laws in Slovakia had a substantial analysis in more than two categories at once which fundamentally breaks the principle of 'integrated' IA in social, economic and environmental aspects as proposed by the European Commission.

These results of the formal existence of IA in Slovakia without real substance only confirm the notion of Radaelli (2005) who argues that IA policy process is shaped by context in terms of dimensions and mechanisms. He claims that the particularly European continental context of public administration institutions and bureaucracy is different from the Anglo-Saxon where IA originated. In this sense '*efficiency still comes second to formal respect of legitimate procedures in the list of criteria used by bureaucracies*' (Radaelli 2005, p. 11). In addition, a transition country (or a newly accessed country with transition legacy) constitutes yet another specific context. First, the bureaucracy still bears the legacy of 'non-activism' and thus increases the chances for the presence of formalism where the IA process is reduced to a bureaucratic tick-off exercise and a

Table 13.2   Summary of data on evaluation of information in explanatory memoranda on impact assessment

RESPONSIBLE MINISTRY	IMPACT ASSESSMENT										
	1.1. No IA	1.2. Formal IA		1.3. Substantial IA		2. Types of IA					3. References
	No IA	A: Verbal	B: Monetary	C: Partial	D: Complex	2.1. Social (A+B+C)	2.2. Fiscal (A+B+C)	2.3. Economic (A)	2.4. Environmental (A)	2.5. Organizational (A)	
Agriculture (n=6)	0	6	0	0	0	6+0+0	6+0+0	6	6	0	1
Culture (n=1)	0	1	0	0	0	1+0+0	1+0+0	1	1	0	0
Construction & regional dvlpt (n=3)	0	2	0	1	0	3+0+0	2+0+1	3	3	0	0
Defence (n=2)	0	1	1	0	0	2+0+0	1+1+0	2	2	1	0
Economy (n=12)	0	10	0	2	0	12+0+0	10+0+2	12	12	0	2
Education (n=2)	0	1	0	1	0	2+0+0	1+0+1	2	2	0	0
Environment (n=6)	0	4	1	1	0	5+0+0	4+1+1	5	5	1	0
Finance (n=20)	0	17	2	1	0	20+0+0	17+2+1	20	20	0	1
Foreign (n=0)	0	0	0	0	0	0+0+0	0+0+0	0	0	0	0
Health (n=5)	0	4	0	1	0	5+0+0	4+0+1	4	5	0	1
Interior (n=8)	0	0	4	4	0	7+1+0	0+4+4	8	8	0	1
Justice (n=17)	0	10	0	7	0	17+0+0	10+0+7	17	17	0	0
Labour & social affairs (n=5)	0	1	2	2	0	5+0+0	1+2+2	5	5	0	0

241

Table 13.2 (continued)

RESPONSIBLE MINISTRY	IMPACT ASSESSMENT										
	1.1. No IA	1.2. Formal IA		1.3. Substantial IA		2. Types of IA					3. References
		A: Verbal	B: Monetary	C: Partial	D: Complex	2.1. Social (A+B+C)	2.2. Fiscal (A+B+C)	2.3. Economic (A)	2.4. Environmental (A)	2.5. Organizational (A)	
Telecommunications (n=6)	0	6	0	0	0	6+0+0	6+0+0	6	6	0	1
Sum (n= acts)*	0	63	10	20	0	92+1+0	63+10+20	93+0+0	93+0+0	2	6
Sum % (93=100%)	0	67%	11%	22%	0%	99%	68%+11%+21%	100%	100%	2%	6%

Note: EXISTENCE and EXTENT of impact assessment [IA] information (1.1–1.3): 1.1. No IAis attached, 1.2. Formal IA, statements to categories 2.1.–2.5. either in verbal or monetized way, however, without logic or evidence provided, 1.3. Substantial, full assessments of impacts in 1–2 categories from 2.1.–2.5 (partial) or in 3 or more categories (complex).

TYPES of IA: 2.1. Social impact assessment, e.g identification of target groups and their socio-economic, etc. situation, 2.2. Fiscal on state and local authorities level, e.g clear statements like 'no additional costs', 2.3. Economic – e.g. cost–benefit, implementation costs, 2.4. Environmental IA, e.g. issues of sustainable development, 2.5. Organizational and administrative changes and impacts, e.g. reorganization of work, action plans, training, etc.

3. References – studies, analyses, expert opinions, reports, etc. on impacts related to IA categories in 2.1.–2.5.

Source: Calculations by the author.

Table 13.3 Sample characteristics for 93 draft laws: existence and extent of IA

Category		Formal IA		Substantial	
No of Drafts	No IA	Verbal	Monetary	Partial	Complex
93	0	63	10	20	0
drafts=100%	0%	67%	11%	22%	0%

Table 13.4 Types of IA and extent of IA

Types of IA Extent of IA	Social	Environmental	Economic	Fiscal	Organizational
Formal verbal	92 (99%)	93 (100%)	93 (100%)	63 (68%)	2 (2%)
Formal monetary	0	0	0	10 (11%)	0
Substantial partial	1 (1%)	0	0	20 (21%)	0
Substantial complex	0	0	0	0	0

political tool for substantiating a preferred option. Second, newly accessed countries still bear the legacy of heavy legislative activity due to the adoption of *acquis communitaire* which may have contributed in creating a specific context of reduced will to conduct assessments for imposed legislation. Third, the systematic data collection and analysis is still in the process of establishment. Whatever the reason for specific context, ignoring the importance of IA may increase the risk of inadequate basis for decision-making and subsequent poor policies.

Types of IA Information

Table 13.4 shows that all of the draft laws studied from the period 1 May–31 December 2004 have indicated verbal fulfilment in all four categories required by law: employment, fiscal, environmental and economic. However, information on the administrative and organizational assessment of implementation of the draft law is in general absent: only 2% of all draft laws have some indication of implementation. This may be related to the fact that the Legislative Rules do not require this type of assessment, and although the Guidelines do ask for it, it is in such an imprecise and unclear way that it is difficult to find other requirements in the text. Surprisingly, the environmental impact assessment remained solely on a formal level despite the volume and tradition of environmental impact assessments that exist in the developed world.

With the exception of one case, all of the substantial impact assessments have been conducted in the fiscal assessment. Similarly, all of the monetized formal assessments (that is those that do not provide evidence or logic as to how that monetization has been arrived at) have been conducted in the fiscal area. Two possible explanations of this imbalance can be suggested. First, fiscal assessment or in other words, implications for the state budget, was traditionally part of the explanatory memoranda. Thus, civil servants are used to the preparation of this part and know how to tackle it. Second, there exists a requirement for the Ministry of Finance to check the quality of assessments on state budgets. Without a body at the governmental level to check the quality of assessments conducted in other areas, there is only a minimal motivation from the side of the ministries to conduct proper substantial impact assessments in the other categories. Whatever the reason behind the fact that only fiscal impact assessment is conducted in a substantial way, it violates the European Commission's principle of balancing impact assessments among the categories to achieve the highest possible cross-sectoral and inter-linkage effect (European Commission 2004).

As far as the interpretation of individual categories is concerned, the legislative requirements already have a narrower meaning than the recommendations of the European Commission and OECD countries (see the discussion on types of impact assessment in the methodology part and legislative background presented earlier). Furthermore, a narrowing of the individual types of IA occurs when the impact assessments are conducted. For example, all of the ministries limit the discussion of 'employment' strictly to 'employment within the state and public service', and not the labour market in general. Consequently, such an interpretation is considered to increase/decrease the burden of the state budget on staff recruitment or dismissal and has become a political tool in the decision-making. Besides, such an interpretation also fits more appropriately into the category of administrative/organizational impacts. Those ministries that follow the Guidelines and thus look at the economic impact assessment defined as impact on 'citizens, businesses and legal entities' interpret these as living standards of the citizens and 'fitting into the goals of the economic policy', though none of the studied draft laws and explanatory memoranda elaborate on this in more detail (all of the statements are on a formal level, such as 'very positive impact on living standards' and so on). This finding is of particular concern when we consider that during the period under study, five of the most important laws passed were on the reform of the health system and services, yet, none of these indicate any impact on citizens or the economy.

In the follow-up qualitative research, these interpretations will be further confirmed, and more detail for the rationale behind these findings will be sought.

Evidence Based Research

One of the guiding principles set by the European Commission (and 'quality regulation' literature) for the impact assessment process is that of transparency. It states that it must 'be clear to all stakeholders and general public how the Commission [and national governments] assesses the expected impacts of its legislation . . . what are the data and methodology that are used' (European Commission 2004, p. 7). Similarly, other OECD countries emphasize the need for validity and quality control of IAs. For example, in the US the guidelines for IAs specifically ask for an assessment, including the underlying analysis (Hahn 2000). Radaelli (2005, p. 22) argues that legitimacy and credibility is much more important than efficiency. In this sense the stakeholders have the right to know how their views have been incorporated into IAs, how science is validated and by whom and how government produces its numbers. This part of the chapter shows the extent of transparency in the undertaking and/or presentation of the IA by tracing whether explanatory memoranda provide sources (such as existing and/or specially ordered analyses, studies, pilot projects, statistics, opinion polls, reports and so on) and details of the type of analytical methods that have been utilized for the conduct of the analyses. These elements enable the tracing and validating of the results of such an analysis.

The explanatory notes hardly ever give the results of any research or analysis, whether performed internally by civil servants or by independent consultants or entities. The small number of draft acts with this type of information (only 6% of all draft laws, see Table 13.2), have only mentioned that analysis was conducted, without providing details of the analysis itself (such as the title of the research, its main conclusions and data). A note indicating where it can be found is also missing in a number of cases. These analyses, however, provided the basis for the rationale in preparing the draft act rather than being a source of information for the undertaking of impact assessments. No mention is made of the methods of analysis that were used. Similarly, there is no mention of external experts employed in the process of draft law development, despite the fact that explanatory memoranda specifically ask for this information. This is quite a surprising finding when we consider that in a transition country there are many external advisors, experts and institutions who participate in the reforms (ranging from the World Bank's involvement in the health reform, to twinning programmes in the EU, to local advisors and experts, subordinated research institutes and so on).

Some explanatory memoranda discuss the practice in foreign countries and quote data or statistics (or practice) from those. However, the data used from such data sources do not follow proper citing principles and therefore, it is difficult to verify the data that are provided. Reference to the external consultants utilized during the preparation of the draft law was found to be minimal (this occurred on only one occasion), although it is a common practice to employ working groups and external experts for the works on draft legislation. This practice may be simply the result of poor education in quoting and paraphrasing, which is widespread in transition countries. However, violation of the European Commission's transparency principle occurs frequently in this way. This is particularly important if we consider that the decision makers and politicians in both government and Parliament should be reaching agreements and decisions on the basis of the evidence with which they are provided.

Consultations

'*Those affected by European or national regulation have the right to be able to access it and understand it*' (Mendelkern Report 2001, p. ii). The European Commission gives big importance to consultation mechanisms throughout the whole legislative process, from policy-shaping prior to the proposal to final adoption of a measure by the legislature and implementation. Depending on the issues at stake, consultation is intended to provide opportunities for input from representatives of regional and local authorities, civil society organizations, undertakings and associations of undertakings, the individual citizens concerned, academics and technical experts, and interested parties. This is fully in line with the EU's legal framework, which states that '*the Commission should [. . .] consult widely before proposing legislation and, wherever appropriate, publish consultation documents*' (Protocol (No. 7) on the application of the principles of subsidiarity and proportionality, annexed to the Amsterdam Treaty, quoted in European Commission 2002c, p. 4). To this end the European Commission established a new consultation framework outlined in the document *Towards a Reinforced Culture of Consultation and Dialogue* (European Commission 2002c).

In Slovakia, the results of the consultation process (that is the gathering of opinions from relevant public bodies on the draft law, their analyses and the responses of the originating ministry) are presented in a separate document within explanatory memoranda in a very organized manner, usually as a table. This table enlists the name of the institution, its comments and the response of the originating ministry (acceptance/non-acceptance of the comments and reasons for that). Ninety-seven percent of all draft laws within the monitored period presented the results of the consultation process in a very organized way, including summaries of the parties consulted, summaries of opinions, and indications of accepted and non-accepted opinions with reasons. Opinions mostly come from other ministries, subordinated agencies and other public institutions to which the originating ministry is obliged to send (in an electronic form) the draft proposal for opinions. Also, the opinion gathering process is well organized, and methodological guidelines exist for the types of opinions, procedures to follow when the opinions are rejected and so on. In sum, there seems to be no problems with this process.

Nevertheless, the identification of external actors outside the government and their active consultation is still lagging behind. Besides the obligation of agencies to provide comments only three other stakeholders were mentioned in the explanatory memoranda. Seventeen percent of all the draft laws that were considered had comments from the nongovernmental sector, 8% received comments from municipalities and 3% from independent experts. There are several possibilities for such low numbers. Although the Slovak system (revolutionary in the Central and Eastern European context) provides the possibility for the external actors to step into the process (the opinion gathering process is public and accessible via the Internet once the draft law is ready),[10] in practice, it is a rather passive way of consulting and not user friendly for those who would like to be more involved in the process.[11] The provision of information is still relatively passive and difficult to understand for people with no legal knowledge or orientation in the documents.[12] It also comes at too late a stage in the whole process, as most of such materials are already prepared to be approved by the government, and civil servants are reluctant to deal with comments from the public at such a late stage. The biggest problem is that a formal procedure must be observed by the public participating in the process of opinion gathering. In practice this means that the legal formulation of comments, including those from the public, is extremely important. If a comment is to be regarded as 'substantial', it must be signed by at least 500 citizens (or 300 for non-legislative materials). Such a substantial comment must then be dealt with by civil servants, who must also explain why it was or was not accepted. However, if the comment is not substantial, it does not have to be taken into consideration.

Slovakian practice thus corresponds to the international practice as far as the gathering of opinions within the government sector is considered, or so called passive consultation.[13] However, public and active consultation is still not conducted in a way that corresponds with the standards of the EU. Prior to any consultations, it is important to identify the most affected parties for which the issues of equity should be considered (as well as the costs and benefits for those particular groups). This may enable governments to prepare the consultation process adequately, and actively seek input from relevant parties on the basis of sound criteria. Absence of the

precise identification of affected parties may prevent any reliable discussion
of costs and benefits (European Commission 2002c; Mandelkern 2001).

Quality of Information in Substantial Impact Assessments

Having identified those impact assessments in the explanatory memoranda
that fulfil the criterion of 'substantial impact assessment', those that
provide logic and evidence on the quantifications are further assessed for
the quality of the information. Thus, the evaluation in this section of the
chapter focuses on the substantive quality of the government's impact
assessment, its comprehensiveness and the precision of information contained in IAs. The review of information quality uses the indicators of
quality as set by the practice of the Organization for Economic
Cooperation, and the European Commission.

Twenty draft laws that fulfilled the criterion of substantial impact assessment were further analysed in terms of the quality of information they contained. The biggest number of substantial impact assessments was
conducted in the Ministry of Justice and Interior (see Figure 13.2 and Table
13.2), followed by the Ministry of Labour. It is quite interesting to note that
the Ministry of Finance only once conducted a substantial impact assessment. Similarly, the Ministry of Environment has only once conducted a
substantial impact assessment despite the fact that the EIA was already
introduced in 1994.

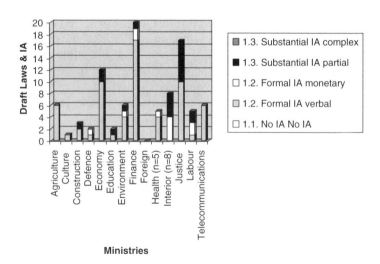

Ministries

*Figure 13.2   Sample characteristics for 93 draft laws according to
individual ministries*

The findings of the evaluation of the quality of substantial impact assessment against the selected indicators match the preliminary findings on the low quality of analysis. The following paragraphs summarize the findings related to the quality of information on impact assessment. In terms of the identification of affected parties, both internal and external, all of the substantial impact assessments identify the state as the prime bearer of any costs or benefits. This hardly provides an improved understanding of the impact of costs and benefits on different groups, which subsequently allows policy makers to address distributional concerns more effectively. Only 10% identify other parties in addition to the state, such as municipalities, state-owned undertakings and so on, which are still parties related to state activities (airport and railways are still in the hands of the state). However, no further thought is given to the impacts on these parties. Private actors, civil society and citizens are not a part of impact assessment.

The Mandelkern Report (2001) identifies cost-benefit analysis as the most rigorous framework for the assessment of impacts, both positive and negative. The primary purpose to assess and preferably quantify the costs and benefits is to assist the ministry (and government) in selecting among alternatives and policy tools (Hahn 2000) and to systematically appraise distributional consequences (social, economic and environmental) of proposed change (Kirkpatrick 2003). In consideration of the analysis and comparison of the costs and benefits associated with the regulation (quantification and so on), it was found that all of the substantial IAs deal with costs, though the assessments are of poor quality. Seventy percent of them deal with the costs of institutionalizing a new post (for example judicial clerk, public defender and so on) or increasing/decreasing a salary to a public official. This high number also explains the greater occurrence of substantial impact assessments in the draft laws of the Ministry of Justice, since their draft laws focused on new institutions within judiciary reform. Only 20% of substantial IAs state benefits, mostly in regards to the state budget. Comparison of benefits and costs is provided in none of the cases. Such incomplete considerations raise serious questions on the way the assessments have been conducted and whether any alternatives have been considered or whether the calculations represent ex post justifications of the preferred solution.

Other methods of identifying costs are also considered, including cost-effectiveness analysis (which does not have to consider benefits), compliance cost analysis (which estimates the likely costs of complying with the new regulation) and so on. This part looks at quantifications but also qualitative estimations of non-monetary impacts to avoid a one-sided cost-focused picture. Naturally, the estimations have to be substantial and not formal, such as statements as 'good', etc. In looking at and weighing up costs and benefits over a time framework (short-, medium- and long-term effects) or in variants (assessment of life-time, risks and so on), only one impact assessment tried to identify long-term effects, without any quantifications. Three impact assessments consider minimum and maximum variants. However, none of the impact assessments dealt with the life-time of the draft law or the risks associated with its implementation and so on. In terms of IA analysis and the comparison of positive and negative impacts of the regulation, a number of IAs were justifying the introduction of a new law by stating that if it was not introduced, sanctions from the EU would cause much higher costs than those linked to the introduction of the measure. However, none of these 'threats' are quantified.

The European Commission in its proposal *Impact Assessment: Next Steps* (2002a) urges the consideration of social, economic, financial, environmental and administrative aspects in an integrated and balanced manner in order to avoid sectorialism. In examining the inter-linkages between the IAs, it is apparent that only fiscal IAs were conducted. The only impact assessment in the social sphere was linked to fiscal impact assessment (and could be considered as such).

In sum, the analytical content of information in the substantial impact assessment attached to the explanatory memoranda is very low. It is limited to quantifications according to the state budget, and most of these are linked to the costs of additional human resources. The practice of considering impact assessment primarily for the public sector seems widespread. Even where there are indications that a more in-depth analysis had been conducted, the civil servants neglected to attach it to the explanatory memoranda and did not refer to it. The nature of the information contained in explanatory memoranda (and impact assessments) suggests that they are made ex post in a bureaucratic manner to fulfil obligations rather than being created during the policy-making process (which would then assist the decision maker to make an evidence based decision). However, this hypothesis, supported by findings in the first stage of the research needs to be tested in the follow-up interviews with civil servants who prepare impact assessments.

IV.   CONCLUSIONS

The results of the empirical study of the sample of draft laws approved by the government in the period of 1 May–31 December 2004 show that the analytical quality of the impact assessments conducted in Slovak ministries is extremely low: just 22% conduct substantial impact assessment, and in the fiscal area only. Thus, most of the draft laws fulfil only the minimal requirement by formally attaching information on impact assessments without providing any informative value. Such poor results raise cause for concern and pose a serious question as to the legitimacy of the decision-making process. At the same time, the presentation of the results of the consultation process is extremely high: 97% of all draft laws present the results of consultations, acceptance and non-acceptance of opinions. However, one has to bear in mind that this is a passive type of consultation. The opinion gathering process occurs mostly among public organizations and although it is open to the public, the activism has to come from the public side.

These results indicate that the continental transitional context of IA implementation matters, and in order to succeed in the implementation of the impact assessment tool some further measures have to be adopted by the government. These include the introduction of clear methodology and guidance in this area. The consultation process is well formalized, with clear guidance and easy-to-complete tables which has enabled the ministries to follow the rules. Also, there is a control mechanism in place that takes care of fulfilling the requirement. On the other hand, in the absence of more detailed guidelines and manuals as to how to conduct impact assessment analysis and in the absence of information on clear categories and indicators for the assessments, the statements of impact assessment remain mere statements on a very formal level, lacking value for the decision maker. Also, there is an urgent need to clearly interpret in a coordinated way the individual categories of types of impact assessment in a much broader sense than is the case today, in order to correspond with the dimensions as identified by the European Commission. These results indicate that there is a need for more sophisticated analytical methods to be employed in assessing regulatory impacts, training for the conduct of these analyses, and a quality checking mechanism that would control the level and depth of analysis conducted. On the other hand, there exists an indication that to a certain extent analytical methods are being utilized in the individual ministries. However, these are not presented in the explanatory memoranda, and further research is needed among civil servants as to the practice of conducting IAs. In any case, the absence of these analyses decreases the legitimacy of decision-making in the governmental sessions (or Parliament) as presumably decisions should be made on the basis of the evidence provided. More work has to be done in order to make explanatory memoranda (and impact assessments) an integrated part of policy- and decision-making, rather than it remaining as a bureacratic tool (which is how it is currently perceived by civil servants).

Naturally, as the whole process of impact assessments was introduced only in 2001, there has to be a period for the development of skills.

However, the current absence of thorough impact assessments results in a technocratic and formalistic approach to the issue, that will not develop the skills of the civil servants. Therefore, it is extremely important to create a system of motivation and sanctions for the undertaking of impact assessments that does not demand sophisticated econometric measures. Even the simple process of asking the right questions in order to prepare for the impact assessment can add value and understanding to policy development, and the level of complexity and effort in it can increase as expertise develops and resources are made available.

ACKNOWLEDGEMENTS

I would like to thank Aare Kasemets from Estonia and Zsombor Kovacsy from Hungary for insightful discussions on the possibility of measuring the quality of impact assessments conducted in Central and Eastern Europe during our meetings in Bratislava in 2003 and Riga in early 2005. I am grateful to the editors of this volume for their useful comments on the earlier drafts of this chapter. Also, I would like to thank Barbora Kahatova for the assistance in the compilation of data.

NOTES

1. The research on this chapter was supported and enabled thanks to the International Policy Fellowship at the Center for Policy Studies at the Central European University, Budapest, Hungary.
2. The draft methodology of this research is based on initial endeavours between K Staroňová (Slovakia), A Kasemets (Estonia) and Zs Kovacsy (Hungary).
3. The European Commission introduced the so called 'better regulation package' in early 2002; see more on the impact assessment website, http://europa.eu.int/comm/secretariat_general/impact/pol_en.htm; OECD (1995) *Recommendation on Improving the Quality of Government Regulation*; and (1997) *Policy Recommendations on Regulatory Reform*; and (2005) OECD *Guiding Principles on Regulatory Quality and Performance* – see, http://www.oecd.org/document/38/0,2340,en_2649_37421_2753254_1_1_1_37421,00.html.
4. For evolution of impact assessment use in the European Commission see Radaelli 2005.
5. The construction of indicators follows the IA dimensions of 'process', 'activities and output' and 'real world outcome', whereas the tests look at 'contents', 'outcome' and 'function'. These approaches are not necessarily mutually exclusive (Radaelli 2005).
6. Staronova, K (2004) offers a discussion on the institutionalization and practice of the policy process stages, arguing that only the stage of policy adoption is formalized in the form of the legislative process.
7. The only exception is environmental impact assessment that has been conducted prior to 2001. The Environmental Impact Assessment Act was adopted in 1994 and reviewed in 2000 to meet EU requirements such as the SEA. In order to comply with also additional requirements such as securing effective public participation a new law on EIA has been submitted to the Parliament in 2005.

8. The most striking contradiction is the use of terminology for impact assessment which is not harmonized in the documents. Legislative Rules use the term 'dopad', whereas Guidelines use the term 'vplyv'. Impact assessment as a concept and process is a relatively new phenomenon and there is still discussion going on about proper Slovak terminology.

9. The Office of Management and Budget in the US has been assigned the task of reviewing draft RIAs produced by agencies and checking the agencies' compliance with its guidelines (Hahn et al. 2000). A similar task is assigned to the Cabinet Office Regulatory Unit in the UK that produces guidelines and manuals. The European Commission also provides a number of handbooks and step-by-step guidelines on impact assessment, such as *Guidelines on IA* (2002), *Handbook on IA* (2002) that were revised in mid 2005. Moreover, as the impact assessment is considered to be an open process, the stakeholders involved in the process ensure that the relevant standards are observed, whereas the overall quality is observed by SG (European Commission 2002a). OECD has prepared a checklist of questions that should be addressed by IA.

10. Free Access to Information Law that came into effect in 2001 opened up the commenting process of draft legislation.

11. For a more detailed discussion on problems in the policy-making process (rather than outcomes) in Slovakia, see Staronova (2004).

12. The draft proposals that are publicly available on the internet are in the form of a legal text in articles, often only providing those articles that amend the previous law. In this way, anybody who is interested in providing comments has to also find the original law, compare the contents of the legal text and answer (provide opinion) in a correct nomotechnical way (legal). Also, the draft laws available for public commenting are organized chronologically rather than thematically which requires anybody who would like to be involved in the process to follow closely what is happening in governmental sessions.

13. Passive consultation refers to the approach of seeking written comment in response to published regulatory information (Deighton-Smith 2004, p. 67). Electronic access to law and commenting is considered to be one of the major tools for both effective passive consultation and transparency by improving its availability and reducing costs of access (Deighton-Smith 2004). For example, on 3 April 2001 the European Commission adopted a Communication on Interactive Policy Making (C(2001) 1014), which aims to improve governance by using the Internet for collecting and analysing reactions for use in the European Union's policy-making process (European Commission 2002c).

REFERENCES

Deighton, Smith (2004), 'Regulatory transparency in OECD countries: overview, trends and challenges', *Australian Journal of Public Administration*, 63 (1), 66–78.

European Commission (2002a), *Impact Assessment in the Commission – Guidelines*, http://europa.eu.int/comm/secretariat_general/impact/index_en.htm.

European Commission (2002b), *A Handbook for Impact Assessment in the Commission – How To Do an Impact Assessment*.

European Commission (2002c), *Towards a Reinforced Culture of Consultation and Dialogue: Proposal for General Principles and Minimum Standards for Consultation of Interested Parties by Commission*, Communication from the Commission, July, Brussels.

European Commission (2004), Commission report on impact assessment, *Next Steps – In Support of Competitiveness and Sustainable Development*, SEC(2004)1377 of 21 October 2004.

Guidelines for the preparation and submission of material for government sessions of the Slovak republic No. 512/2001.

Hahn, R W and Litan, R E (1997), *Improving Regulatory Accountability*, Washington D.C., Brookings Institution Press.

Hahn, R W and Litan, R E (March 2003), *Recommendations for Improving Regulatory Accountability and Transparency*, Working Paper, Joint Center.

Hahn, R W, Burnett, J K, Chan, Y I, Mader, E A and Moyle, P R (2000), *Assessing the Quality of Regulatory Impact Analyses*, Working Paper 00-1, AEI – Brooking Joint Center for Regulatory Studies, January.

Jacobs, Scott (1997), 'An overview of regulatory impact analysis in OECD countries' in OECD *Regulatory Impact Analysis: Best Practices in OECD Countries*, Paris, OECD.

Kirkpatrick, Colin and Parker, David (2003), *Regulatory Impact Assessment: Developing its Potential for Use in Developing Countries*, Manchester, Centre on Regulation and Competition.

Legislative rules of the government as amended by the government ruling No. 1118 from 1999 and No. 1130 from 2001 [Legislatívne pravidlá vlády SRč. 241/1997 v znení Uznesenia vlády č. 1118 z decembra 1999 a Uznesenia č. 1130 z novembra 2001].

Mandelkern Group Report (2001), *Final Report*, Brussels, 13 November. Available at, http://www.cabinetoffice.gov.uk/regulation/docs/europe/pdf/mandfinrep.pdf.

OECD (1997a), *Law Drafting and Regulatory Management in Central and Eastern Europe*, Paris, SIGMA Papers No. 18.

OECD (1997b), *Regulatory Impact Analysis: Best Practice in OECD Countries*, Paris, OECD Publications.

OECD (2005), *OECD Guiding Principles on Regulatory Quality and Peformance*, Paris, OECD Publications.

Radaelli, Claudio M (2005), 'How context matters: regulatory quality in the European Union', in *Journal of European Public Policy*.

Staroňová K (2004), 'Public policy making in Slovakia', *NISPAcee Occasional Papers*, V (3), 3–18.

Zubek, Radoslaw (2005), 'Complying with transposition commitments in Poland: collective dilemmas, core executive and legislative outcomes', *West European Politics*, 28 (3), 592–619.

14. Challenges of regulating integrated impact assessment: the case of Slovenia

Mojca Golobic and Franc Zakrajšek

I. INTRODUCTION

Sustainability concerns ideally should be integrated in all fields of public action and regulation, above all in spatial planning and environment protection. This chapter discusses the options for such implementation. Policy actions have diverse consequences: not all of them are intended or even considered. It can be assumed that any policy with formal instruments for the implementation of its objectives[1] will have some impacts on the environment. Even the measures explicitly intended for environmental protection can cause adverse impacts on some component or part of the environment. For example, nature protection areas can cause excessive pressure on neighbouring areas (Pfefferkorn et al 2005). The ability to predict and understand these consequences enables us to either avoid the unwanted effects or to reach an agreement in society to accept them. This means that the possible impacts have to be assessed before the action actually takes place.

Present legal regulation in most Western countries requires environmental impacts of projects to be systematically assessed. While the appraisals on a project level have already a considerable tradition and history, the need to assess the hierarchically higher documents (plans, programmes and policies) was recognized more recently, partly in response to the limitations of a project level approach (Owens et al 2004; Haq 2004). The theory and practice of assessment show a very wide scope in terms of what could be the subject of assessment as well as which aspects need to be assessed (Owens et al 2004). Although the initial attempts of EU regulators reflected this complexity, particularly in considerations regarding the scope of strategic environmental assessment (SEA) application (Resolution 93/C 138/01), the resulting Directive 2001/42/EC limited the scope of assessment to *certain* plans and programmes, explicitly omitting the defence and civil protection documents and budget plans as well as the highest levels of policy and law making documents. On the other hand, the SEA Protocol to the UNECE convention on EIA in a trans-boundary context (2003) includes these aspects as non-binding. This limitation of the scope of assessment is probably a good indicator of the challenges that the regulators face when trying to formalize such a complex set of issues. These challenges have been discussed extensively in scientific and decision-making communities and will hopefully inform the further regulatory attempts of other forms of assessments, which are still under consideration (see, for example, Caratti et al 2004; Dalal-Clayton and Sadler 2004, 2005).

The intent of this chapter is to contribute to these discussions using the experience gained from a relatively long (strategic) environmental impact assessment practice in Slovenia, as well as from the recent attempts to legally regulate strategic impact assessment. The paper will present some evidence confirming that regulating SEA is not a trivial task. Regulation inevitably requires simplification and formalization, which can easily impede the complex and inclusive nature of SEA (or SA), especially in its integrated form. The experience from Slovenia shows that even a long and rather successful tradition of impact assessments does not guarantee an easy and effective transfer into legislation. While the practice has led to the integrative type of assessment, which is focused in improvement of the decision-making process, the regulation seems to focus on the ex post type, with the product (the report) as a base for granting the environmental consent. As such the procedure is more the aim in itself, more intended to grant the discretion power to environmental authorities, than a means to achieve the environmentally sound policies (Kontic 2005). The Slovenian example also shows that learning from the spatial planning procedures could be a more fruitful way towards integrated SEA than simply expanding the EIA experience to a strategic level. The differences between the last two seem more fundamental than differences between spatial planning and strategic environmental assessments. The latter share some important common characteristics, such as close intertwinement with the decision-making process and the requirement to negotiate conservation requests with development needs.

II. CHALLENGES IN REGULATING THE ASSESSMENT PROCESS

Effective regulation of the integrative assessment process needs to resolve (among others) three main questions. First, what are the main aspects of assessment (scope)? Second, which actors are involved, and what are their roles and responsibilities? Third, what methods and techniques should be applied (and how can public participation be ensured)? Each of these questions is now considered.

Scope of the Assessment

The assessment should ultimately help to answer the question of whether the proposed policy action together with its potentially negative outcomes is acceptable. In the case of EIA, the acceptability of a project can usually be established unambiguously (for example by referring to the emission limits), while the necessity of the project is never questioned. However, the situation is quite different on the strategic level. The answer to the question of which impacts a society is willing to accept depends on what the gains are that the society will receive in exchange. If there are few or no benefits, the acceptability of environmental costs is much lower. So, the question can be answered positively only when the social benefits outweigh the environmental costs. The benefits and the social demand for them therefore inevitably (explicitly or implicitly) become a part of the assessment (Jiliberto 2004). The question of the necessity of the proposed policy intervention cannot be answered by the initiator (as is the case with the projects submitted to EIA) but must be addressed to the society as a whole. Benefits are often not limited to profit: they (should) also include general economic growth, new jobs, improvement in social and human capital and so on. All these are public interests. On the other hand, an economically failed plan or programme may place a huge burden on the public good, regardless how low its environmental impacts might be. The institution of prevailing public interest (as applied by the documents regulating the Natura2000 programme) clearly highlights this problem: there may be several, and conflicting public interests, each related to a sustainability objective. Any assessment on the strategic level therefore very soon extends beyond the environmental sector (Haq 2004) and calls for more comprehensive approaches to address natural, social, cultural and economic aspects of the environment, as well as geographical and generational equity considering the distribution of costs and benefits.

The other reason why the impact assessment can (and indeed) should scrutinize the policy action objectives as well as the wider value systems in society, is that these do bias the assessment to some extent. Drawing on the case of the UK's transport policy assessment (NATA), Owens et al argue that the general policy climate and dominant discourses in any given policy sector can pre-empt or permit certain kinds of analyses (Owens et al 2004). While this is unavoidable, it should be recognized and clarified by the assessment process.

Roles and Responsibilities

Despite their clear social relevance, environmental impact assessments remained a relatively isolated field, independent from development planning and programming, and entrusted to (mainly natural science) experts. This separation has a historical background: before the so called environmental crisis, the results of which are also the EIAs, economic (feasibility) appraisals were the only type of assessment applied to projects and plans. The motivation for these assessments has been clearly on the side of the developer, for whom the acceptability of an intervention was the matter of profit. It took a huge shift to turn the optic the other way round and put the environment at the centre of project acceptability. The recognition that environmental costs are not included in market price also shifted the decision-making arena from market to state regulatory mechanisms. However, neither the market nor the politics seem to be able to achieve the ideal goal of decoupling economic gains from environmental costs (von Schomberg 2002).

While this antagonistic situation between a (private) developer, who is concerned about the profit, and the community, who is concerned about the negative externalities, is rather clear on the project level, these interrelations become much more complex on the strategic level. There would normally be many different actors involved in the preparation and assessment of a policy action: the institution responsible for plan or programme preparation (initiator), the assessors, the authorities responsible for the approval and the (various groups of) public, with sometimes overlapping, ambiguous and changing roles. But when it comes to the legal regulation of a procedure, clear distribution of roles and responsibilities becomes an important issue. The question here is, 'Who can legitimately decide upon what basis?' (von Schomberg 2002).

The answer to this question depends much on the aim and the results of the assessment and the ways it informs the policy- (or decision-) making. SEA can be a recommendation, a guideline for public action or a formal consent to a policy document. If assessment is considered to be a final check of a document before the consent is granted (so called ex post or consent-related SEA), then the policy document draft needs to be submitted to a relatively independent assessment procedure performed by disinterested assessors. Such a straightforward relation between the assessment and decision-making is typical for project EIA. However, the strategic assessment can only seldom be an unambiguous ascertainment, but rather it is guidance for balancing several public interests and optimization of the policy action. This balance is obviously a dynamic one, and the procedure towards it is in reality far from a linear flow of rational decision-making

(Dalal-Clayton and Sadler 2005). The assessment can therefore hardly offer support if it is a one-off exercise, performed by experts in a confinement.

Slovenian regulatory attempts obviously derive from the EIA practice and regulation, when focusing on the SEA as an administrative procedure where environmental authorities grant (or refuse) consent to a policy document. The sole base for this decision should be the environmental report, completed by a licensed scientific institution. The dominating role is thus given to the approving body and scientists, while the role of other actors, notably the general public, is inferior. This distribution of roles does not really fit the concept of integrated assessment, since there is no room for optimization or consensus. By shifting the responsibility and discretion power away from the elected decision makers and from democratic towards technocratic decision processes, it resembles the unpopular elite or 'eco-dictatorial' type of deliberation about sustainability (von Schomberg 2002; Haq 2004).

Methodological Issues

The question of methodology is not as obviously related to the legal regulation of assessment but it is crucial to ensure the quality of results. The methodologies and tools should be used to help to obtain a firm knowledge base for decisions. This information is usually presented as a quantitative or qualitative estimation of costs and benefits for each of the alternative options. The SEAs are usually dealing with relatively abstract and general policy statements, where neither the technology of intervention nor the territory of action is determined. In such a situation the impacts can hardly be identified with any level of reliability, let alone quantified, and the empirical proofs cannot be provided. Holistic and intuitive techniques (expert interviews and panels, Delphi) have been prevailing in practice to overcome the problems of lacking reliable quantitative data sets and difficulties with the definition of clear cause–effects relationships. These problems shook the trust in the reliability of existing methods and weakened the legitimacy of decisions, based on resulting findings.

However, these facts do not diminish the need to assess the strategic decisions from the aspect of their environmental impacts. They led on the one hand to the shift of focus from the assessment of impacts to the assessment of the process (for example analytical strategic environmental assessment, ANSEA; Caratti et al 2004) and on the other hand to other ways to ensure the legitimacy of outcomes (von Schomberg 2002; Owens et al 2004). These include transparent procedures, continuous involvement of actors, explanation and discussion of assumptions, uncertainties and methodological questions. This implies new requirements for methods and tools: besides producing 'hard numbers' it is at least as important that they provide a common platform and forum for communication and inclusion of all concerned parties.

The SEA toolbox is becoming more diverse: besides traditionally used impact matrices and indicators, forecasting and scenario development have become a regular part to support future, strategic and quality type of thinking (Dalal-Clayton and Sadler 2004) and risk analysis to deal with uncertain events. Overlay or GIS techniques, originating in land-use planning, provide a semi-quantitative and at the same time practically useful decision-making support, but are applicable only when the policy intervention is location sensitive. Quantitative methods have not lost their appeal since they enable comparison of different aspects (environmental, economic and social) and offer a straightforward input for decision makers. Traditional quantitative methods, such as cost-benefit analysis, are being complemented by indirect assessments (hedonic pricing, contingency evaluations) to include non-financial costs. Alternative quantitative approaches, such as ecologic footprint gain increasing attention (von Schomberg 2002). With a high level of uncertainty however, these methods are much less effective: on the contrary, their apparent exactness may even be misleading.

The issue that is still not adequately resolved is the methodology support for the participation of stakeholders. The requirements to identify and engage the relevant value systems and to display greater sensitivity to the roles and identities of actors (Owens et al 2004) show that these issues are still a weakness of assessment procedures. These requirements cannot be fulfilled by considering stakeholders and the public as objects of research, but only by granting them an active role of a subject, co-responsible for decisions. In the context of complex and controversial issues it is only through public deliberation that technical analysis can gain the essential empirical inputs concerning the selection, definition and prioritization of selection criteria (Stirling 1999). The interactive methodologies, supported by the information and communication technology (Internet), can help to achieve this kind of interaction even on the most strategic levels, where traditional methods such as focus groups and workshops are less applicable. It is important that the involvement is enabled throughout the process, in exploratory, alternative testing and decision-making phases (Carver 1997).

III.   CASE STUDY: THE ASSESSMENT OF SLOVENIAN TRANSPORT POLICY

Assessment theory and practice in Slovenia has quite a long and productive history. Most plans for major (public) undertakings have been assessed in terms of their environmental impacts since the 1970s. The major loan giver (the bank of Ljubljana) explicitly requested that the environmental aspect be assessed among other aspects (health hazard, economic and technical feasibility and so on). Although without a legal base, this institution functioned remarkably effectively, and from today's perspective seems an extremely progressive one. To comply with the recommendations of the assessment, the developers often had to improve their projects in terms of technology, intensity or location. In a few cases the projects were even abandoned due to the negative results of the appraisal. Among the most contradictory ones were the proposal for an oil refinery in the surroundings of Ljubljana and a chemical factory on the coast near Koper. The assessments were formalized in 1993 with the Act on Environmental Protection, which introduced project and strategic environmental impact assessments (EIA and SEA). EIA has been a regular part of permitting procedure since 1996, when the bylaws determined the eligible projects, methodology and scope of EIA. The practice of EIA soon showed that the previous and hierarchically higher decisions (strategies, plans and programmes) narrowed the decision space so that the negative impacts could not be avoided. These findings led to a rather extensive practice of strategic assessments despite the lack of regulatory framework, which would include SEAs in a formal procedure. The new Act on Environmental Protection was passed in 2004 (partly with the precise aim to implement the EU Directive 2001/42/EC) and recently also the bylaw (Decree laying down the content of environmental report and on detailed procedure for the assessment of the effects on certain plans and programmes on the environment 2005). The contents of these two documents do not suggest that lessons were learned from past experiences, which could have contributed towards solving some of the aforementioned issues (Kontic 2005).

On the other hand, the procedures, similar to the integrated type of SEA, developed within the spatial planning procedure. Indeed, most of the interventions requiring environmental assessment had to be included in the spatial planning procedure. The tradition of integrated planning approach led to the comprehensive consideration of impacts on the natural, social and cultural environments, development potentials and other users of space. Probably the biggest public project in Slovenia, the highway programme, triggered amendments to the spatial planning legislation (Amendments to the Act on spatial planning 1996), which introduced the main elements of SEA (development and assessment of alternative proposals) in the planning procedure.

Transport policy is a convenient case to discuss the questions and hypotheses addressed in the first part of the paper, not only because of its complex impacts, but also due to its influence on the practice and regulation of impact assessments in Slovenia. European transport policy (TEN-T) caused significant improvements in accessibility and connectedness after 1991. These effects were even larger in the countries that recently joined the EU: some sections of the Slovenian road network experienced a 200% increase in the amount of traffic in the first few months after accession. A high increase in the use of private cars is also expected, especially if counter measures are not taken. Although the positive economic effects of the improved transport connections cannot be denied, the environmental effects of the traffic, such as greenhouse gas emissions and habitat fragmentation are also well known (Dalkman and Bongart 2004). Most of the negative impacts of the structural funds are related to the construction of new transport routes (EU-SUD 2003).

The Slovenian transport policy was only recently articulated as a coherent set of programmes and measures in a policy document (Resolution on transport policy of Slovenia 2004). However, separate parts of the policy were developed and assessed earlier in different forms.

Assessment of the Highway Plan

The Slovenian highway plan (National programme for highway construction 1994) was the first policy document to be systematically and consistently assessed, and has been in many respects a model for other similar endeavours, as well as for amendments of spatial legislation. This plan proposed to build 540 km of missing highways in the 5th and 10th TEN corridors crossing Slovenia. By approval of the plan Parliament secured the financial resources for its implementation. It was first approved in the year 1994, followed by subsequent amendments of which the last extends the deadline for completing the plan to the year 2013. The initiative for the assessment came from the National Office for Spatial Planning, which was responsible for the spatial planning of the project and also implemented the assessment as a part of planning procedure. The overview of the main steps followed in this process is presented in Figure 14.1. Although the assessment was focused on the project and not on the network level, it was a strategic one because there was still a lot of space for different alternatives within the proposed corridors. The assessment was conceived as a comparative study of alternative routings for each of the individual road sections. The scope of the assessment covered five aspects: impacts on regional and urban development; technological (transport) efficiency; environmental impacts; economical efficiency and social acceptability (Novak 1995). Similar aspects, namely cost benefit ratio, ecological risk, urban development impacts and 'additional criteria' were considered, for example, for assessment of the German federal transport infrastructure plan (Dalkman, Bongart 2004).

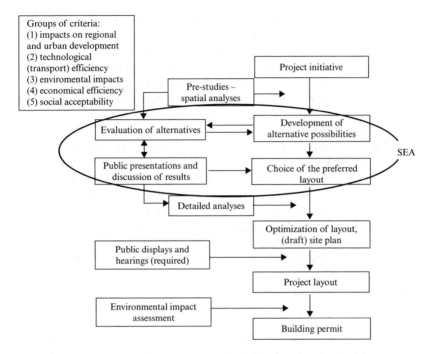

Figure 14.1 The summarized process for highway planning in Slovenia (the part of the process, which corresponds to strategic assessment, is within the circle)

After ten years of continuous implementation of the highway programme, the amount of experience with comparative studies of alternative proposals is also significant. 'Classical' types of assessments, such as those of environmental impacts and economic efficiency have been quite successfully implemented, while the other issues proved to be a difficult task, mastered with varied success. Assessment of impacts on regional and urban development, for example, usually considered only direct impacts on the existing built structures and stopped short of considering development potentials. They reflected one of the main weaknesses of the assessment practice: weak theoretical and methodological ability to consider the longer time dimensions as well as more complex cause–effects relations, such as secondary and indirect impacts. Application of more complex tools such as scenarios or integrated infrastructure land-use change models could be used to improve the results.

The other weakness was the assessment of social acceptability, which disclosed most of the problems regarding public participation. The aim of this assessment was somehow naively set to determine in advance, which of the proposed alternatives would have 'higher social acceptability'. This idea proved unfeasible, partly because it usually failed to recognize that the acceptability might be different for each part of society (national/regional/local/a specific interest group), and partly because the society (and local communities in particular) proved not to behave as a research object but took a rather active role in the process, influencing it according to their ideas of acceptability. In some cases, the local community took its position the first day the project began, and did not change it until their option was eventually implemented (although this was recognized as rather unfavourable by all experts involved). The process of highway planning and comparative assessments also generated a relatively new phenomenon of so called 'civil initiatives'. These were groups of people who considered that their interests were not adequately represented by formally involved actors and so they organized themselves around an existing (or newly developed) alternative. This type of organization of society is now a common way of entering into public debate.

Assessment of the High-speed Rail Plan

During a decade that was dedicated to the accelerated construction of highways, the other parts of the Slovenian transport policy, notably the railway programme, have been largely neglected. However, the proposal to build a high-speed rail connection in the 5th TEN corridor across Slovenia brought the railway to the focus of attention. The first attempts to provide the framework (scope, methodological guidelines and so on) for a strategic environmental impact assessment have already been made (see Table 14.1).

These studies have shown that the Ministry for Transport, which is responsible for the project, is clearly not the only one to provide arguments for the project. It also became apparent that the need for this project (as well as its costs and benefits) cannot be adequately assessed independently from the whole transport policy, since issues such as the locations of connecting nodes and the complementary infrastructure need to be considered. The debate also revealed the interconnectedness between technical, development and environmental issues and the problems of the general level of policy. Since the technology of the project (the speed of the train and the type of the transport) is not defined yet, the assessment of benefits (development effects) is impossible, which in turn makes it difficult to assess the acceptability of imposed costs (environmental impacts). If the speed of the train will only allow one stop in Slovenia (Ljubljana), then Slovenia only plays the transit role and the benefits are questionable, and no environmental damage is acceptable. However, even in such a case the

Table 14.1   Proposed framework for an SEIA process, as developed within the exploratory phase of the high-speed rail case study

Phase of SEIA		
Main steps	Actors	Results

Identifying the need for SEIA (screening)

Legislation overview, obtaining expert opinions, public discussion	Ministry for environment, initiator of plan/ programme, public	Issued provision for SEIA, guidelines for further procedure

Scoping

Appointment of (group of) experts obtaining expert opinions, public discussion	Ministry for environment, initiator of plan/ programme, authors of environmental report, public	Scope and focus of SEIA; guidelines regarding contents, methods, reference frames and so on

Assessment of objectives

Overview of strategic documents on national and international level, identification of objectives (economic, social, environmental, territorial)	Ministry for environment, initiator of plan/ programme, authors of environmental report, public	Identification and assessment of development objectives (hierarchy of objectives; assessment of relevance, coherence and compatibility with environmental protection objectives)

Note: It is important to verify whether the objectives written in the official text correspond to the objectives of society. Public debate is needed with active participation of public, interest groups

Assessment of impacts (of alternative options)

Identification of basic assumptions underlying alternative options, overview and analysis of alternative options, forecasting outcomes of each alternative option, identification of impacts, evaluation of impacts	Initiator of plan/ programme. Authors of environmental impacts report, public, revisers, local communities	Environmental vulnerability study, cost-feasibility study, comparative assessment of alternatives: – environmental impacts,

Table 14.1 (continued)

Phase of SEIA		
Main steps	Actors	Results
		– economic feasibility, – technical suitability, – impact on regional and urban development

Note: Questions related to alternatives: is identification (or development) of alternatives a part of the SEIA? Of which phase? On which level(s) do they need to be developed? Who is responsible for providing alternatives: initiator, other involved actors, authors of environmental impacts study? How many alternatives are reasonable? Do we have to have them?

Single criteria methods (such as financial valuation) are usually not very applicable at the strategic level. On the other hand, multi-criteria evaluation methods are not well developed.

Assessment of compliance and comprehensiveness of plan/programme

Revision	Revisers (independent experts)	Solving open methodological issues, overview and evaluation of work done and the results, suggestions for improvements

Monitoring of plan/programme implementation and goal achievement

Definition of indicators for monitoring	Ministry for environment, initiator of plan/ programme. Authors of environmental report, public, revisers	Defined set of indicators

long-term perspective may disclose other relevant consequences in terms of generating new metropolitan urban areas and revitalization of relations with the Balkan countries. The assessment must consider different levels of decisions, territorial scales and time horizons with good interflow of the results.

IV. ASSESSMENT OF TRANSPORT POLICY

The effects of policies are generally low if compared to the effects of spontaneous trends and driving forces, such as globalization, increased competitiveness between cities and regions, increased productivity, lifestyle changes and so on. Nevertheless, the national transport policies can to some extent ameliorate or exacerbate these impacts, and the need for assessment of the highest level of decisions has been increasingly present (Communication from the Commission on Impact Assessment 2002; Impact assessment guidelines 2005). Contrary to the assessments of projects and plans, there is almost no experience in assessments on the policy level in Slovenia. One of the reasons is that Slovenia lacks the tradition of policy analysis of any kind. A specific reason in the transport sector was the lack of an articulated transport policy. The first transport policy assessment has been therefore attempted in the frame of an on-going research project, which aims to develop a knowledge support tool for policy development.[2]

The project results include a knowledge base, accessible on the Internet, with several functionalities to support policy assessment. The main focus of assessment is on the operational level with policy measures as main objects of assessment. The knowledge base consists of expert assessments of the relations between policy measures (so called 'instruments') and a set of sustainability objectives. A measure corresponds to a specific policy action with well defined objectives and an implementation mechanism, usually within a time and budget frame. The measures are identified based on the analysis of the logic of policy action (A practical guide to program and policy evaluation, 1999). In the case of the transport policy, these measures fall into three groups of actions (see table 14.2).

Each of the measures is stored in the database with a formalized description of its main characteristics: code, title, description, objective, target group, level of implementation, sources for implementation, time frame, expected (or identified) outcomes, date and author of entry, references. The reference frame for assessment is described by a set of spatial planning policy objectives as set forth by the Spatial Development Strategy of Slovenia (SDSS).[3] These objectives were chosen because the project specifically aimed at the assessment of impacts on spatial development. The document adequately considers the general sustainability objectives and adapts them to Slovenian context, by setting the conditions for balanced economic, social and cultural development while providing for conservation of the human environment, nature, heritage and the quality of life. There are 38 objectives, grouped in 12 thematic areas, comprehensively covering the main aspects of sustainable development.

Table 14.2   Types of transport policy measures

I: Public transport	• measures for improving accessibility and effectiveness of public transport
II: Financial measures for infrastructure use	• financial stimulations for more environmentally friendly freight transport
	• introduction of the system of comparable pricing of infrastructure use
	• agreement on the level of external costs to be included in tolls
III: Infrastructure development	• finalization of the construction of highway network in 5th and 10th corridors
	• preparation of studies for the high-speed train corridor
	• construction of the second rail between Koper and Divaca
	• modernization and electrification of rails in 5th and 10th corridors
	• construction of 3rd pier in Koper port
	• planning, implementation and stimulation of development of intermodal logistic centres and freight terminals

The assessment process is based on the compilation of expert evaluations. The first phase identifies the relation (relevance) of an instrument to a certain objective. This phase basically corresponds to a traditional inter-action matrix. The second phase produces an individual evaluation for each of the identified correlations. Since the objectives were originally not explained or accompanied by indicators, these were added in the course of the project to provide a guideline for assessors, to unify the understanding of impacts and to help find existing references (studies, agency registers and so on) to policy effects. The evaluation is made in a semi-quantitative manner, where the level of the impact is assessed on a scale from -5 (strong impact, leading against the objective) to $+5$ (strong impact, leading towards the objective). The direction of the impacts does not imply a value judgment of the assessor, but correspondence to the objective in question. The most important part of the evaluation is the comment, providing a short argumentation for the given score together with a reference. The evaluations are directly filled in the forms available on-line. At any moment, all existing evaluations are available to all users of the tool. All inputs are stored in the database, and after several rounds of evaluations are made, the joint (average) score is calculated.

V. TOWARDS A FRAMEWORK FOR INTEGRATED POLICY ASSESSMENT

As mentioned earlier, the policy analysis is not a very developed field in Slovenia. Besides the lack of experience, there are other circumstances, making these efforts even more difficult. Due to the on-going transition (from ex-Yugoslavia to independent Slovenia, from a socialist-planning system to market economy, from a non-EU country to member state and so on), the Slovenian policy documents have almost all been renewed over the last decade. There are very few policies which have been in place long enough to be assessed ex post, and even fewer (if any) with a reasonably consistent measurement of their effects. Ex ante and integrated forms of assessments therefore seem to be the most relevant approaches.

The knowledge support tool, presented in the previous chapter can therefore be a useful tool to foster the integrated policy assessment practice. The initial input into the knowledge base was provided by a group of experts from relevant research fields with considerable insight and experience in assessments of the effects of policy instruments. Later on it is planned that the support tool will be taken over by the Ministry for Environment and Spatial Planning, who will use it as a knowledge base in the policy development procedure, that is, in negotiations with other policy sectors when proposing new policy measures. During these processes the knowledge base will be complemented by additional inputs. This could be done by the officers at the Office for Spatial Development, their contracting experts or external experts; even by the general public. As such, the tool is adapted and supports the assessment as a continuous process and a part of the policy-making process.

The additional value of the approach is that it enables an integrated evaluation of measures of different sectoral policies, and identification of their antagonistic or synergetic impacts. This methodology also allows the use of several different reference frames and corresponding sets of sustainability objectives and targets. It also allows a rather flexible approach to assessment, combining mid-term and ex ante approaches and exploration of all types of knowledge.

Clearly the approach does not allow for an in-depth assessment as required for SEA. Its use is therefore most relevant in the screening phase, where the policy measures with potential impacts are identified to be subjected to a complete SEA; and in the scoping phase where relevant aspects, level of assessment and potential relations to other policy measures have to be determined.

VI. CONCLUSIONS

It does seem than neither market nor politics (regulation) succeeds to provide adequate forums and sufficient mechanisms for an integrated sustainability assessment. The review of the practice of policy assessment in Slovenia, of which just a small part is presented in this contribution, shows that it provides a rich and adequate pool of experience to inform the establishment of regulation in this field. Since the attempts to do this in Slovenia (as well as in the EU) are well underway, we consider it timely to contribute to the discussion. The first set of issues discussed in this chapter is related to the distinction between the optimization and the consent-related aims of the assessment. The smooth and transparent functionality of the latter type should be enabled whenever the need to influence the policy *outputs* is of primary concern (this might be the case with certain types of documents with direct legal consequences). However, the aim to influence *processes* and their *outcomes* should be considered the most important merit of integrative strategic assessments (Haq 2004; Jiliberto 2004). This means that the assessment procedure should strive to optimize the plan or programme from the economic, environmental, social and territorial aspects. The assessment process should therefore start early on and develop in together with the concerned document (policy, plan or programme). If performed in the last phase before the document is finalized, the assessment can only contribute to cosmetic improvements (or alternatively, completely block the process).

The second group of issues refers to the legitimization of the decisions. Decision makers can rely less on scientific truth-producing mechanisms when setting the norms for sustainability. The role of public participation in granting legitimacy is getting higher priority. Although the issues might be highly complex and abstract, this should not restrict opportunities for people to participate. Adequate platforms, methods and tools should be developed to enable effective participation of a wide general public in the deliberative processes.

SEA procedure provides a viable framework for both policy optimization and legitimization aims. But as the open questions regarding its regulation indicate, the strong roots in the normal science, rational decision-making and modern society (Nilsson and Jiliberto 2004) place the focus on (over)regulation of norms and procedures. Instead the attention should be shifted to the development of the 'third arena' of decision-making (von

Schomberg 2002), which would provide a more pluralistic platform where trade-offs could be identified, discussed and decided upon on the interface between typically independent discourses of science, economy, politics, law and so on. The required methodological support includes foresight and back-casting, adaptive development of systems, reflection on technology and inclusive deliberation of targets and trade-offs. The last part of the chapter presents a policy and decision-making support tool, which could contribute to the activation of such an interface.

NOTES

1. The term 'policy action' will be used in this contribution to describe a course of public action, determined by objectives and supported by a set of instruments for implementation.
2. The title of the project is, 'Assessment of territorial impacts of sectoral policies: towards a decision support model'; the client is Office for Spatial Planning of the Ministry of Spatial Planning and Environment.
3. Spatial development strategy is the main strategic spatial planning document, adopted by the National Assembly of the Republic of Slovenia, in force since July 2004. The document is available in English on-line, http://www.gov.si/upr/doc/SPRS_eng.pdf.

REFERENCES

'A practical guide to program and policy evaluation' (1999), French Council for Evaluation, Scientific and National Councils for Evaluation, Paris.

Bundesamt fur Bauwesen und Raumordnung (2004), 'Integrated tools for European spatial development', Final Report, ESPON 3.1.

Caratti, P, Dalkmann, H and Jiliberto, R (2004), *Analysing Strategic Environmental Assessment: Towards Better Decision Making*, Edward Elgar, Cheltenham & Northampton.

Carver, S (1997), 'Open spatial decision making: evaluating the potential of the WWW', in Kemp, Z (ed.) *Innovations in GIS 4*, Taylor & Francis, London, 267–78.

Dalal-Clayton, B and Sadler, B (2004), 'Strategic environmental assessment: a sourcebook and reference guide to international experience', International Institute for Environment and Development, London.

Dalal-Clayton, B and Sadler, B (2005), 'Sustainability appraisal: a review of international experience and practice (draft report)', International Institute for Environment and Development, London.

Dalkman, H and Bongart, D (2004), 'Case study – the German federal transport infrastructure planning', in Caratti, P, Dalkmann, H and Jiliberto, R (eds) *Analysing Strategic Environmental Assessment: Towards Better Decision Making*, Edward Elgar, Cheltenham & Northampton.

European Commission (1993), 'Resolution 93/C 138/01 of the Council and the Representatives of the Governments of the Member States', Official Journal of the EC, no. C 138, vol. 36, 17 May 1993, s. 70.

European Commission (2001), 'Directive 2001/42/EC of the European Parliament and of the Council of 27 June 2001 on the assessment of the effects of certain plans and programmes on the environment', Official Journal of the European Communities, 21.7.2001, Brussels.

European Commission (2002), 'Communication from the Commission on impact assessment', COM (2002) 276 final, Commission of the European Communities, Brussels.

European Commission (2005), 'Impact assessment guidelines', SEC (2005) 791, European Commission, Brussels.

EU-SUD (2003), 'Managing the territorial dimension of EU policies after enlargement: expert document', EU Working Group on Spatial and Urban Development.

Haq, G (2004), 'Background and context of a strategic environmental assessment', in Caratti, P, Dalkmann, H and Jiliberto, R (eds) *Analysing Strategic Environmental Assessment: Towards Better Decision Making*, Edward Elgar, Cheltenham & Northampton.

Jiliberto, R (2004), 'Setting the ground for a new approach to SEA', in Caratti, P, Dalkmann, H and Jiliberto, R (eds) *Analysing Strategic Environmental Assessment: Towards Better Decision Making*, Edward Elgar, Cheltenham & Northampton.

Kontic, B (ed.) (2005), *Celovito Presojanje Vplivov Na Okolje* (Strategic environmental impact assessment), Jozef Stefan Institute, Ljubljana.

Ministry for Transport of the Republic of Slovenia (2004), 'National programme for highway construction' (Nacionalni program izgradnje avtocest), Ljubljana.

Ministry for Transport of the Republic of Slovenia (2004), 'Resolution on transport policy of Slovenia' (Predvidljivo v skupno prihodnost), Ljubljana.

Nilsson, M and Jiliberto, R (2004), 'SEA and decision making sciences', in Caratti, P, Dalkmann, H and Jiliberto, R (eds) *Analysing Strategic Environmental Assessment: Towards Better Decision Making*, Edward Elgar, Cheltenham & Northampton.

Novak, J (1995), 'Nacrtovanje cestnega prostora' (Planning the highway space), in Ministry for Environment and Planning (ed.) *Oblikovanje Avtocestnega Prostora*, Office for Spatial Development, Ljubljana.

Owens, S, Rayner, T and Bina, O (2004), 'New agendas for appraisal: reflections on theory, practice, and research', *Environment and Planning A*, 36, 1943–59.

Pfefferkorn, W, Egli, H-R and Massarutto, A (eds) (2005), *Regional Development and Cultural Landscape Change in the Alps: From Analysis and Scenarios to Policy Recommendations*, Geographica Bernensia, University of Berne, Berne.

Republic of Slovenia (2005), 'Decree laying down the content of environmental report and on detailed procedure for the assessment of the effects on certain plans and programmes on the environment' (Uredba o okoljskem poročilu in podrobnejšem postopku celovite presoje vplivov izvedbe planov na okolje), Official gazette (Ur.l. RS) 73/2005.

Stirling, A (1999), 'The appraisal of sustainability: some problems and possible responses', *Local Environment*, 4 (2), 111–35.

UNECE (2003), 'Protocol on strategic environmental assessment to the Convention on environmental impact assessment in a transboundary context', UNECE.

von Schomberg, R (2002), 'The objective of sustainable development: are we coming closer?', Foresight working papers series no. 1, European Commission, DG research, available at, www.cordis.lu/rtd2002/foresight/home.html.

15. Strategic environmental assessment and sustainability assessment in the Netherlands

Geert P.J. Draaijers and Rob Verheem

I. INTRODUCTION

The EU Directive on Strategic Environmental Assessment (SEA), which came into force in July 2000, makes environmental assessment mandatory for certain plans prepared by governmental authorities. Such an assessment should be performed for plans which set the framework for future projects that require an environmental impact assessment (EIA) and for those which require an 'appropriate assessment' of their implications for sites with nature development objectives. This is not a new requirement in the Netherlands. During the last 20 years, already a lot of experience has been gained on SEA. In this paper some key elements for effective SEA are discussed as well as the implementation of the EU Directive on SEA into Dutch legislation.

Sustainable development becomes increasingly important as an objective for both government and the business community in the Netherlands, as part of a wider international trend. In the *National Strategy for Sustainable Development* (Ministry VROM 2002) it is stated that a method should be developed to assess the impact of governmental plans on sustainable development. Several experiments with sustainability assessment (SA) were conducted, and learning experiences were published. At the same time experience with SA was gained from SEAs in which sustainability issues were raised. Based on the aforementioned experiences, the Netherlands Commission for Environmental Assessment (NCEA) defined some key elements for effective SA (Working Group on Sustainability Assessment 2006). Some of these elements are discussed in this chapter.

II. STRATEGIC ENVIRONMENTAL ASSESSMENT IN THE NETHERLANDS

The EU Directive requires that prior to the preparation of the SEA report the terms of reference (TOR) are set in consultation with the relevant environmental authorities. The SEA report also needs to be discussed with these authorities, as well as with the public. The adopted plan should be motivated and its implementation monitored.

Compared to the requirements set by the EU Directive, the existing SEA approach in the Netherlands included the following additional steps:

- The start of the plan process is published in newspapers. In this way it is guaranteed that the public is aware that something is going on.
- The public is consulted when setting the terms of reference for the SEA report. It is found that the public regularly comes up with good and surprising alternatives to be included in the SEA study. Moreover, public participation in the scoping phase has been found to improve the support for the finally adopted plan.
- The NCEA advises in the scoping phase on the topics the SEA report should cover. It also assesses at a later stage whether the information in the SEA report is complete and correct. To ensure that its opinions are unaffected by any administrative responsibilities or political considerations, the NCEA is situated outside and independent from government.
- The SEA report includes an alternative that is best from an environmental perspective. This challenges the proponent of the plan to be creative.

As a starting point for the implementation of the EU SEA Directive, the Dutch government took as a basis that the extra steps in the Dutch SEA process were extremely important, yet no longer required as mandatory steps, but rather as voluntary elements to be included by competent authorities where needed. Twenty years of SEA experience should be sufficient for those authorities to be able to judge where extra steps would be required. There is one exception: creating transparency through a mandatory publication at the start of the plan process was judged of such importance, that it was maintained as a mandatory requirement.

When asked for advice on this suggested approach, the NCEA compared the proposal with the practice experience in SEA (see Figure 15.1 for more details). On the basis of this experience it was proposed to maintain the core elements of the existing SEA approach for a limited set of plans, i.e. those plans that were so controversial that it should be safeguarded in all cases

Since 1987 more than 100 SEAs have been carried out for a variety of sectoral and spatial plans in the Netherlands dealing with, for example, electricity generation, waste management, drinking water supply and infrastructure. From these practical experiences some key elements for effective SEA became apparent. Most important is that SEA should strengthen decision-making in meeting the principles of 'good governance': sufficient transparency, participation and reliable information at all stages of the process leading up to the decision. To achieve this objective any good SEA system should include the following process elements:

Transparency

All steps leading up to the decision and the decision-making itself must be accountable. To achieve this, results of assessments must be made public and available in time, to everyone, before the decision is taken. Description of alternatives and justification of choices will ensure transparency in the consideration and balancing of interests.

Participation

All main stakeholders have to be sufficiently involved throughout the decision-making process, for example by including public consultation exercises. Participation especially matters when plans are controversial.

Information

The information on which public consultation and decision-making are based should be reliable and acceptable for all stakeholders. Openness and the opportunity to make comments and objections are important elements in this. However, this may not be enough when the decision to be made is highly controversial. An independent quality control of the assessment procedure, as part of the decision-making process, may be desirable in certain cases. This should be ascertained in advance.

Figure 15.1   Key elements of effective SEA

that full public participation and independent review is included, not only to win support for the decision, but also to give them a sound legal footing.

This advice was partly followed. In November 2005 Parliament agreed on a governmental bill on the implementation of the EU SEA Directive in Dutch legislation. It includes a basic minimum approach for most plans and programmes – following the requirements of the EU Directive – and an extended approach for plans and programmes affecting nature areas protected under the Birds and Habitats Directive. In the extended approach the quality of information in the SEA report is assessed by the NCEA. At the same time Parliament agreed that a covenant should be made between the competent authorities, the Ministry of Environment and the NCEA on arrangements for the 'voluntary' steps in the SEA process, such as early public participation and independent review, to prevent delay in decision-making by unnecessary discussions on the design of this process.

Now the EU SEA Directive is implemented into Dutch legislation, Parliament will start work on a bill to tune current environmental impact assessment (EIA) with SEA legislation. This bill most probably will be presented in the second half of 2006.

III. SUSTAINABILITY ASSESSMENT IN THE NETHERLANDS

Generally, sustainable development is defined as creating a sufficient ecological, economical and social situation to meet the needs of present generations without hampering the needs of future generations (WCED 1987). What is to be regarded 'sufficient' can be assessed based on present-day preferences and an estimate of future preferences. Achieving sustainable development can be considered a major challenge for present-day decision makers, which up to now were frequently judged only on achieving sectoral policy targets. Sustainability assessment (SA) involves informing and structuring the process of decision-making in such a way that administrators can develop and justify plans or projects from the perspective of sustainable development. Below, some key elements of effective SA are discussed on the basis of two sources: the Dutch National Strategy on Sustainable Development and the two advices that have been issues so far by the 'Working group on sustainable development', that was supported and facilitated by the NCEA.

Key Elements for the Content of SA

Probably the most important and also most difficult part of SA is to define what is considered a 'sustainable development'. In practice different visions may exist on what is meant by sustainable development. Some people take the ecological domain as a basis for sustainability, whereas others consider the ecological, economical and social domain equally important. Another obstacle is the subjective character of sustainability regarding the perception of the main qualities for existence: which qualities do we consider most important? Which qualities do we want or have to leave for future generations and for people living in other regions or countries? Is it allowable to replace existing values by new ones, or should we always protect what we have?

An objective definition of sustainable development is hard to give, and value judgments are unavoidable. Therefore, sustainable development should to a large extent be based on consensus among stakeholders rather than scientifically defined. One of the issues to be resolved is whether

Table 15.1   Framework for sustainability assessment suggested in the national strategy on sustainable development of the Netherlands

	Ecological aspects	Economical aspects	Social and cultural aspects
Here and now			
Elsewhere			
Later			

improvements need to be made in all sustainability domains or whether exchange between the different domains is allowed. Exchange might include, for example, allowing some economic decline in favour of (large) improvements in the ecological domain, or vice versa.

In the Netherlands, the following framework for SA has been suggested in the *National Strategy on Sustainable Development* (Ministry VROM 2002) (see Table 15.1). It contains a 3×3 matrix with one axis displaying the three dimensions of sustainability and the other axis showing its spatial and temporal dimensions. Sustainable development would then be a development that scores well on all nine boxes.

From this matrix it becomes apparent where the challenge for SEA lies. Most SEAs generally only concentrate on the ecological dimension of sustainability 'here and now' and generally do not include effects for future generations ('later', i.e. 50 years and beyond) or for other regions or countries ('elsewhere', in particular developing countries). In contrast, the central question in SA is whether a plan or project will be an improvement on all domains of sustainability,[1] or whether risks exist for unwanted transfer of effects to other times, regions and/or sustainability domains.

SA should give insight into the possibilities to reduce or prevent these risks. In this respect, SA does not necessarily need to include a quantitative assessment of effects. In many situations, a sound qualitative discussion on whether an option scores better or worse is sufficient. Thus, the focus should not be on effects but on risks linked to insufficient goal achievement and possible trade-off effects to other dimensions of sustainability, future generations and/or other regions or countries (Working group on sustainability assessment, 2001).

It should be accepted that for certain issues it is possible to indicate a 'hard' threshold or limit that should not be exceeded, e.g. toxic substance levels in drinking water that will kill people. It should be the role of science to inform the stakeholders' dialogue where these limits exist. In Dutch practice so far, however, it has shown that these kinds of hard limits only exist for a minority of issues: for the rest, stakeholders have to agree amongst themselves.

Up to now, no generally accepted set of indicators exists to be used in measuring goal achievement and unwanted side-effects in sustainability assessment, partly, because such a standard set of indicators is not useful. The practical feasibility of sustainability assessment will be larger if a limited set of plan- or project-specific indicators is directed towards the specific plan or project under consideration and accepted by all stakeholders.

In assessing these indicators, national or provincial governments' standards need to be considered. If standards are lacking or unsuitable (e.g. based on reaching too low a minimum quality[2]), it is advisable to define standards by looking from a sustainability perspective. Although such standards may not be achievable in the short (or even longer) term, they may give insight where sustainable development has roughly been reached and where more effort will be necessary. Standards should be scientifically based where possible, and otherwise defined in discussion with the main actors involved.

Final reporting on the results of the SA does not primarily focus on the indicators set (Verheem 2002). Indicator values should be 'translated' towards information that is understandable and relevant for decision makers, e.g. where achieving objectives in one domain hampers their objectives in another domain. In particular, the strategic choices to be made to achieve sustainable development and the dilemmas hampering making these choices should be indicated. Moreover, the possibilities for action and solution should be addressed (SER 2002).

Key Elements for the Process of SA

The main focus of the SA process should be to assist in achieving well structured and well informed deliberations between parties involved in the design of a plan or project. It must not be an ex post evaluation but the primary objective should be to facilitate consultation and to consider conflicting interests during the decision-making process. The process itself is as important as the substance (content) of the assessment (Verheem 2002).

Decision-making procedures generally differ with government level, and with the subject of the plan or project. It therefore seems ineffective to use a fixed procedure for SA. On the other hand, a procedure that does not commit anyone to anything is not very useful either. As with SEA, a set of minimum requirements for SA should be based on the principles of good governance. The core of a good SA process will therefore be the same as that of a good SEA process, with some additional elements to deal with the more integrated and multi-disciplinary nature of SA.

An SA should be made on the basis of a dialogue between all stakeholders, with science indicating the hard limits not to be crossed. Cooperation between parties needs to be guaranteed in all steps considered crucial to SA, such as problem definition, goal formulation, setting review framework (i.e. what is to be considered 'sustainable'), design of alternatives, selection of analytical approach and reporting. To facilitate dialogue and prevent delay due to discussion on the validity of information, independent advice on scope and quality of information may prove useful, especially in the case of controversial plans or projects.

Sustainability assessment thus implies a process of cooperation between people from different disciplines (e.g. environmental, economic and social science). In practice, this will not always be easy because people will not always be capable of looking beyond their own sectoral problems and policy targets (where integrated assessments are required), are not always used to work in multi-disciplinary project teams, and often use their own terminology and definitions of sustainability, with a resulting confusion of tongues (Verheem 2002). Preventing decision-making along sectoral lines and developing a common language are considered prerequisites for sustainability assessment.

IV. CONCLUSIONS

SEA and SA can be regarded as the extremes of a continuum of impact assessment tools (OECD DAC 2005), SEA being an environmental, short- to mid-term assessment, while SA is a short- to long-term integrated assessment of economic, social and environmental issues (although SEA is often used as the 'umbrella-term' for the whole continuum). Both instruments will have their value in specific situations: SEA is more focused, yet less comprehensive; SA is integral, yet more complex. However, both have great potential to increase the quality of discussions on possible directions of development and to contribute to the democratic quality of policy-making through weighting alternatives, consequences, costs and benefits and thus making the (often complex) process of policy-making more transparent for citizens.

In the Netherlands the main challenge for SEA is to find out if the new, simplified framework, while offering more flexibility for governments, will still provide sufficient safeguards for environmental issues to be considered in strategic thinking. The main challenge for SA is to make it a more widely used tool that is comprehensive, yet pragmatic.

An overall challenge for both instruments is to clarify the relationship with other instruments for impact assessment (e.g. EIA, cost benefit analysis, social analysis), and – even more ambitious – how these instruments can be integrated into one.

NOTES

1. i.e. the ecological, economical and social and cultural domain.
2. The reduction percentages for greenhouse gas emissions agreed upon in the Kyoto Protocol, for example, are based on attainability, not on sustainability.

REFERENCES

Ministry VROM (2002), *Nationale Strategie voor Duurzame Ontwikkeling* (National Strategy for Sustainable Development – Exploring Government Policy), January 2002.

OECD/DAC (2005), *(First Draft) Good Practice Guidance on Strategic Environmental Assessment (SEA)*, SEA Task Force, Paris, OECD.

SER (2002), *Advies over de Verkenning van de Rijksoverheid in het kader van de Nationale Strategie voor Duurzame Ontwikkeling* (Advisory report on the outlook of the national government on the National Strategy for Sustainable Development), Publication No. 7, May.

Verheem, R A (2002), *Recommendations for Sustainability Assessment in the Netherlands*, in Environmental Impact Assessment in the Netherlands: views from the Commission for EIA in 2002, June.

WCED (1987), *Our Common Future*, Brundtland Report, World Commission on Environment and Development (WCED), Oxford University Press.

Working Group on Sustainability Assessment (2001), *Aanbevelingen voor een duurzame ontwikkelingsbeoordeling* (Recommendations for sustainability assessment), December.

Working Group on Sustainability Assessment (2006), *Aanbevelingen voor een duurzame ontwikkelingsbeoordeling* (Recommendations on sustainability assessment), January.

16. Exploring the feasibility of sustainability impact assessment procedures for federal policies in Belgium

Tom Bauler, Marco Wäktare and Alessandro Bonifazi

I. INTRODUCTION

Since September 2004, Belgium has been building the first steps towards institutionalizing an evaluation scheme[1] at its federal level which aims to integrate evaluation patterns of a regulatory impact assessment with the Belgian sustainable development (SD) agenda (Belgian Federal Government 2004-a). While the very basic inter-departmental responsibilities attached to this resulting sustainability impact assessment (SIA) have been clarified by the initial regulation, all other parts of this future SIA scheme appear to be very loosely determined. This chapter takes stock of some of the results of a research project,[2] which explores whether and how such an SIA scheme could be applied to the federal level of Belgian government. It provides a description of the first steps of the research project and more specifically, it addresses issues related to the supply and the demand sides of SIA. The supply side is covered through an analysis of major points to take into account when designing such an assessment. Issues related to the demand side were identified through face-to-face interviews which aimed to gain knowledge of the understanding, dangers and opportunities, experiences and expertise, as well as the institutional challenges, perceived both by stakeholders and civil servants. The results of the interviews are discussed in detail in the chapter.

II. THE BELGIAN CONTEXT

The basic inter-departmental responsibilities attached to a Belgian federal SIA mechanism were clarified by the initial regulation which also established the creation of 'sustainable development cells' for each ministry (Belgian Federal Government 2004-a). These departmental cells are in charge of the implementation of the actions stemming from the federal sustainable development strategy, among which, are the planning and execution of SIAs. The cells are departmental working groups consisting of representatives of the political cabinets and civil servants. Apart from these basic institutional principles, all other parts of this SIA scheme appear to be very loosely determined for the time being (Thomaes et al 2005).

In Belgium, besides the embryonic SIA initiative and a number of traditional ex ante assessments (for example budgetary checks), two ex ante assessment procedures have been recently introduced. They are considered by some stakeholders as reference points for the insertion of SIA into the federal regulation procedure. First, the Kafka-test (Belgian Federal Government 2004-b), implemented in October 2004, is mandatory for policy proposals submitted to the Federal Council of Ministers. Its objective is to encourage administrative simplification through the determination of the administrative burden of regulations: it mainly consists of a check-list and a form to be filled in by the author of regulatory initiatives. The Kafka-test is viewed by some as a potential future procedural anchor for SIA to enter into the regulatory decision-making process.

Second, RIA (regulatory impact assessment) at the Flemish regional level has recently been implemented (at the beginning of 2005) as the first RIA mechanism in Belgium (Ministerie van de Vlaamse Gemeenschap 2005). In the tradition of improving regulatory processes (including the elaboration of the regulation itself), RIA is employed to assess policy options, to identify the costs linked to the policies and thus, in general terms, to better inform decision makers. The RIA at the Flemish regional level is held to be one possible procedural and methodological blueprint for SIA at the federal level, despite the fact that the initial motivations for both assessments are complementary rather than substitutable.

III. THE EXPLORATION OF THE POTENTIAL SUPPLY AND DEMAND FOR SIA

A comprehensive literature study (Wäktare 2004; Lussis 2005; Risse 2004) consolidated the apprehension that SIA, as it is understood for this project (strategic, integrated, ex ante, participatory) is still in a very early phase of development. Institutionalized and operational evaluation processes, which make explicit and coherent reference to integrated assessment in a context of sustainable development appear to be rather few. However, the literature study strongly confirms that many initiatives are being developed in different

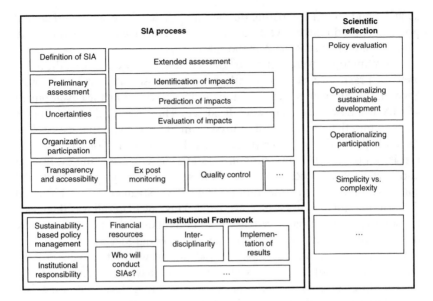

Figure 16.1   Overview of methodological, institutional and scientific issues for developing an SIA-framework

countries and international institutions, which can be understood as forerunners of SIA (Pope 2003; Dalal-Clayton and Sadler 2004). The development of SIA practice gives rise to numerous questions, which necessarily emerge when elaborating a framework for SIA in Belgium. Some of these questions are on the methodological level, others on the level of the institutional embedment of SIA, still others point to the need for more fundamental scientific reflection. Based on the literature study, the research partners developed a diagrammatic representation of the determinants of SIA (see Figure 16.1). This was then developed into research themes and issues to be taken into account when developing SIA methodologies.

The issues related to the demand side were identified through face-to-face interviews in order to define the needs and supporting capacities of policy makers and stakeholders in using SIA and, to preliminarily assess the institutional integration of SIA at the Belgian federal level. As matter of fact, from the point of view of operationalization, the federal authorities could choose to integrate the SIA instrument into existing evaluation processes. Therefore, it is crucial to identify how policy makers and experts evaluate the institutional, methodological and financial feasibility of SIA. Twenty-three interviews[3] were conducted with potential 'users' and providers of SIA. These included both experts (academic and private consultants, public agencies and so on) competing on the supply side of the 'SIA market' and political and administrative actors who will be involved in the later execution of the SIA (that is the demand side).

Five main topics were focused on during these interviews. First, the interviewees' previous experiences with 'impact assessments' were addressed. Second, the interviewees' expectations and fears regarding the development of SIA as a new policy tool were discussed. Third, policy domains and/or programmes that should be submitted to an SIA were identified, as well as the evaluation criteria underlying an SIA. Fourth, the major methodological issues of an SIA (including integration character, ex ante evaluation and participatory processes) were addressed and finally, the institutional challenges linked to the integration of the SIA instruments into the actual decision-making process were considered. This raw material was then used to identify, on a comparative basis, commonalities and differences among the point of views of the different types of potential SIA users.

It appeared throughout most of the interviews that in general, the differences were not as pronounced as one would have expected them to be, even if differences in the perception of SIA are generalized somewhat according to the institutional embeddedness of the interviewee, his or her organization's mission and his or her function in the organization's organigram. Thus, it could be concluded[4] that there are some common understandings of SIA, both in terms of its strengths and weaknesses, but also with regard to the opportunities and threats it raises. Simultaneously, it is the implementation of SIA, the institutional layout of SIA, and the procedural design, which appear to be rather polarized among the interviewees.

The following sections will focus more specifically on the determinants that have a closer link to the aspects that have been covered during the face-to-face interviews. They are related to SIA development (referring to the interviewees' past experiences with SIA), preliminary SIA and screening (related to the policy domains interviewees wish to submit to SIA) as well as methodology and institutional challenges.

IV.   SIA DEVELOPMENT

Integrated evaluations exist in many forms, at several institutional levels and in different degrees of refinement. Some authors (for example Dalal-Clayton and Sadler 2004) suggest that the adoption of assessments characterized by a sustainability dimension gained prominence following the employment of strategic environmental assessment (SEA), itself building on environmental impact assessment (EIA). So, developments stemming from the environmental side were one way that SIA emerged. Another path of evolution could have been through the inclusion of environmental and social dimensions in economic assessments, or by the widening of regulatory assessments. In 2003 the European Commission replaced the individual assessments it had formerly institutionalized in its General Directorates with an over-arching, integrated mechanism called impact assessment (European Commission 2002, 2004). Finally, in general, it appears that virtually all the existing integrated assessment processes refer to some extent to sustainable development as being one of their main objectives to strive for in their definitions. However, specific sustainability-related aspects (for example integration, differing temporal and spatial scales, irreversibilities, uncertainties and so on) are far from being the strongest determinants of the assessment methodologies themselves.

An overview of integrated impact assessments from different institutions (UK RIA, Flemish RIA, Swiss Impact Assessment and EC Impact Assessment) identified several common characteristics and goals. First, a common goal for all these assessments is the improvement of the quality and coherence of policy design. However, some guidelines put more stress on the sustainable development dimension (Swiss Federal Office for Spatial Development 2004), mentioning that the policies and projects should be designed in the most sustainable way. Second, all assessments focused on the identification and assessment of impacts, with some paying particular attention to specific targeted groups (for example children in the Flemish RIA). Third, other common features are the participatory design of the mechanisms, and the prominence given to transparency. A fourth major challenge of these assessments is related to the inherent uncertainties, which may occur at four different levels (Heyerick et al 2004). The first level is technical uncertainty (that is the malfunctioning of evaluation methods, for example through lack of data). Second is methodological uncertainty (such as the wrong choice of methodology, for instance cost-benefit analysis where multi-criteria analysis would have been more consistent). Third is epistemological uncertainty (which could result in the vague definition of the objectives of the assessment) and fourth, fundamental uncertainty (the impossibility to determine the future). One of the specificities of SIA is to increase the preponderance and depth of fundamental uncertainties over the other types of uncertainties while at the same time generating a reinforcement of epistemological uncertainties (mainly driven by the intrinsic complexity of sustainable development policies).

Considering the many existing interpretations on the origins and objectives of SIA, an important entry step to the exploration of the demand for SIA was to gather knowledge about the expertise and experience of the interviewees with regard to evaluation in general, and SIA-type characteristics of evaluation processes in particular (that is participatory evaluation schemes, ex ante evaluation and integrated evaluation). None of the interviewees was aware of a fully-fledged SIA-type evaluation having been realized in his/her organization (that is evaluations having satisfactorily met the three pillars of SIA evaluations mentioned before). Simultaneously, none of the interviewees was aware of SIA experience or practice in Belgium. However, most interviewees had knowledge of the existence of ex ante policy evaluations at other levels, notably the European Impact Assessment scheme, while impact assessments without explicit integration of an SD perspective appeared to be conducted in various organizations. In these cases, the evaluations conducted were oriented towards the organization's main competence (for example towards the environment, economics or business). The integration characteristic seemed thus to be rarely, if ever, met. It appeared also that only limited experience exists with ex ante evaluations and where this was the case, interviewees acknowledged that they neither followed a strict methodological framework, nor relied on a formalized and institutionalized evaluation process.

In a more general sense, it appeared that the expertise and practice of integrated evaluations (the evaluation culture) is deeper at regional than at federal level (except for the Brussels Region). The Walloon Region largely appears to have taken advantage of evaluation requirements stemming from European development funds (for example structural funds), which resulted in the trickle down of integrated evaluation into other regional policy developments. In parallel, Flanders is currently exploring the first steps of an extensive regulatory impact assessment (RIA) scheme in accordance with international developments in this field. In this regard, the interviews consolidated the researchers' vision of a rather poor expertise with impact evaluations at the federal level (see also Jacob and Varone 2003). It further occurred that in the current situation, the upcoming SIA process[5] would be embedded in a setting with particularly embryonic expertise and experience with evaluation. As a matter of fact, neither the SD cells (which are foreseen by the current state of law to be conducting the evaluations at federal level), nor the programmatic horizontal SD administration (which is foreseen to act as a methodological help-desk and quality-controller) can rely on any type of expertise on evaluation.

More generally, asked about the probable reasons for this situation, some interviewees mentioned that the over-arching lack of evaluation exercises, and more specifically of SIA-type evaluations, could be due to three main reasons. First, the politicized policy-making processes in Belgium: the role of ministerial cabinets often expands from a mere initiator of policies to a developer of policy and this is not fertile ground for evaluations which would engage further liability of political actors. Second, the generalized trend at the federal level in Belgium towards programmatic law making (resulting in policies that embrace numerous policy measures which are not necessarily linked to a single policy issue) renders evaluations particularly difficult and thus dissuasive. Finally, the recurrent budgetary cuts in most policy sectors diminish the availability of resources for evaluations. Thus, civil servants prefer to invest scarce resources in policy implementation, instead of allocating even a small share of the policy budget to evaluate and/or monitor the induced impacts.

In conclusion, it can be ascertained from the interviews that one can hardly speak of a strong and shared evaluation culture in Belgium at any level of the policy process. However, it has to be acknowledged that the existing embryonic evaluation culture (which is confined to a few people and/or institutions) is to be found at regional level rather than at federal level. In parallel, the research team generally encountered a particularly strong demand to strengthen the development of evaluations in Belgium. The evident lack of evaluation capacities was identified as a potential hindrance for the necessary development of a more objectified policy-making process, including the development of a more SD-oriented policy configuration. However, the desirability of the development of evaluation was conditional: in the current Belgian institutional setting, which is felt to be strongly complicated and occasionally inefficient in implementing and monitoring its policies, the development of evaluation should neither render the policy cycles more complex, nor demand resources to shift from the necessary policy implementation phases.

V. IDENTIFICATION OF POLICY DOMAINS FOR SIA

Because of time and resource constraints, not every policy proposal can be subject to a detailed and in-depth impact analysis. The costs of ex ante policy assessment have to be justified by the potential for avoiding or mitigating negative policy impacts, as well as strengthening any positive effects. Therefore all of the studied aforementioned evaluation instruments and processes contain some form of preliminary assessment and use a number of rules, criteria or thresholds to determine a selection procedure to identify which policy proposals should be further examined, and hence undergo SIA.

Within the different experiences considered, preliminary assessments range from a very short and general overview of potential impacts, to a more intensively constructed methodology implying some consultation with other departments or even with the general stakeholders. The more detailed the preliminary assessment, the better it can be used to scope the subsequent extended assessments. Similarly, screening with standardized and rigid approaches (like inclusion or exclusion lists) is simple and rapid to employ but might appear to be unrealistic and insufficient in the light of the complexity of SD assessments.

The second part of the interviews was thus directed towards understanding how interviewees acknowledge the scope and scale of SIA, what implicit definition they would give to SIA, and where SIA should be positioned in the policy-making cycle. Most interviewees attached particular importance to the procedural and institutional aspects of this question.

With regard to the procedural and substantive challenges underlying the selection of policies that should undergo SIA-type evaluations (that is the screening and scoping stage), most of the interviewees thought that policy decisions with potential relevance for SD were too numerous and heterogeneous to draw up a positive (or negative) list of policy issues and themes. Interviewees advocated enlargement of the pool of policy decisions which could potentially be submitted to SIA to all issues (environmental, financial, scientific and so on) and all levels (including programmes, regulation, plans, policies). However, in order to select relevant policy decisions, most interviewees advocated both the use of criteria and the notion of 'important' decisions. However, important decisions were not necessarily, in the eyes of the interviewees, those decisions that present a high potential for important impacts. Furthermore, interviewees saw no prominence in restricting SIA to policy decisions of strategic level, such as programmes and plans. Interviewees saw no use either to limit SIA to policies that are directly and unambiguously linked to the formal SD agenda (in Belgium, this agenda would be the Federal Plan for SD). Simultaneously, some interviewees strongly advocated to include the 'déclarations gouvernementales' (that is a government's formal plan of intentions covering its entire legislative period) in the pool of eligible policy decisions for SIA.

VI. MAJOR METHODOLOGICAL ISSUES WITH SIA

Existing practices are relatively unclear about how to put into effect the impact assessment and impact evaluation, both methodologically and procedurally. Generally they offer a non-elaborated range of methods to adopt or adapt according to priorities, resources and other contextual circumstances. Several existing analytical methods, quantitative or qualitative, can be used for assessing the impacts of a proposal, which differ in concept and coverage (for example cost-benefit analysis, cost-effectiveness analysis, multi-criteria analysis, risk assessment, causal chain analysis, comparative value analysis, utility analysis and so on). Applying a single evaluation method to all evaluation situations appears very difficult, considering that SIA is a tool for evaluating a range of different policies diverging widely in scope, scale and depth of impacts and that each policy proposal under scrutiny involves adapting the objectives of the evaluation according to the challenges of the policy with regard to SD issues. Rather than rigidly applying one single method of evaluation (for example cost-benefit analysis), a main part of the methodological challenge of an SIA process is to allow for the best possible correspondence between the object of the evaluation and the method and process to be used. Thus, to a certain extent, SIA will have to be adapted procedurally and methodologically to the object of the evaluation. The development of a resilient methodological meta-framework is thus one of the challenges for the present project (Boulanger 2005).

From the background of the interviewees' current experiences with evaluations, they were thus asked to discuss eventual solutions to the challenges of implementing SIA at the level of impact identification, impact assessment and impact integration. This question divided the panel into two (broad) categories. Some of the interviewees called for a quantitative approach to SIA methodologies while others wanted its methodologies to develop in a qualitative direction. It appeared that this dichotomy was mainly based on different understandings about the use and utility of SIA.

Those who argued in favour of hard 'facts', even when acknowledging the intrinsic difficulties linked to quantifying impacts in an SD perspective, argued for a further rationalization of the Belgian policy-making cycle. One could thus infer that they had gained former experience that only hard figures could influence the outcome of policy negotiations and that a quantitative SIA could be a way to translate the SD agenda into figures and hence into action. The calls for quantitative methodologies were particularly strong when interviewees addressed 'extended' impact assessments. On the other hand, those who showed an interest in soft, qualitative SIA methodologies advocated that the main driver for SD necessarily is societal capacity building that induces a general awareness and acceptance of the issues included in SD agendas. This capacity building element could, from their viewpoints, be achieved through participation in the SIA. Hence they advocated for soft, participatory and more qualitative methodologies (such as scenario building).

Still on the level of methodology elaboration, interviewees wanted the impact evaluation methodologies to be able to identify impacts along a series of criteria, which could be seen as rather straightforward SD criteria. These include inter-generational justice and equity, precaution, integration, spatial generalization and so on.

Most interviewees spoke of SIA as an evaluation based along the lines of the three pillars[6] of SD (so, incorporating economic, environmental and social elements). They also mentioned the quest for equilibrium. Generally, interviewees argued not to interpret the call for balanced policies too narrowly (that is balanced according to the three pillars of SD), but rather to seek a balance of impacts on the level of the entire policy agenda (as opposed to the level of single policies). Some interviewees from environmental stakeholder groups also mentioned the fact that the broadening of SIA to the three pillars could eventually reduce, or at least endanger, the importance of environmental impacts and criteria in decision-making processes, and hence endanger the environmental agenda.

When the interviewees were asked to state their vision on participation in SIA, most developed a rather strong view in favour of the opening of SIA to relevant actors in the policy process. However, a clear consensus or typology as to how to translate this call for more participation into practice could not be detected. Most interviewees acknowledged that SIA needs to be participatory right from the start of its development and from the first steps (the screening or scoping phase) onwards. Some interviewees feared that resources that would allow the serious implementation of participation could fall short, and rather argued to orient resources in the first place in favour of a consequential transparency. Simultaneously, some interviewees addressed the importance of steering participation towards discussing policy alternatives rather than mitigation measures, implying by this that participation should be concerned with the most important and 'political' steps, rather than participation on technical issues. A clear picture with regard to the nature of the participants could not be identified. This element appeared again to be linked to the general representation the interviewees had about SIA. For some interviewees, SIA was to be an essentially administrative process with a rather limited opening to stakeholders but with a rather consequential inter-departmental collaboration. For others, SIA needs to be a wide open stakeholder dialogue where the administration would assume the role of facilitator and mediator.

However, it was generally felt that opening SIA to extensive participation could endanger the setting of the current Belgian policy-making process. As a matter of fact, the current Belgian policy processes were felt by many as being strongly consensus-seeking and based on inter-departmental and inter-ministerial negotiation (including the involvement of lobbyists on each side of the negotiation table). Introducing formal participation in the early stages of these policy cycles could endanger the entire construct, and perversely reduce the insight of stakeholders into the policy-making process by misplacing negotiations into the dark.

VII.   INSTITUTIONAL CHALLENGES

The assessment processes that were studied evolved in different institutional contexts, whereas only some of the features can directly be adapted to the Belgian setting. Belgium is characterized by many competences allocated at federal and regional levels, where federal policies could also have some influence at the regional level. An impact assessment for the Belgian federal level should ideally be organized in such a way that it does not make the whole process more complicated and it should take time constraints into account. Another relevant issue is the determination of the organization of the assessment and people responsible for it. Many impact assessments in other countries or organizations are the responsibility of the author of the policy proposal, with the help of a coordinating and supervisory body if needed. Furthermore, there is also the issue of identifying the stakeholders to involve, either in a participatory or consultative way. So far it seems that consultation rather than active participation has been the norm in the assessments analysed (as is the case of the Flemish RIA).

As SIA is an administrative exercise, the institutional organization of SIA should be a major point of debate. It emerged during the interviews that most interviewees were addressing the main aforementioned challenges to establish SIA in Belgium in terms of institutional and organizational issues.

Generally, interviewees regretted the virtual non-existence of integrated policy-making in Belgium, as well as the lack of experience in integrated policy development. The culture of departmental segregation, intra- and inter-ministerial competition and negotiation as well as the influence of ministerial cabinets into policy-making were identified by almost all interviewees as major hindrances to more integrated policy-making, and by extension as the major barrier to the installation of a strong SIA scheme within the federal policy actors. Therefore, viewpoints were shared that SIA could only have a clear impact if it could count on long-term permanent support from the highest-level politicians and civil servants. It was felt that this is not yet the case in the current federal government, neither for SIA nor for SD. Eventually, a strong SIA will also need to empower stakeholders in order to develop a more balanced and symmetrical power relationship among policy and decision makers.

As just mentioned, interviewees felt the opportunity for two rather different institutionalizations of SIA: one being rather strictly internal to administration; the second being external. In the former case, which prevailed among our interviewees, institutions would need to further develop their own capacity in conducting evaluations in order to establish ownership both of the evaluation process and of the outcomes. Regarding the current state of evaluation culture in federal administrations, this was felt to need temporary external assistance. In this sense, interviewees also felt the need for a series of effective coordination mechanisms on the level of the federal administrations but also between the federal level and the regional authorities. The latter could play an important role, at least as observers to the evaluation exercise, notably because a non-negligible part of the impacts of federal policies will be of regional competence (typically environmental and land-use impacts were cited).

A major issue raised by virtually all interviewees was the special attention to be devoted to the timeliness of the evaluation process. At best, SIA should be developed in parallel to the policy-making process and feed the latter constantly. Many interviewees feared that SIA might come too late in the policy process, at a point when most decisions were already widely closed, when analysed alternatives to the policy under scrutiny would be fake and where the major stakes were already distributed among the influential. In this regard, some interviewees proposed to institutionalize SIA along the lines of existing assessment processes. Currently, before being submitted to the ministerial council (or Parliament), policies undergo a budgetary check (usually by inspecteurs des finances), as well as a check with regard to the administrative burden of the policy implementation (for example the Kafka-test). These assessments, limited in scope and rather non-evaluative, are attached to the appendices of policy proposals. A considerable number of interviewees saw a way to institutionalize SIA in these practices.

VIII.   CONCLUSION

From this introductory exploration of the feasibility of a Belgian SIA mechanism for the federal authorities, it appears that many challenges need to be addressed before SIA will become an institutional reality. The problems are, not least, related to the political-administrative context within which the idea of SIA grew. During the last few years, several adjustments and reorganizations have happened at federal political-administrative level. Within these reformed structures, several entities specifically created for the purpose of developing sustainability policies (for example through integration of policies) have now become part of the federal landscape. The functions of and (power) relations between these actors are not always clear and are subject to the strategic behaviour of people. This became evident during some interviews and other forms of contact. It is logical behaviour within any administrative-political context but it may have effects during the later stages of operationalizing SIA.

ACKNOWLEDGEMENTS

This chapter is based on an intermediary report prepared for the aforementioned Belgian SIA research project. The authors are therefore grateful to the following researchers: Paul-Marie Boulanger and Benoît Lussis, Institut pour un Développement Durable, Ottiginies, Belgium; An Heyerick and Erik Paredis, Universiteit Gent, Centruum voor Duurzame Ontwikkeling, Gent, Belgium; Nathalie Risse, Université Libre de Bruxelles, SMG, Brussels, Belgium; Pieter Thomaes, Universiteit Gent, Centrum voor milieurecht, Gent, Belgium; Frédéric Varone, Université Catholique de Louvain, AURAP, Louvain-la-Neuve, Belgium.

NOTES

1. This evaluation scheme is called in French, 'Etudes d'Incidences des Décisions sur le Développement Durable – EIDDD' and in Flemish, 'Duurzame Ontwikkeling Effecten-Beordeling – DOEB'.
2. The project was financed from July 2004 to February 2006 by the 'Belgian science policy' under the 'Scientific support plan for a sustainable development policy' (www.belspo.be).
3. Interviews took place with three politicians, five high-level civil servants, three institutional auditors, three academic and private experts and nine experts from stakeholder organizations.
4. However, we want to be cautious in generalizing this statement. Indeed it appeared through the interviews that most interviewees did not have a very precise technical knowledge of SIA. This can be explained by the fact that SIA is a relatively new field in the management of public administrations and policies, and does not yet have any systematic application in Belgium. Interviewees were either extrapolating from their know-how developed from other forms of policy or programme evaluation, or they relied on their secondary knowledge of SIA-type evaluations as they occur in other institutions (namely at the European level).
5. As foreseen in the 'Arrêté royal portant création des cellules de développement durable au sein des services publics fédéraux', 22 September 2004, Brussels, Belgium.
6. In parallel, most of the interviewees agreed that they could find such a 3-dimensional representation a very limited and unhelpful approach to SD.

REFERENCES

Arnstein, S R (1969), 'A ladder of citizen participation', *Journal of the American Institute of Planners*, 8 (3), 217–24.

Belgian Federal Government (2004-a), *Arrêté Royal Portant Création des Cellules de Développement Durable au Sein des Services Publics Fédéraux*, 22 September 2004, Brussels, Belgium.

Belgian Federal Government (2004-b), *Fil Conducteur pour le Test Kafka*.

Boulanger, P M (2005), 'Integration in sustainability impact assessment: meanings, patterns and tools', Working Paper for the Research Project 'Methodology and feasibility of sustainability impact assessment. Case: Federal policy making process', Institut pour un Développement Durable, Ottignies, Belgium.

Dalal-Clayton, B and Sadler, B (2004), 'Strategic environmental assessment: an international review', final draft, London, International Institute for Environment and Development (IIED).

Dalkmann, H, Herrera, R J and Bongardt, D (2003), 'Analytical strategic environmental assessment (ANSEA) developing a new approach to SEA', *Environmental Impact Assessment Review*, 24 (4), 385–402.

Devuyst, D (2001), *Sustainability Assessment: The Application of a Methodological Framework*, VUB, Human Ecology Departement.

Devuyst, D (ed.) (2001), *How Green is the City: Sustainability Assessment and the Management of Urban Environments*, New York, Colombia University Press.

European Commission (2004), 'Commission report on impact assessment: next steps – in support of competitiveness and sustainable development', SEC(2004)1377, 21 October, European Commission, Brussels.

European Commission (2002), *Impact Assessment in the Commission*, European Commission, Brussels, http://europa.eu.int/comm/secretariat_general/impact/index_en.htm.

Federal Office for Spatial Development, Department of Environment, Transport, Energy and Communications (2004), *Sustainability Assessment: Conceptual Framework and Basic Methodology*, Switzerland.

Heyerick, A, Paredis, E, Wäktare, M (2004), 'Sustainability impact assessment, an overview of methodological, institutional and scientific questions', preparatory document for the PODO-II project sustainability impact assessment (SIA) users committee of 5 October 2004, Universiteit Gent, Centrum voor Duurzame Ontwikkeling, Gent, Belgium, Université Libre de Bruxelles, IGEAT-CEDD, Brussels, Belgium.

Jacob, S and Varone, F (2003), *Évaluer L'action Publique: État des Lieux et Perspectives en Belgique*, Academia Press, Gent.

Lussis, B (2005), 'EU extended impact assessment overview', Working Paper, Institut pour un Développement Durable, Ottiginies, Belgium.

Ministerie van de Vlaamse Gemeenschap – Kenniscel Wetsmatiging (2005), 'Handleiding, Richtlijnen voor de opmaak van een Regulerings Impact Analyse'.

Pope, J, Annandale, D and Morrison-Saunders, S (2004), 'Conceptualising sustainability assessment', *Environmental Impact Assessment Review*, 24 (6), 595–616.

Radaelli, C M (2003), 'Innovations, quality, and good regulatory governance'. Background report on the conference on impact assessment in the European Union, Brussels.

Risse, N (2004), *Revue de la Littérature et Synthèse de L'état de L'art en Évaluation Environnementale Stratégique*, ULB, Service de Mathématiques de Gestion, Bruxelles, Belgique.

Thomaes, P, Lavrysen, L, Paredis, E (2005), 'Institutional and juridical integration of SIA in the Belgian federal government's structure', Working Paper, Ugent, Belgium.

UNEP (2002), *Environmental Impact Assessment Training Resource Manual*, Second Edition, UNEP.

Wäktare, M (2004), 'L'analyse d'impact de la Commission Européenne, revue de la littérature et analyse de cas', Université Libre de Bruxelles IGEAT-CEDD.

Wilkinson, D, Fergusson, M, Bowyer, C, Brown, J, Ladefoged, A, Monkhouse, C and Zdanowicz, A (2004), *Sustainable Development in the European Commission's Integrated Assessments for 2003, Final Report*, IEEP, London.

Index